Research on Adulthood and Aging

SUNY Series in Aging
Sheldon S. Tobin and Edmund Sherman, Editors

Research on Adulthood and Aging: The Human Science Approach

L. EUGENE THOMAS, EDITOR

State University of New York Press

Published by
State University of New York Press, Albany

Printed in the United States of America

For information, address State University of New York
Press, State University Plaza, Albany, N.Y., 12246

Library of Congress Cataloging-in-Publication Data

Research on adulthood and aging : the human science approach
    L. Eugene Thomas, editor.
        p. cm. — (SUNY series in aging)
    Bibliography: p.
    Includes index.
    ISBN 0-7914-0068-9. -- ISBN 0-7914-0069-7 (pbk.)
    1. Gerontology.   2. Aging--Social aspects.   3. Middle age.
    4. Adulthood.   I. Thomas, L. Eugene, 1932-   . II. Series.
HQ1061.R45   1989
305.2'6--dc19   88-31873
                                                                            CIP

10 9 8 7 6 5 4 3 2 1

I would like to acknowledge my indebtedness to Bernice Neugarten, who introduced me to qualitative research concepts many years ago, and Robert Peck who more recently helped me develop the *iccha* to learn new research methods that articulate with the human science paradigm.

Contents

Preface

One of the criticisms leveled at contemporary American social science is that it is methodologically sophisticated but content poor. Certainly the social sciences have put major emphasis on using "strong methodology" but whether this has led to an impoverishment of our questions about and understanding of adulthood and old age is the question. This book takes the stance that there are new territories to be explored by new approaches, that there is another position between rigorous operational science (positivism) and individual subjectivism. That position is labelled *human science*.

Here are qualitative methods for obtaining and analyzing subjective information or inner experiences of aging. One author calls it, "Gerontology with a Human Face." This gives emphasis to the difference between the research agenda for aging posed by the book and that often found in the work of head counters and talliers of yeses and noes in questionnaire studies.

There seems to be a gap between the research methods that focus on how to obtain information and the process of generating good questions. Here one learns that the research in the human sciences studying aging asks different questions than might be raised by more conventional social science. For example, questions are generated about how a long-lived individual extracts meaning from a life or how older persons maintain meaning in their lives in a society that is changing from industrial production to an information society.

Good science consists of asking good questions as well as having good methods by which to answer them. There is little doubt that this book is asking good questions, but we should keep in mind that a good question in this book is a question that probes the understanding of human existence. The chapters of this book are primarily oriented toward understanding the experience of "adulthood and aging." The key word is *experience*, for that limits the inquiry to that of which we are aware. Most of the information exchange in the human organism is not decoded by the brain. We are oblivious to such processes as digestion, the mineral exchange in bones or the processes of reading out the cellular DNA to build and repair the body. We are not aware of these processes and how they may change with age within ourselves. "Human Science" is not concerned with these, but with that part of our existence of which we are aware or about which we are self-conscious. Human science is concerned with exploring experience, and this book explores the experience of aging. The individual becomes the observer, not the observed.

The tenor of the book encourages us to talk to different kinds of people in different settings, analyze dialogues and explore subtleties that reflect the human experience that is often recorded in literature as poetry or fiction. Without a doubt, this opens the door to exploring the interior of later life and the editor believes that removing the stricture of the "positivist paradigm" opens the door to exploring in more detail the subjective dimensions of life as we develop and age.

This territory has been unexplored except by a few psychoanalysts and a few figures in literature who wrote from their individual experiences. It is also the territory that was declared to be off limits by the behaviorists who announced their abhorrence for the covert and denied that the subjective could be or should be explored by science. In contrast, these chapters offer us encouragement to explore conversations, interviews and biographies for insights that individuals have into the way life flows and the forces that shape the flow.

What was minimized in past research on aging is the role of intentions, personal strategies and the interpretations that individuals place upon the flow of their lives. Human science aims to make science out of the subject's interpretations or the meanings that are attached to events. Although this book offers reassurance that useful maps of middle age and old age can be drawn from the approaches that are described, we don't yet have much experience with the landmarks and the suggested surveying instruments. The new settlers represented by the authors of chapters invite us in to share what they believe to be a fertile territory for social scientists, the inside view of middle and late life. Since this is the space within which we live our lives, it deserves our attention.

James E. Birren

Introduction

Chapter 1

The Human Science Approach to Understanding Adulthood and Aging

L. EUGENE THOMAS

The chapters in this book represent a wide diversity of research strategies and substantive topics. What they have in common is their "unconventionality," in terms of standard social science research practices. This unconventionality is not random or arbitrary, however. Underlying each of these papers is an attempt to conduct research from the human science perspective.

In this chapter I will seek to clarify the nature of the human science paradigm, and indicate how the following research reports fit within this paradigm. Rick Moody, in the concluding chapter, will focus more on the substantive findings from the studies, identifying cross-cutting themes and issues. He will also touch on the "emancipatory" implications of this research in his concluding remarks.

Before going into the more technical aspects of the human science paradigm, it might be well to point out several unique characteristics of this approach, which will become immediately apparent to the reader in glancing over the chapters of this volume. To the social scientist accustomed to the style of most professional journals, perhaps the most startling difference is that researchers speak in the first person, rather than the anonymous third person. This difference is not accidental, but flows from the basic view that objective, context-free knowledge is impossible in the social sciences (if anywhere), and the use of "objective" terminology contributes to deception and mystification.

Substantively, the most striking difference that will be noted in these contributions is the absence of statistical analysis and tests of significance. Although quantitative analysis isn't ruled out in the human science framework, the research based on this paradigm tends to deal with linguistic data. While the focus of the research contained in this volume is based upon linguistic data, the reader will note that a wide variety of data sources are used, ranging from the more usual interview format, to analysis of literary texts and participant observation.

The main purpose of this book is to argue that there are viable alternatives to the "orthodox" positivist methodology, and to provide examples of research utilizing these methods in seeking to understand adulthood and aging. I will first outline in broad strokes what the human sciences paradigm is, and then use the research in this volume to illustrate the range of methods that are opened up to the social scientist working within this framework.

What is Human Science Research?

The emerging post-positivist approach has been given different names in the various social science disciplines, including: humanistic psychology, interpretative social science (sociology) and hermeneutics (humanities). The term "human science" has been chosen for this book because it is more generic, and appears to be gaining acceptance in a range of disciplines.[1]

Use of the term "human sciences" dates back to Dilthey's 1883 work on that topic (Makreel, 1975). He used the term *Geisteswissenschaften* in distinction to the natural sciences, *Naturwissenschaften*, insisting that the two domains dealt with different types of knowledge, and required distinct methods of inquiry.[2] The natural sciences strive for explanation (*Erklaren*) based on perception of physical reality, with the aim of predicting and controlling phenomena. The human sciences, on the other hand, seek to attain understanding (*Verstehen*) based on expressions of life. One does not expect to utilize the methods of the human sciences to "understand" a garbage can, nor should one expect to use the methods of the natural sciences to "know" human meaning and experience.

It is beyond the scope of this chapter to outline the philosophy of science arguments that have centered on Dilthey's formulation of the scope and methods of the human sciences. For the present purpose it is sufficient to note that his identification of the importance of meaning as a focus of the human sciences, in distinction to the knowledge claims and methods of the natural sciences, has proven to be central to the post-positivist approaches in the social sciences.

Considerable progress has been made in moving beyond Dilthey's original formulations in devising methods for studying human sciences phenomenon. In particular, the field of hermeneutics, developed as a means of interpreting religious texts, is increasingly being used by the social sciences as a means of moving such inquiry beyond the subjectivism of private minds into the social and cultural realm (cf. Rabinow & Sullivan, 1979). By engaging in the "hermeneutical circle," whereby a particular text is interpreted in light of the larger context, and conversely, the larger meaning is interpreted in light of the particular text or action (Ricoeur, 1971), the researcher is better equipped to understand and interpret the text.

One of the tenets of the human science approach is that the subject matter under examination should determine the methods used, rather than vice versa. Further, it is not possible for the researcher to rely upon method-ological orthodoxy to insure the adequacy of knowledge claims—the method utilized must be, as it were, custom tailored to the problem under investigation. The methods utilized can draw upon the humanities (as with hermeneutics), as well as the more orthodox social science procedures, since the issue of human understanding is as broad as the human experience. Needless to say, it is not possible to spell out definitively what the methods of human science are. The one characteristic these methodologies are likely to have in common is that they work with linguistic data (Polkinghorne, 1983). As will be seen in the following chapters in this book, these data can be taken from a wide variety of sources, including literary and historical material, as well as the more traditional interview data.

But Is This Science?

Implicit in most criticism of human science research is the question of whether it has validity and reliability, the basic criteria that we have come to associate with scientific research. Whatever else it merits, if the human sci-ence approach is not able to establish that it can meet these criteria, then it is not likely to find a place in the social sciences.

In answering this question we must be careful that assumptions of the positivist philosophy of science are not smuggled in. Habermas (1977) has helped clarify this issue by noting that rather than being value free, all types of scientific investigation bring with them "metalogical" interests. The natural sciences assume a causal-analytical method whose "interest" is predictive knowl-edge. Study of the human realm does not follow from a "knowledge-constitutive interest" in prediction, but can be either that of understanding (the herme-neutic sciences) or emancipation (critically-oriented science).[3] In either case the aim is not to predict and control, in the manner of the natural sciences.

In addition to Habermas's distinction of the interests of scientific investi-gation, Chapman (1966) has made a useful distinction between the kinds of knowledge produced by the different types of scientific investigation. He notes that Descartes posited only two types of knowledge: "apodictic," or certain knowledge, which was the aim of the natural sciences, and "problematic" knowl-edge, which was fallible (akin to "doxa," or opinion) and therefore "unscien-tific." Chapman suggests that there is a middle type of knowledge, "assertoric," which is validated by the living context in which it is embedded.

Although he doesn't use the term "assertoric," this would appear to be the type of knowledge produced by the hermeneutic method developed by Ricoeur (1981). A text (or an action), he suggests, can have a "plurivocity" of meanings. One makes a first guess as to its meaning, and then seeks to validate this meaning by determining if it is more probable than competing claims. This hermeneutical circle is continued until the most plausible construction of the text is arrived at. In the social sciences (as perhaps in all realms) there is no final arbiter or judge—in fact, the process is more like judicial reasoning than the logic of empirical verification.

It will be remembered that according to Dilthey, the focus of the human sciences is understanding (*Verstehen*). To understand a phenomenon does not necessarily mean that one is able to predict it. Indeed, there is reason to believe that at the level of understanding human meaning, prediction might well be a theoretical impossibility. Schutz (1962) has argued that meaning is only imputed to experiences and events in retrospect. At the time of living through them their meaning is unclear; only as events recede into the past is the ego able to lift them out of the stream of consciousness and give them meaning.

From this line of argument, it would appear that prospective prediction of the meaning that experiences have for an individual is not only practically impossible, but theoretically inappropriate as well. Thus it is inappropriate, for example, to reject Elizabeth Kubler-Ross's (1969) concept of anticipatory grief, or Levinson's (1978) model of the "seasons" of the life cycle, because they do not predict behavior. If this research provides understanding of human experience, the requirement that it be able to predict behavior is inappropriate. The only legitimate question is whether it provides better understanding of this human experience than competing explanations, not if it provides for prediction and control of behavior.

To return to the question of validity and reliability of human science research, the conclusion would be that the truth claims of each piece of research must be judged, not by adherence to methodological orthodoxy, nor by the ability to predict behavior. Rather, the criteria must be in the area of the "assertoric," that is, a careful consideration of whether more convincing arguments can be made for the validity of this research than can be made by competing claims.

Neugarten (1985), in commenting on the interpretative approach to the study of gerontology, summarized the human science approach as well:

> The goal is not to discover universals, not to make predictions that will hold good over time, and certainly not to control; but, instead, to explicate contexts and thereby to achieve new insights and new understandings. (p. 292).

Some Examples of Human Science Research

At the present time those researchers utilizing the human science paradigm are mostly isolated, and their work does not frequently appear in established research journals. In the following chapters the reader will find a collection of studies utilizing this paradigm in seeking to understand the experience of adulthood and aging. It is hoped that these reports will provide the reader with a glimpse of alternate research strategies, and help to further open the field to innovative and exciting research methods.

The contributors to this volume illustrate both the wide range of disciplines converging toward this form of post-positivist social science research, and an equally wide range of research strategies and data sources which can be employed. The first three chapters utilize the method which is perhaps least familiar to social scientists—hermeneutics. Hermeneutics has a long tradition in the humanities and was originally used in the interpretation of sacred and other texts (Polkinghorne, 1983). Harris's chapter, in which he analyzes a biblical text dealing with the issue of generational relationships, is firmly within this historical tradition. More recently the hermeneutical technique has been introduced into the social sciences (beginning with Dilthey, but more directly by Ricoeur, 1971, 1981), and provides a method for critically analyzing linguistic data of different sorts. Berman and Chinen utilize hermeneutics in their analyses of vastly different textual material—Berman analyzing the personal diaries of a contemporary literary figure, and Chinen analyzing the published works of two eminent philosophers. In their analyses they utilize the "hermeneutical circle"; that is, they analyze the texts within the larger social and historical contexts, and in turn judge the contexts in light of the particular texts.

Participant observation, on the other hand, has a long tradition in the social sciences, particularly in anthropology and sociology. Gubrium's research represents a more traditional application of this method, while seeking to gain the human science objective of understanding the meaning that experiences have for those being observed. Gergen's research illustrates more subjective involvement and identification with the research population. In her use of the "dialogic" method, the distinction between researcher and informant has purposely been blurred. Thus, although the method utilized here is not as unfamiliar to social scientists as that of hermeneutics, the stance of the researcher vis-a-vis her research subjects is a clear break from the positivist research tradition.

Intensive case studies are also familiar to social scientists, although they are generally looked down upon as being less "scientific" than their more rigorous counterparts. Working within the anthropological tradition (which has utilized this method perhaps more than any of the other social science disciplines, with the possible exception of social work), Rubinstein engages in an on-going relationship with his respondents in constructing his case studies. Ferguson utilizes the more traditional interview format in her research, but supplements the resulting case studies with careful and systematic analysis of the interview protocols. Scheibe also makes use of the case study in his chapter, but he couples this with a remarkable combination of literary texts and other sources, including published autobiographies, history, film and poetry. Scheibe's work illustrates the blurring of the distinction between the social sciences and the humanities in the human science approach, in which methodology is subordinate to the overriding aim of gaining understanding of lived experience.

The final three chapters represent more familiar social science methodology. Eisenhandler and Thomas and Chambers utilize open-ended and semi-structured interviews to understand the experience of elderly persons, while Wood includes personal diaries and structured instruments as well. Their analyses of the interview protocols, however, is less traditional. Working with the linguistic data of interview protocols, they engage in what is really a hermeneutical analysis—this is particularly clear in the Thomas and Chambers chapter, in which they seek to understand the protocol texts in light of the cultural contexts of India and England, and conversely the context of aging in these countries in light of the concrete texts. And in each of the chapters the authors are engaged in what might well be termed "phenomenological" analysis, in that they have sought to understand the world through the eyes of their informants, rather than testing hypotheses generated from other sources and imposed upon the data.

The studies in this volume, then, represent a wide range of research strategies and methods of data analysis. They illustrate the wide latitude offered by the human science paradigm, both in the methods that may be used, and the issues that are amenable to investigation. Indeed, the removal of the strictures of the positivist paradigm opens up to the researcher the whole realm of the subjective dimensions of life. The only limitation is the researcher's ingenuity in devising methods that are consistent with the topic under investigation. Given this latitude, there is reason to hope that we can make progress in understanding the meaning of the lived experience of adulthood and aging. If this proves to be the case, then giving up our safety nets of methodological orthodoxy will be a price well worth paying.

Notes

1. As an indication of the inclusiveness and growing acceptance of this term, an interdisciplinary Human Science Research Conference has been held annually for the past several years at universities in this country and Canada (the 1989 conference is scheduled to be held in Denmark). Although attended mostly by psychologists and educators, the conference draws sociologists, anthropologists, historians and representatives from other humanities disciplines.

2. Ironically, the term *Geisteswissenschaften* is a German rendition of John Stuart Mill's term "moral sciences." Its translation back into English has been somewhat problematic. Earlier the term was rendered "human studies"or "cultural sciences," but in recent years "human sciences" has tended to be the preferred translation (Polkinghorne, 1983).

3. It should be noted that in his formulation Habermas (1977) goes beyond Dilthey's formulation. Dilthey, he claims, had not succeeded in extricating himself from his postivist dogma of objectivity. It is not possible, Habermas argues, for the researcher to maintain a stance as the uninvolved observer. To try to do so leads only to abstract theory and sterile knowledge.

References

Chapman, H. M. (1966). *Sensations and phenomenology.* Bloomington, IN: Indiana University Press.

Habermas, J. (1977). *Knowledge and human interests.* London: Heineman.

Kubler-Ross, E. (1969). *On death and dying.* New York: Macmillan.

Levinson, D. J. (1978). *The seasons of a man's life.* New York: Knopf.

Makkrell, R. A. (1975). *Dilthey: Philosopher of the human studies.* Princeton, NJ: Princeton University Press.

Neugarten, B. L. (1985). *Interpretative social science and research on aging. In A. S. Rossi (ed.), Gender and the life course.* New York: Aldine.

Polkinghorne, D. (1983). *Methodology for the human sciences.* Albany, NY: State University of New York Press.

Rabinow, P. and W. M. Sullivan (1979). The interpretative turn: Emergence of an approach. In P. Rabinow & W. M. Sullivan (eds.), *Interpretive social science.* Berkeley, CA: University of California Press.

Ricoeur, P. (1971). The model of the text: Meaningful action considered as a text. *Social Research,* 8(3):528-562.

Ricoeur, P. (1981). *Hermeneutics and the human sciences.* New York: Cambridge University Press.

Schutz, A. (1962). On multiple realities. *In Collected Papers, Vol I.* The Hague; Martinus Nijhoff.

The Hermeneutical Approach

Chapter 2

May Sarton's Journals: Attachment and Separateness in Later Life

HARRY J. BERMAN

May Sarton is a poet and novelist who has made a unique contribution to those interested in the study of lives. She wrote a series of four personal journals while she was between the ages of fifty-nine and seventy-one (Sarton, 1973; 1977; 1980; 1984).[1]

Sarton's journals are "personal journals" in that the life of the author is the prime subject (Fothergill, 1974), as distinguished from other journals in which the author is primarily reporting events, such as those describing expeditions (Lewis & Clark, 1953; Schlissel, 1982) or chronicling political affairs (Cuomo, 1984). Although there are several other contemporary personal journals which document the day-to-day experience of older people (see especially Horner, 1982; Olmstead, 1975; Scott-Maxwell, 1968/1979; Vining, 1978), there is no other instance of a series of recent, published personal journals spanning an entire decade of later life. Because of their potential for illuminating inner experience in later life, Sarton's journals warrant examination by scholars interested in the life course.

The Analysis of Journals

One assumption underlying this chapter is that "psychology needs to concern itself with life as it is lived" (Allport, 1942, p. 56). Studying life as it is lived implies directing scholarly attention to inner experience and to the meanings that people impart to the events of their lives. Personal journals have the potential to capture such meaning-making as it happens. Journals are also

---

1. Since completion of work on this chapter, a fifth journal, *After the Stroke*, has been published. It covers the events of Sarton's life at age 74.

uniquely suited for tracking changes in mood and can reveal inconsistencies, as well as consistencies, in self-concept.

An appropriate way to analyze personal journals is with an approach that can be characterized as qualitative psychological research (Fischer, 1987) or as phenomenological human science (Wertz, 1984). Wertz has argued this approach "begins with a bracketing or suspending of preconceptions and a fresh immersement in the lived reality to which the description refers" (1984, p. 42). After beginning with immersion in the text there follows a process of analysis and interpretation. As Taylor (1979) has pointed out, successful interpretations are those that clarify the meaning which was originally present in the text in a confused, fragmented, cloudy form. For human science researchers interested in the study of the life course, interpretations should serve not only to clarify the text in its own terms, but should also show how the text relates to developmental theories.

There is a mutuality in the exchange between the author of a journal and a human science researcher. The journal author gives the researcher a communication about some facet of experience which may not be expressed in available theory. At the same time, the researcher's theories and concepts may provide a more encompassing perspective than was available to the author (Berman, 1987).

The journals of May Sarton present an opportunity for examining one person's lived reality and analyzing her experience in light of relevant developmental theories.

Background

May Sarton was born in Belgium in 1912 and came with her parents to the United States in 1916 to escape the war. She was educated in Cambridge, Massachusetts, and in Belgium at schools that emphasized the pleasure and excitement of study, love of poetry, and the dignity of the inquiring mind. For three years she was part of the Civic Repertory Company in New York and for another three years directed her own theater group. This group failed when Sarton was twenty-four, at which time she committed herself to a life of writing poetry and novels. A useful summary of her early life appears in a 1972 biography (Sibley, 1972).

To understand the events in the four published journals familiarity with two previous works, *Plant Dreaming Deep* (1968) and *Kinds of Love* (1970), is important.

Plant Dreaming Deep, a memoir of Sarton's move from Cambridge to Nelson, New Hampshire, describes the life she created in that rural community. The move was precipitated by the deaths of both of her parents, her mother in 1950 when Sarton was thirty-eight and her father six years later. She had remained quite involved with her parents through her thirties. They helped her financially and she viewed their home in Cambridge as her home, although she actually lived in an apartment she shared with her long-time friend, Judith Matlack. Within a week of her father's death "the house had been sold, and within two months dismantled, the books gone, everything torn apart of the fabric of my parents' lives together," (Sarton, 1968, p. 22). At age forty-six, as a single woman and "orphan," Sarton decided to buy a house for the first time. Her choice was not to remain in Cambridge, but rather to move into a dilapidated eighteenth-century farmhouse in the Monadnock mountains of New Hampshire. In *Plant Dreaming Deep*, written eight years after this move, she recounts the difficulties of getting established in the house, bringing order to the grounds and becoming accepted in the town. She describes her deep feeling for the people who came into her life and conveys the texture of her life, that of a person committed to work, but who is also a great lover of people and of nature. The content of *Plant Dreaming Deep* resembles that of the journals which followed it over the succeeding decade. It addresses, as the journals do, the themes of solitude, friendship, the beauty and power of the natural world and the struggle to create both her self and her work. Its narrative style, however, sets it apart from the journals: it does not recount events as they unfold but rather sets forth an organized distillation of eight years' experiences. It has a logical form, the descriptions move out in widening circles to encompass house, garden, neighbors and community and conclude with a characterization of her self in this place. Also, there is a dramatic structure to the narrative of the fall and subsequent rise in her fortunes over the eight years which makes the work resemble a novel. Viewed in this way *Plant Dreaming Deep* tells the story of a woman who took on the challenge of establishing a solitary life in a remote place, who endured considerable difficulty, who learned much from the natural beauty of rural New England and from the strength of character of its inhabitants, but whose life also had deep roots in other places and in a past not shared by her neighbors.

Her next work, *Kinds of Love*, was Sarton's most complex and ambitious novel to that point. Set in Willard, a small New Hampshire town modeled on Nelson, and drawing heavily on the people she encountered there, the novel is about what happens when an older couple who are long-time summer residents resolve to stay through the winter months. Portrayals of many kinds of love are woven into the story: love between old friends, between a husband and wife late in life, between a mother and an emotionally disturbed adult son; love of nature; the love of young lovers; and the love of people for their community. The novel also deals with courage in facing the "ordinary" adversities of poverty, illness and old age. As Bakerman (1982) has noted, a central theme of this novel is the crucial importance of the life-long work of the making of a self: "What is interesting after all is the making of a self, an act of creation, like any other, that does imply a certain amount of conscious work" (Sarton, 1970, p. 32).

Both these works are linked to *Journal of a Solitude*. In *Journal of a Solitude* (1973) Sarton wrote that *Plant Dreaming Deep* presented a false view of the kind of person she was, that it presented her as a "wise old party" (p. 142) and failed to convey "the anguish of her life," particularly her "rages" (p. 12) and her "destructive angers" (p. 206). One of Sarton's aims in *Journal of a Solitude* was to present a more authentic version of herself than she believed was presented in *Plant Dreaming Deep*.

In *Journal of a Solitude* Sarton also reflects on *Kinds of Love*, particularly the review in *The New York Times*, which was devastating: "This novel, flawed in style and flabby in content, is filled with characters but does not bring the reader in to share the depth of their experiences" (cited in Blouin, 1978, p. 134). Although there were other, favorable reviews, the *Times* review was emotionally bruising and financially harmful. In *Journal of a Solitude* Sarton deals with the aftermath of this event; later, In *Recovering*, she deals with a similar rejection of *A Reckoning*. A further link between *Plant Dreaming Deep*, *Kinds of Love*, and the journals is that in all four journals Sarton discusses various elements of her life after her decision to move from Cambridge.

Attachment and Separateness

Because a special value of Sarton's journals for developmentalists is the presentation of day-to-day experience and developmental potentials during an entire decade of later life, all four journals will be considered jointly. Nonetheless, it is important to recognize that each journal was published separately and can be read independently. Also, the journals are discontinuous. There are periods during the twelve years spanned by the four books of which nothing is written. During those periods Sarton was engaged in creative work which required her to set aside journal writing. Unlike journal writers such as Pepys, Sarton used journal writing not principally as a record-keeping activity but rather as a form of creativity leading to published works that necessarily begin and end at discrete points in time. Table 1 is provided in order to clarify the time periods covered in the four books, Sarton's age during those periods and the major issues they contain.

When the four journals are considered together one theme is especially prominent: the dilemma of attachment and separateness.

Tension between the desire for attachment and the desire for separateness is central to human development (Becker, 1973; Freud, 1955; Gilligan, 1982;

Table 1
Chronology of Sarton's Journals

Journal	Dates	Sarton's Age	Major Issues
Journal of a Solitude (1973)	9/15/71- 9/30/72	59-60	Critical rejection of her work Relationship with X Anger, depression
A House by the Sea (1977)	11/13/74- 8/17/76	62-64	Success of *As We Are Now* (1973) Happiness at living by the sea Physical illness Feeling old
Recovering (1980)	12/28/78- 11/30/79	66-67	Judith Matlack's senility Rejection by lover Critical rejection of *A Reckoning* (1978) Mastectomy Recovery from losses
At Seventy (1984)	5/3/82- 5/2/83	70-71	Seventieth birthday Dealing with success Feeling young despite age

Kegan, 1982). This tension arises in infancy (Mahler, 1970), then is present in late adolescence in the tension between intimacy and isolation (Erikson, 1950) and emerges again in adulthood as the tension between love and work (Levinson, Darrow, Klein, Levinson, & McKee, 1978).

Sarton recognizes this tension as a fundamental feature of human life: "The two greatest yearnings of humans may be the yearnings for inclusion and the yearnings for distinctness" (Sarton, 1980, p. 142). The power of the journals lies not in merely acknowledging the importance of the tension between attachment and separateness for people in general, but rather in tracing the emotional upheavals created by these incompatible desires in a particular life.

For Sarton the tension between attachment and separateness arises in two contexts. The first is in connection with her repeated attempts to establish a lasting, intimate love relationship and the second is in her need for solitude in order to work.

Intimacy.

In *Recovering* Sarton wrote:

> The value of loving someone passionately, often a person very unlike oneself,
> is that one is taken literally out of one's self on a journey into unknown
> territory. As in a journey to a foreign country there is culture shock; one
> often feels lonely, even attacked by differences. One is also all the time in a
> state of strange excitement, there are glorious moments, unforgettable scenes
> that make one tremble with joy and surprise, and there are days of great
> fatigue when all one longs for is home, to be with the familiar that does not
> ask for stretching to understand it, which can be taken for granted. Where
> one can rest. And above all where one is accepted as one is, not stammering
> in an unfamiliar language, not trying desperately to communicate from one
> ethos to another (Sarton, 1980, p. 204).

During the period covered in the four journals, Sarton records three
such journeys through passionate love relationships, all with other women of
her age. Sarton is aware of the stereotypical responses elicited by her desire
for intimacy at her age and with another older woman. She wrote:

> Americans are terrified of the very idea of passionate love going on past
> middle age. Are they afraid of being alive? Do they want to be dead, i.e. safe?
> For of course no one is ever safe when in love. (1973, p. 80)

And she acknowledged the prevalent notion that

> to be in love at our age is ludicrous and somehow not proper, that passionate
> love can be banished after sixty. . . . That is one of the myths that has been
> around a long time, but it was never true (1980, p. 205).

Similarly, she is aware that in acknowledging her homosexuality she runs
the risk of having everything she writes analyzed through the lens of sexual
preference, of having her novels reduced to one theme:

> What the fear of communism did to destroy lives and to confuse the minds of
> the innocent to an unbelievable extent under Senator McCarthy's evil influ-
> ence, the fear of homosexuality appears to be doing now. . . . I have hoped to
> provide a bridge between women of all ages and kinds. . . . The vision of life
> in my work is not limited to one segment of humanity or another and it has
> very little to do with sexual proclivity. It does have to do with love, and love
> has many forms and it is not easy or facile in any of them (1980, pp. 80-81).

Nonetheless, she takes the risk and writes openly about her intense passion, her need for intimacy and her desolation when it cannot be achieved.

Sarton's struggles with her passions give insight into the dynamics of intimacy regardless of the ages or genders of the partners in the relationship. The object of passionate love "focuses the world" (1980, p. 204) and provides a "gentle river of communion that runs along under all the days" (1980, p. 239). Such a person can stave off "the quicksand that isolation sometimes creates, a sense of drowning, of being literally engulfed" (1973, p. 107) and can "bring the world to life" (1977, p. 214). For Sarton such a person serves, additionally, as a muse for poetry. Despite her deep friendships with people mentioned by name in the journals and despite her many admirers, Sarton needs an intimate relationship to spur on poetry: "Poetry does not happen for me without a muse" (1984, p. 304). And, in fact, during the time period covered in the journals, successive love relationships resulted in the poems in *A Durable Fire* (1972), *Halfway to Silence* (1980) and *Letters from Maine* (1984).

But intimacy is achieved at a cost: inauthenticity, not being true to one's self, in effect, the loss of identity. To Sarton, for whom the creation of a true self is the central purpose of life (see below), such inauthenticity is intolerable:

> The thing is that art doesn't brook a censor and in the relation to those we love if it is not in perfect harmony we have to censor ourselves, keep the demons at bay. Then the censorship in one area ends by taking over all areas (1980, p. 113).

Also, she recognizes that because of her work she is likely to be misperceived by potential lovers who project their image of May Sarton on to the real person:

> [T]wice in my life people who discovered me through the work, who came to me as admirers and became intimate friends ended by being unable to accept the whole person, the flawed human being, because they had somehow fallen in love with an image beside which the reality of a living, suffering being who is not perfect, who is temperamental, who "has no surface" as someone once said of me, became disillusioning (1980, p. 123).

Sarton's journals track the mood swings and varying self-evaluations set in motion by the opposing pulls of her desire for intimacy and her desire to be true to herself. They are particularly valuable in providing descriptions of the feelings that arise when the pendulum swings toward the self, that is, the feelings that accompany a decision to break off a love relationship, an event which occurs three times during the twelve years in these journals:

> For a week or more I have been in a state of extreme excitement, as though on the brink of revelation. It began at once as soon as I had decided to bring

myself to the point of decision and to break off, not to cling out of need and desperation to something that perhaps was never there. The central person focuses the world and when there is no one to be that, one is at first terrified. Once the decision is made that had to be made, one is free at last to go home to the self, that self which has been censored, without even being aware of it by the effort to please, and to become acceptable to the one one loves (1980, pp. 204-205).

The decision to break off a relationship is accompanied by an adjustment in self-concept. At age sixty, after the break-up of the relationship which forms an undercurrent to *Journal of a Solitude*, she wrote that she longed for one person with whom everything could be shared, but was "slowly making peace with the knowledge that this will never happen" (1973, p. 157) and that the time had come for her to have many loves and no love (1977, p. 262). Yet she did find another such person. Five years later, in *Recovering*, she was dealing with the painful aftermath of that relationship. In a moving passage she wrote that the "door has closed forever on passionate communion with another human being" and that her mutilated body (the body she was left with after a mastectomy) was the physical evidence of that fact (1980, p. 138). But, again, four years later, at age seventy, Sarton was in love and once again contending with the competing pulls of the desire for intimacy and the desire to be true to herself.

Thus, over the twelve years covered in the journals, there are successive self-descriptions about being the kind of person who will never be intimate with another, and successive predictions that the door to passion had closed forever. Yet each time the door is again opened.

From the perspective of a reader who knows how the "story" turns out it is tempting to view Sarton's statements about her fated isolation as self-deception or as unjustified appeals for sympathy. After all, each time her predictions are proven wrong. But while she was keeping her diaries, Sarton, of course, could not know how the story would turn out. When she wrote that she would never love again she was trying to make sense of her life at that moment, to create a self-image that was true to her recent experience. Any such image can only be a temporary construction, though. The journals exemplify the way in which people try to make meaning out of experience and weave such meanings together to create the story of their lives (Spence, 1982; Cohler, 1982; Gergen, 1983; Kaufman, 1986), a story which is subject to constant revision.

Solitude

Both Levinson (Levinson, et al, 1978) and Erikson (1950) have noted that in adulthood one manifestation of the tension between attachment and separateness is the conflict over what is owed to others versus what is owed to oneself. One arena in which this conflict arises is in balancing the competing demands of family and of work. In adulthood family involves attentiveness to others' needs and the fostering of others' growth. Work may also involve meeting others' needs (see especially Levinson's discussion of mentoring), but it serves principally as a channel for the realization of self. The tension between obligations to others and obligations to oneself in the arena of family and work is particularly prominent in Sarton's journals.

Sarton's "family" obligations do not consist of taking care of husband, children or aging parents. Rather her family obligations are her obligations, first, toward her successive lovers, and second, toward her many friends and admirers. She feels these latter obligations very strongly and knows that she is enriched by the visits and numerous appreciative letters she receives.

But meeting the needs of lovers and responding to friends and admirers keeps her from her work, her writing, which requires solitude. Solitude is not only essential for her work, which provides her livelihood, it is also essential for the creation of the self which is realized through her work.

> It's not that I work all day; it is that the work needs space around it (1977, p. 157).

> For more than a year now I appear to have been fighting for myself, fighting to recover the creative being in me, fighting in essence to stay alive, not to become silted down in "obligations" that are escapes from the far harder obligations to write poems and books (1980, p. 134).

Citing Scott-Maxwell (1968/1971), Sarton wrote that the activity of creating the self is a sacred duty (1980, p. 134) and quoted her father's journal:

> The main purpose of a man's life is to give others what is in him. Such a matter is not a question of selfishness or unselfishness. . . . We only have what we are and we only have what we give (1980, p. 35).

Therefore, Sarton is compelled to seek solitude so that she can do her work and realize her true self.

Much of the impact of the journals derives from the descriptions of what solitude is like: its extraordinary possibilities and its terrible costs:

> I am here alone for the first time in weeks to take up my "real life" again at last. . . . When I am alone the flowers are really seen; I can pay attention to them. They are felt presences (1973, p. 11).

> We are one, the house and I, and I am happy to be alone—time to think, time to be (1973, p. 81).

> There are compensations for not being in love—solitude grows richer for me
> every year (1977, p. 61).

The creative possibilities afforded by solitude do not mean that it leads
to continuous inner harmony. Quite the contrary, Sarton's solitude (particularly during the period of *Journal of a Solitude*) meant that she was open to
"attacks from within" (1973, p. 16).

> My need to be alone is balanced against my fear of what will happen when I
> suddenly enter the huge empty silence if I cannot find support here. I go up
> to Heaven and down to Hell in an hour (1973, p. 12).

There are many expressions in the journals of her desperate loneliness,
"loneliness like starvation" (1977, p. 202), loneliness because she cannot live
with the person she loves (1980, p. 239). And her solitude is experienced as
painful when she thinks about having sole responsibility for all housekeeping
and maintenance chores, tasks which can become particularly difficult during New Hampshire and Maine winters.

Solitude is also experienced as painful when there is no one with whom
to share joy. For example, in 1972 Sarton was alone when she received in the
mail copies of her book of poetry *A Grain of Mustard Seed* (Sarton, 1971).
About that experience she wrote: "I felt let down to be alone with this new-
born babe, to have no one to whom I could show it" (1973, p. 87).

The "attacks from within," the loneliness and self-criticism are not merely
fleeting thoughts which are then put aside. The entries for months at a time
are dominated by unhappiness. However, even in the midst of periods of
unhappiness she maintains an optimism about the ultimate usefulness of her
ordeal and forces herself to be open to negative feelings because of her faith
that "the courage to despair" (1973, p. 22) is essential to creativity.

> Sometimes one has simply to endure a period of depression for what it may
> hold of illumination if one can live through it, attentive to what it exposes or
> demands (1973, p. 16).

Sarton's valuing of solitude, despite the pain associated with it, makes
her work expecially meaningful to readers who are also leading lives of solitude or who wish for such lives. In the journals she records her gratitude that
people take comfort from her determination to make a solitary life be a rich
one, but she is also aware how easily such a life can be romanticized. She is
particularly critical of young people to whom she may represent "a role model
that is dangerous rather than helpful" (1980, p. 32). She does not want to be
misconstrued as advocating solitude for its own sake. Rather, "if one does

choose solitude it must be for a purpose other than mere self-seeking" (1980, p. 32). From the perspective of her life at age seventy she recognizes that "we all have our nostalgias for the giving up of the world" (1984, p. 26). She warns her readers and correspondents repeatedly during the twelve years covered in the journals that the solitary life should not be envied and it especially should not be pursued by the young:

> I did not begin to live alone till I was forty-five, and had "lived" in the sense of passionate friendships and love affairs very richly for twenty-five years. I had a huge amount of life to think about and to digest, and above all I was a person by then and knew what I wanted of my life (1977, p. 135).

And much as she needs her separateness she recognizes that total independence is not desirable:

> At what price would total independence be bought? That's the rub! I am conscious of the fruitful tension set up between me and anyone for whom I care. . . . I learn by being in relation to (1973, p. 107).
>
> Perhaps the idea is not detachment as I used to believe but rather to be deeply involved in something is to be attached (1984, p. 12).

And in a letter to a young admirer she wrote:

> Agreed that human relationships are often painful, always may be collisions, but through them we grow. How do we grow otherwise? You yourself say in this letter, "It is in my times alone that I straighten things out" . . . exactly. But there would be nothing to straighten out if you had no relationships (1980, p. 33).

Sarton expresses the irreducible and unsolvable dilemma of attachment and separateness much as it is recounted by the men in Levinson's (Levinson et al., 1978) study and expressed in Levinson's idea of the interpenetration of self and world. People learn about themselves through their involvements with others, involvements which place demands upon them for time and energy. But those involvements, if left unchecked, can draw a person totally away from the self. A measure of separateness must be preserved in order to develop the self and, thereby, be able to give to others the best one has to offer.

Conclusion

Stability and Change

The analysis presented above was based upon elaboration of a single theme found in all four journals, the dilemma of attachment and separateness.

Consequently, the analysis highlighted the stable aspect of Sarton's personality. In each of the books there are descriptions of struggles to achieve intimacy without sacrificing authenticity and of attempts to strike a satisfactory balance between obligations to self and obligations to others.

There is considerable evidence of other aspects of stability during the period covered in the journals. The personal values Sarton expresses are consistent, particularly in the idea that the creation of self is the central purpose of life. During these years, also, interests and "loves" developed earlier in life continue. Most notable among these are her intense love for her gardens and her misery when they do not thrive; her deep emotional response to flowers; her attachment to her dog and cat and their importance in relieving loneliness; and her vivid memories of her elders, the now-deceased members of her parents' generation who shaped her character.

Though Sarton's central concerns, values and interests remain quite stable, the journals record changes in her predominant mood and sense of self-esteem. The first journal, *Journal of a Solitude*, is dominated by anger, tension and depression and questioning of self-worth. The second and third journals cover extensive periods of unhappiness, but the unhappiness of these books lacks the energy, the *Sturm and Drang*, of the first journal. In particular, in *A House by the Sea*, the second journal, Sarton explains that she feels old, that she has made her contribution, and that her life is basically finished. However, at the end of the decade, in *At Seventy*, Sarton's expressions of emotional distress are less intense and her periods of unhappiness are less protracted. Her life at that point is dominated by her sense of satisfaction with her achievements, her commitment to continued work and her reflections on what it is like to be an active, respected seventy-year-old. It is important to recognize that external events, not aging per se, helped shape this change. During the period covered in the journals Sarton went from being a relatively unnoticed novelist and poet to being a widely-recognized and honored exemplar of the woman writer.

The Flexible Life Course

Sarton's journals have a special relationship to the model of ego development propounded by Erikson and to the idea of the aleatoric change described by Gergen.

Sarton's journals *fixate the meaning* (Geertz, 1983; Ricoeur, 1979) of an experience which Erikson brought to our attention in his sixth stage of development: the dilemma of intimacy versus isolation. More specifically, the journals show the way that identity is put at risk in the course of trying to establish close relationships and they describe the anger and unhappiness that accompany unsuccessful approaches toward intimacy.

The journals also illuminate the dilemma that Erikson labels generativity versus self-absorption and that Levinson terms the polarity of attachment and separateness. This dilemma consists of balancing responsibilities for the care of others, particularly family, against the responsibility for the care of oneself. Sarton repeatedly addresses the way in which relationships with others and the obligations they entail sustain the self, but how in a life which consists exclusively of meeting obligations toward others, the self becomes diminished and ultimately less capable of serving others.

Erikson's theory of ego development is so widely taught and cited that it has virtually become a part of our culture. However, the eight ages of man set forth in the original presentation (Erikson, 1950) and reiterated subsequently (Erikson, 1980; 1982) lend themselves to oversimplification. They have come to be viewed as stages that are met and passed through in a lock-step order one after the next. But Erikson made it clear that each of the developmental dilemmas which comes into prominence at a particular chronological age is subject to pre-working and reworking. In other words, all developmental issues are potentially "up-for-grabs" at any age. Even if we accept with Erikson the notion of the prominence of questions about intimacy in early adulthood, that does not imply (nor would Erikson argue) that such questions are absent in later adulthood. Similarly, even if we accept, with Levinson, the likelihood of the conflict between love and work in the lives of mid-life men, that does not imply that this theme cannot also be central to the lives of older women.

The idea of the flexibility of the life course which is implicit in Erikson is a central element of Gergen's recent contributions to our understanding of human development (Gergen, 1977; 1980). Gergen proposes the term "aleatoric change" to express the idea that there is very little about human development in adulthood that is pre-programmed and that much of the research that supports either a stability model or an ordered-change model of development is a consequence both of the prevailing methodologies used to study persons and of historical circumstance.

Sarton's journals illustrate the aleatoric nature of development in two ways. First, in their emphasis on the dilemma of intimacy versus isolation, they highlight the way that a developmental issue which ostensibly predominates in early adulthood can quite readily become a central focus of later adulthood. It is not necessary to view Sarton as off-time or retarded in her development, from an aleatoric perspective she is manifesting an age-irrelevant developmental potential.

Second, Sarton's journals illustrate the way that self-conception and the story of one's life are constantly reshaped through interactions with others and by the flow of events. The journals present successive versions of what she sees as her true self and her fate. A special value of the journals is that Sarton has not tried to explain away or edit out inconsistencies but rather has let the inconsistencies stand. They serve as a testament to the way that our views of our selves can change over time. As Vaillant has written, "maturation makes liars of us all" (Vaillant, 1977, p. 197).

Kegan has succinctly stated, "the activity of being a person is the activity of meaning-making" (1982, p. 11). Meaning-making consists, in part, of the continuing and interrelated processes of constructing a version of the self and creating the story of one's life. Personal journals are one source of data about these processes. This chapter has presented one interpretation of a set of personal journals which have a unique value for those interested in the study of the life course. The richness of these books, however, warrants further research from a human science perspective and justifies the development of a set of complementary interpretations that explore the many issues raised in them.

References

Allport, G. (1942). *The use of personal documents in psychological science*. New York: Social Science Research Council.

Bakerman, J. (1942). Patterns of love and friendship: Five novels by May Sarton. In C. Hunting (ed.) *May Sarton: Woman and poet*. Orono, MN: National Poetry Foundation-University of Maine at Orono.

Becker, E. (1973). *The denial of death*. N.Y.: Free Press.

Berman, H. (1987). Admissible evidence: Geropsychology and the personal journal. In S. Reinharz & G. Rowles (eds.), *Qualitative gerontology*. N.Y.: Springer.

Blouin, L. (1978). *May Sarton: A bibliography*. Metuchen, NJ: The Scarecrow Press.

Cohler, B. (1982). Personal narrative and life course. In P. Baltes & O. Brim, Jr. (eds.), *Life-span development and behavior* (Vol. 3). N.Y.: Academic Press.

Cuomo, M. (1984). *The diaries of Mario M. Cuomo*. N.Y.: Random House.

Erikson, E. (1980). *Identity and the life cycle*. N.Y.: Norton.

Erikson, E. (1982). *The life cycle completed: A review*. N.Y.: Norton.

Fischer, C. (1987). The quality of qualitative research. *Theoretical & Philosophical Psychology, 7*, 2-11.

Fothergill, R. (1974). *Private chronicles: A study of English diaries*. London: Oxford University Press.

Freud, S. (1955). Beyond the pleasure principle. Standard Edition (Vol. 18). London: Hogarth Press (Originally published, 1920).

Geertz, C. (1983). *Local knowledge: Further essays in interpretive anthropology.* N.Y.: Basic Books.

Gergen, K. (1977). Stability, change and chance in understanding human development. In N. Datan & H. Reese (eds.), *Life-span developmental psychology: Dialectical perspectives on experimental research.* N.Y.: Academic Press.

Gergen, K. (1980). The emerging crisis in theory in life-span development. In P. Baltes & O. Brim, Jr. (eds.), *Life-span development and behavior* (Vol. 3). N.Y.: Academic Press.

Gergen, K. (1983). Narratives of the self. In T. Sarbin & K. Scheibe (eds.), *Studies in social identity.* N.Y.: Praeger.

Gilligan, C. (1982). Adult development and women's development: Arrangements for a marriage. In J. Giele (ed.), *Women in the middle years: Current knowledge and directions for future research and policy.* N.Y.: Wiley.

Horner, J. (1982). *That time of year.* Amherst, MA: University of Massachusetts Press.

Kaufman, S. (1986). *The ageless self: Sources of meaning in late life.* Madison: University of Wisconsin Press.

Kegan, R. (1982). *The evolving self.* Cambridge: Harvard University Press.

Levinson, D.; Darrow, C.; Klein, E.; Levinson, M.; & McKee, B. (1978). *The seasons of a man's life.* N.Y.: Knopf.

Lewis, M. & W. Clark (1953). *The journals of Lewis and Clark.* Edited by J. Bakeless. N.Y.: New American Library.

Mahler, M. (1970). *The psychological birth of the human infant: Symbiosis and individuation.* N.Y.: Basic Books.

Olmstead, A. (1975). *Threshold: The first days of retirement.* N.Y.: Harper and Row.

Ricoeur, P. (1979). The model of the text: Meaningful action considered as a text. In P. Rabinow & W. Sullivan (eds.), *Interpretive social science: A reader.* Berkeley: University of California Press.

Sarton, M. (1968). *Plant dreaming deep.* N.Y.: Norton.

Sarton, M. (1970). *Kinds of Love.* N.Y.: Norton.

Sarton, M. (1971). *A grain of mustard seed.* N.Y.: Norton.

Sarton, M. (1972). *A durable fire.* N.Y.: Norton.

Sarton, M. (1973). *As we are now.* N.Y.: Norton.

Sarton, M. (1973). *Journal of a solitude.* N.Y.: Norton.

Sarton, M. (1977). *The house by the sea: A journal.* N.Y.: Norton.

Sarton, M. (1978). *A Reckoning.* N.Y.: Norton.

Sarton, M. (1980). *Halfway to silence: New poems*. N.Y.: Norton.

Sarton, M. (1980). *Recovering: A journal*. N.Y.: Norton.

Sarton, M. (1984). *At seventy: A journal*. N.Y.: Norton.

Sarton, M. (1984). *Letters from Maine*. N.Y.: Norton.

Schlissel, L. (1982). *Women's diaries of the westward journey*. N.Y.: Schocken.

Scott-Maxwell, F. (1979). *The measure of my days*. N.Y.: Penguin (Originally published, 1968).

Sibley, A. (1972). *May Sarton*. N.Y.: Twayne.

Spence, D. (1982). *Narrative truth and historical truth: Meaning and interpretation in psychoanalysis*. N.Y.: Norton.

Taylor, C. (1979). Interpretation and the sciences of man. In P. Rabinow & W. Sullivan (eds.), *Interpretive social science*. Berkeley, CA: University of California Press.

Vaillant, G. (1977). *Adaptation to life*. N.Y.: Little, Brown.

Vining, E. (1978). *Being seventy: The measure of a year*. N.Y.: Viking.

Wertz, F. (1984). Procedures in phenomenological research and the question of validity. In M. Anastoos (Issue ed.) *Exploring the lived world: Readings in phenomenological psychology*. Carrollton: West Georgia College Studies in the Social Sciences, *23*, 29-48.

Chapter 3

Biblical Hermeneutics and the Aging Experience

J. GORDON HARRIS

Hermeneutics (*ermeneia*) provides crucial rules and techniques for interpretation, translation or explanation of data.[1] Though it has a long history, from Homer to Schleiermacher, it has only recently been adopted into social sciences.[2] Social science research has recognized that principles used for Bible interpretation provide a framework that will help its discipline become more self-reflective in the conduct of critique. Hermeneutical principles isolate biases within the explanatory process which hinder discovery of truth.

This essay focuses on a biblical text, Genesis 9:18-29, utilizing the hermeneutical circle to illustrate the importance of bracketing preconceptions in such a way as to allow the text and its historical context to emerge. In a positive sense, the essay illustrates how explanation of data can be enhanced by taking into account the paradigm of old age.

Hermeneutical Developments and Preunderstanding

Historical insights have made biblical hermeneutics more aware of potentially limiting preunderstandings. Discoveries increasingly have led scholars to study the relationship between interpreter and culture as well as interpretation and culture.[3] For example, rival schools in the first century C.E. clashed over whether to interpret the Bible by a literal or allegorical method. Allegorical interpretations prevailed and opponents were ostracized as heretics. Church authority provided the stability which gave interpreters the license to find multiple meanings in a text. This method dominated Bible interpretation until the Reformation, when reformers utilized a more literal approach to seek one, primary meaning and replace the authority of the Church with that of the Bible.

The Enlightenment spawned a series of other insights. Eighteenth-century philosophers, in the spirit of Kant, dealt expressly with the act of understanding language. Schleiermacher and Dilthey led this phenomenological approach. Nineteenth-century German historians directed the discipline to consider texts as documents of history. These approaches sparked recognition of a hermeneutical circle which suggested that an interpreter's preunderstandings influence conclusions about data.[4] Allowing for that circle of interpretation demanded more than an effort to find a "real" or "single" meaning of a thought or event. Rather, the process called for reading presuppositions of interpreters as well as texts or data. Each movement increasingly examined the role that preunderstanding plays in collecting and discerning the meaning of data.

Preunderstanding and Ageism in Bible Interpretation

Recognizing the role preunderstanding plays in gathering and explaining data confirms the interpretive nature of research. Even the gathering of gerontological data is vulnerable to bias intrusions. For example, ageism sometimes appears unconsciously in methodological presuppositions. Researchers may assume negative expectations for elderly and hence stress the frailty of the old. Others assume that aging brings perpetual activity and middle-aged vigor and so conclude that older adults have never been happier.[5] They attribute negative aging experiences to ageism in society.

Biblical interpretation occasionally shows age bias in its conclusions. Interpreters may understand a passage in light of exaggerated negative or optimistic aspects of aging. More often, however, ageism appears in omission of aging issues within a text rather than in direct statements against older people. Still, potential biases about aging need to be isolated to guard against misunderstanding a passage, although accurate appropriation of aging as a paradigm guards against interpretation distortions.

Discussing aging questions within a text sometimes captures biblical concerns better than so-called scientific approaches. Recall that ancient literature elevates older persons and identifies experiences of old age with blessings from God. Familiarity with aging issues often increases the ability of modern interpreters to recover the ancient agenda of the writer. The so-called scientific approach at times unconsciously follows the agenda of a modern youth-oriented society. Consciously looking for significant statements about old age may loosen an interpreter's ties with the present and allow one to understand better the profundity of an ancient document.

Guidelines for Utilizing Aging Paradigm

Utilizing an aging paradigm for interpreting passages does not give an interpreter the right to impose old age concerns on texts. Rather, commentators may consider aging insights only when these fit a passage's inherent form and meaning. Discovery of this dimension, however, helps interpreters move closer to the goal of removing ageism from key presuppositions. Such a methodology enables commentators to recover aging themes and to reemphasize a generation's fears about aging.

Interpretation which takes aging concerns into account accepts aging as a legitimate paradigm of theology.[6] It assumes that aging plays a significant role in human experience. The paradigm recognizes potential contributions old age can make to understanding issues of faith. It explains Scriptures in a more pluralistic and inclusive manner.

Such a methodology, however, must not be used uncritically. Interpreters first must carefully reconstruct the ancient context of a passage and its primary intent(s). The passage also must be analyzed as to its canonical function and meaning. Nevertheless, interpreters complete their study of a text only when they examine it in light of current concerns. In certain texts they must examine aging concerns before they can determine the text's primary thrust. Theologians need not develop a gray theology. Rather, interpreters need to understand passages more inclusively by considering their implications for old age.

Example Utilizing Old Age Paradigm

Genesis 9:20-27

A story about Noah demonstrates how experiences of aging increase the understanding of a passage. The event seems to be set after the flood. Noah plants vineyards and becomes intoxicated on the wine of his harvest. He falls into a drunken stupor in his tent and is lying there asleep and exposed. His three sons come into his tent with different attitudes and results: Ham/Canaan is cursed; Shem and Japheth are blessed.

Commentators raise technical questions about the passage. They point out that incomplete details limit interpretation of the story. Consequently, they find it difficult to decide on the focus of the story. Commentaries discuss the following issues:

— Was Noah the first to plant a vineyard?
— Was he the first to become intoxicated on wine?
— Was Ham or Canaan the son who looked on his father's nakedness?
— What did the passage mean by the statement "look on the nakedness" of another?
— How did Ham/Canaan relate the incident to his brothers after seeing his father?
— If Ham committed the sin against his father, why was his son Canaan cursed?

Attention to aging concerns in the passage does not diminish these questions, but it does encourage an interpreter to focus on the story's central events and messages. Two issues benefit from intergenerational experiences. The first question asks: What was the sin of Noah? Drunkenness? Nakedness? A second relates directly to it: What sin of his son (Ham/Canaan) could prompt a severe curse on Canaan?

I. EMBARRASSMENT IN OLD AGE

The story takes the form of a family narrative even though it focuses on the fortunes of three branches of the human race. Sons of Noah are portrayed as primogenitors of people involved in the political life of Canaan. Though control of Canaan dominates the curse, Noah, the primal ancestor, plays an important role in the events. In a general sense the story provides a literary bridge between the flood narrative and table of nations in Genesis 10. Nevertheless, intergenerational issues in the story demand study of its allusions to family roles. Discussion of Noah's sin needs to consider his role as representative of the older generation. Unfortunately, many commentaries do not elaborate on these dynamics.

Commentaries offer numerous explanations for Noah's radical change of behavior in Genesis 9:18-27. Unlike the righteous and blameless Noah of Genesis 6:9, this Noah drinks too much and passes out lying exposed and vulnerable in his tent. A sample of explanations indicates the variety of opinions and preunderstandings.

1. *Noah became intoxicated out of naiveté.* This argument points out that the narrative includes a remnant of an "inventor saga" (9:20). As the first one to plant a vineyard, Noah could not have suspected that drinking wine would have made him drunk. Hence, he was overpowered by an unknown force.[7]

2. *Noah maintained his sexuality by drinking wine.* Cohen maintains that Noah, like his neighbors, believed that wine increased the procreative abilities. He, like Lot and his daughters, drank wine to fulfill the divine command to populate the earth. So Noah committed no indiscretion by getting drunk and by exposing himself.[8]

3. *Noah became intoxicated because his values deteriorated with age.* Ross points out that the story of Noah follows the pattern of Genesis which in every case describes a deterioration from beginning to end. Noah began as a righteous and blameless person and in old age ended life in a degraded condition. The story illustrates the effects of wine—drunkenness and nakedness.[9]

4. *Noah made himself vulnerable and embarrassed his family.* The narrative is not condemning drunkenness as much as it is using it as an example of a father who embarrasses his family by drinking too much and exposing him-

self. The question the narrative asks is an intergenerational one. Even when a parent acts the fool, does this give a child permission to devalue that parent?

Other views of the incident do not adequately get to the central focus of Noah's behavior. The naiveté argument attempts to justify behavior that the passage does not condemn. Though the account parallels an "inventor saga," that emphasis fades as the account continues.

Likewise, an argument that Noah was increasing his procreative abilities through drinking wine represents another attempt to interpret the Bible in light of comparative religions material. The passage itself does not mention this concern. This explanation does little to clarify the sin of Noah's son.

The third argument assumes an ageist posture. To describe changes in Noah's behavior as a deterioration from youthful righteousness prescribes an "ageist" pattern for the Noahic cycles. That argument assumes a significant passing of time between Genesis 6:9 and 9:20. Despite arguments of Ross, personal life cycles found in Genesis do not fit his deterioration scheme, nor does the passage focus on Noah's standards of behavior as much as it does on the responses of his sons to that behavior. It borders on ageism to attribute the drunkenness and nakedness of Noah to a deterioration of his values as he aged.

Though some help can be found in each interpretation, the fourth argument best explains intergenerational dynamics in the incident. The story assumes that parents at times embarrass grown children and make themselves and family members vulnerable to ridicule. Experience shows that older people behave unwisely at times. Age never guarantees wisdom. This interpretation unifies the two elements of the passage and leads to the second issue.

The second issue deals with the following questions. Does parental indiscretion give children grounds for dishonoring a vulnerable elder? Would a child behaving in this way violate the fifth commandment to honor parents (Ex. 20:12) and laws related to it (Deut. 5:16; Lev. 19:3; Ex. 21:15,17)? These concerns focus discussion on a second intergenerational concern: What was the sin of Noah's son which warranted the curse on Canaan?

II. The Disrespectful Child

Commentators discuss Ham's impropriety in a variety of ways and propose a number of solutions. The severity of the curse on Canaan and his descendents indicates to them that the text considers his acts an affront to decency. What caused the affront is discussed along the following lines:

1. *The son's act includes sexual exploitation or elder abuse.* As early as the Talmud, sages understood the account of Ham's act as an allusion to sexual abuse. Tha sages record an argument on this matter between Rav and Samuel (B. Sanhedrin 70a). One maintained that Ham castrated Noah and

the other suggested that he abused him sexually. Ibn Ezra commented on v. 24: "Scripture has not revealed what was done."[10]

Some commentators quote parallel stories from Canaanite myths that tell how the god El-Kronos emasculated his father. They point out that a Hittite legend mentions a Kumarbis who severed the genitals of his father, the god Anu. The Midrash portrays Ham as laughing at his father as did Kumarbis. Both Ham and Kumarbis are cursed for their deeds. These commentators assume that Ham/Canaan's atrocity was not mentioned because it was a repulsive crime of sexual abuse.

Other modern commentaries note that the son may have done more than view the nakedness of his father. The phrase "look upon the nakedness" occasionally refers to sexual relations (Lev. 20:17). On this basis some interpreters assume that the son performed some sexual act with his father.[11]

2. *The son does not harm Noah and is only a clan primogenitor.* Some commentators view this passage as a harmonization of stories about two primogenitors of separate clans living in Canaan and/or Northern Africa. Since Canaan was cursed by Noah, Canaan, not Ham, must have violated his father. Since the deeds of the two are harmonized in the text, the problem remains otherwise unresolved.[12]

3. *The son ridicules the religion of Noah.* Though this view is not as widespread as the other two, as long ago as Calvin writers have suggested that Ham was laughing at Noah in rebellion; he ridiculed Noah himself and therefore also what Noah believed.[13]

4. *The son hurts Noah by having intercourse with his father's wife (incest).* Since the punishment was so great, one commentator suggests that Ham uncovered the nakedness of his mother when he looked on the nakedness of Noah.[14] Some justification for this view can be found in the terminology of Leviticus 18:7-8, 11. Nevertheless, arguing from silence or from parallel terminology leads to subjective conclusions. Solid exegesis interprets a passage from data that appears in the document.

5. *The son shows disrespect for his father.* The phrase "looking on his father's nakedness" herein is interpreted as desecrating a natural and sacred barrier between child and parent. Aging concerns emphasize the enormity of such violations of filial duties. Ham committed an outrage by leaving his father exposed. He aggravated it by telling his brothers. They then honored their father by discreetly covering his shame and protecting his honor. Ham tarnished his father's dignity by leaving him exposed and vulnerable and by telling others of his father's plight. A faithful child would have covered his father's nakedness and would have protected his honor from further ridicule.[15]

Respect for father, even an intoxicated one, is a wide-spread ancient social value. An Ugaritic (Canaanite) epic, "The Tale of Aqhat," requires taking care of a drunken father among duties that a son should perform for this father (2 AQHT:I Col.: 11, 31-32, ANET, 150).

Commentators need not explain Genesis 9:20-27 as an example of elder abuse. Arguments of sexual exploitation, incest or religious ridicule do not recognize the importance of filial obligations. Such viewpoints search for additional reasons for the curse on Canaan. Recognition of the primogenitor roles of Ham/Canaan does not exclude consideration of intergenerational implications in this incident. To speculate about some outrageous behavior or to leave the event unresolved ignores available evidence.

An interpreter sensitive to aging issues will recognize the importance of filial respect for the welfare of elders. The commentator thereby will note that the passage addresses neglect by adult children of parental emotional and physical needs in old age. Such an interpreter can accept lessons from the passage as it exists. The approach combines insights about aging with historical grammatical exegesis to clarify interpretation options.

SUMMARY OF INTERPRETATION

Clarification of Genesis 9:20-27 provides an example of how addressing experiences of aging helps an interpreter move beyond technical questions and sensationalism to focus on important themes of a text. Answers to basic questions of this text point out that the elderly sometimes behave in foolish ways. Foolishness, however, does not negate filial responsibilities to respect and honor even weak and exposed parents.

The punishment of Canaan (subjection and slavery) may seem severe unless interpreters take into account the role filial respect plays in social stability. Noah's curse reinforces its crucial status. When understood in this way, the passage undergirds unconditional support for aging, dependent parents. A drunken Noah embarasses his children. Still, respect which Shem and Japheth render their vulnerable father becomes an example for other adults who likewise care for frail and imperfect elders.

Breaking an interpreter's hermeneutical circle demands careful study of data that exists as well as isolation of preunderstandings that can distort the explanation. Asking accurate and appropriate questions of the text in light of aging experiences helps eliminate age bias. It is important to discover what the text means as well as what it meant and the two questions are not as separate as they may at first appear.

Implications for Social Science Interpretation

Explanation of social data, likewise, can be influenced by an interpreter's hermeneutical circle. For example, failure to question thoroughly preunderstandings of a project can lead scientists into gathering inaccurate data and into stating false conclusions. Western society generally misinterprets the experience of aging to such a degree that researchers must take extra precautions to achieve some measure of freedom from these views. On top of this, aging issues are personal ones that rarely are viewed objectively. Social research, therefore, must follow a rigorous discipline or it also can present speculative or misguided interpretations. At least three principles remain crucial:

First, researchers must carefully examine preunderstandings before gathering or interpreting data. The interpreter must be the first object of study. Once a researcher/interpreter understands how a hermeneutical circle dominates the assumptions of a research project, a scientist may state and bracket those preunderstandings and perceptively analyze its data. Secondly, results from social research must be examined only in light of available evidence. To do otherwise leads to speculation and flawed conclusions. Third, evidence must be evaluated in the context of a variety of aging experiences as related by those who age. This provides a larger context for gathering data and determining assumptions for researchers. Once these three principles go into effect, a researcher can interpret more accurately experiences of aging and learn from them as well. Such methodologies increase the self-reflective quality of social research and thereby improve the results of its critique.

Notes

1. Cf. D. G. Burke, "Interpret; Interpretation," *International Standard Bible Encyclopedia*, (ISBE) *2*, 861-863. James A. Sanders, "Hermeneutics," IDB, supplementary vol., 402-407; Walter C. Kaiser, *Toward an Exegetical Theology*. (Grand Rapids, MI: Baker, 1981), 17-40; and Donald S. Ferguson, *Biblical Hermeneutics, An Introduction*. (Atlanta: John Knox Press, 1986), 4-6.

2. E.g., W. Dilthey, "The Rise of Hermeneutics," F. Jameson, tr., *New Literary History: A Journal of Theory and Interpretation, 3*, No. 2, (1972):229-244; John B. Thompson, *Critical Hermeneutics, A Study in the Thought of Paul Ricoeur and Jurgen Habermas* (Cambridge: Cambridge University Press, 1981), 150-181.

3. Cf. D. P. Fuller, "Interpretation, History of." ISBE, *2*, 863-874.

4. Ferguson, 6-22; Thompson, 36-70; and Paul Ricoeur, *Essays on Biblical Interpretation*, (Philadelphia: Fortress Press, 1980), 49-57.

5. Thomas R. Cole, "The 'Enlightened' View of Aging: Victorian Morality in a New Key," Hastings Center Report (June, 1983), 34-40, argues that ageism appears in the debunking of myths of aging as well as in deep prejudices against the elderly. He disagrees with the views of Robert N. Butler [*Why Survive* (New York: Harper and Row, 1975), 11-12].

6. See David Maldonaldo, "Towards a Theology of Aging in the Christian Community" (Unpublished ms. delivered at NICA, Washington, D.C., November 11-13, 1985), 2ff. W. Paul Jones, ["Theology and Aging in the 21st Century," *Journal of Religion and Aging*, *3*, Nos 1/2 (1986):30-31] outlines several features of a "Gerontheology." Stephen Sapp, [*Full of Years: Aging and the Elderly in the Bible and Today*. (Nashville: Abingdon Press, 1987), 20-25], discusses ethical dimensions that arise out of this reflection. Cf. also J. Gordon Harris, *Biblical Perspectives on Aging: God and the Elderly*, (Philadelphia: Fortress Press, 1987), 3-10.

7. Cf. S. R. Driver, *The Book of Genesis*, Westminster Commentaries (London: Methuen & Co., 1904), 109, and D. C. Allen, *The Legend of Noah* (Urbana, IL: Illini Books, 1963), 73.

8. H. H. Cohen, *The Drunkenness of Noah* (Alabama: University of Alabama Press, 1974), 3-8.

9. Cf. Allen P. Ross, "The Curse of Canaan," *Bibliotheca Sacra* (1980): 226-27.

10. See U. Cassuto, *A Commentary on the Book of Genesis, II*, tr. Israel Abrahams (Jerusalem: Magnes Press, 1964), 150-151 and W. Gunther Plaut, *The Torah, Genesis, A Modern Commentary* (New York: Union of American Hebrew Congregations, 1974), 83-86. Note also discussion in Jack P. Lewis, *Study of the Interpretation of Noah and the Flood in Jewish and Christian Literature* (Leiden: Brill, 1968), 153.

11. See Terry Fretheim, *Creation Fall and Flood*, (Minneapolis, MN: Augsburg, 1969), 119. Gerhard von Rad, *Genesis*, Old Testament Library (Philadelphia: Westminster, 1961), 133, assumes that some horrible deed is concealed by the narrator.

12. E.g., E. A. Speiser, *Genesis*, Anchor Bible, 61-62 and Gene Rice, "The Curse That Never Was, (Gen. 9:18-27)," *Journal of Religious Thought, 29* (1972):5-6.

13. Cf. John Calvin, *Commentaries on the First Book of Moses Called Genesis*, I (Grand Rapids, MI: Eerdmans, 1948), 302, and Robert Candlish, *Studies in Genesis* (Grand Rapids: Kregel, 1979), 158-59, and James M. Boice, *Genesis*, 1 (Grand Rapids: Zondervan, 1982):321.

14. Cf. F. W. Bassett, "Noah's Nakedness and the Curse on Canaan: A Case of Incest," *Vetus Testamentum 21* (1971):232. Bassett argues that Canaan was cursed because he was born as a result of the incest.

15. *Commentaries on Genesis* by G. Ch. Aalders, Bible Students Commentary, (Grand Rapids, MI: Zondervan, 1981), 203, W. Brueggemann, Interpretation (Atlanta: John Knox, 1982), 90-91, C. Westermann, *Genesis 1-11*, tr. John J. Scullion, (Minneapolis: Augsburg, 1984), 488-489 indicate that the primary focus in the story is upon respect for one's father. Westermann concludes that the statement when Ham "saw his father's nakedness" can only be taken literally in this narrative.

Chapter 4

From Quantitative to Qualitative Reasoning: A Developmental Perspective

ALLAN B. CHINEN

The general thesis of this volume is that human science methodologies are essential for a complete understanding of adult development. In the present chapter, I discuss the complement of the thesis: I argue that a developmental approach is essential for understanding the human sciences—and the natural ones, too. In particular, I argue that quantitative and qualitative modes of understanding mature at different times in the life cycle. Abstract, scientific thinking peaks during the first half of life, while rigorous, humanistic reasoning flowers in the second (Lehman, 1953; Frenkel, 1936; Buhler, 1968).

Dramatic examples of this pattern come from prominent scientists: Nobel laureates like Jonas Salk, Jacques Monod and Linus Pauling turned toward humanistic social concerns later in life. But the second careers of such individuals are often considered inferior to their first ones, and their later work is sometimes dismissed as pontification. The shift from quantitative to qualitative thinking is therefore often attributed to decline in abstract reasoning or "fluid intelligence" (Botwinick, 1977). However, a handful of remarkable individuals have produced widely different work in youth and maturity, with both periods acknowledged to be highly significant. I propose to look at two such unusual individuals, in an attempt to analyze the complex and intriguing developmental relationships between quantitative and qualitative reasoning.

The two individuals are philosophers—Ludwig Wittgenstein and Alfred North Whitehead. The reason for studying philosophers rather than scientists is that philosophers habitually reflect and comment upon their reasoning, so their writing directly reveals how they think. Both men also lived in a deeply scientific period—indeed, Wittgenstein helped shape the doctrine of scientific positivism. But both ultimately turned from the purely scientific model. Their shift from quantitative to qualitative reasoning is all the more dramatic.

While other research has looked at creativity and productivity over the life cycle (Simonton, 1985; Dennis, 1966; Lehman, 1953), most studies have been quantitative—counting up the number of works produced, and the frequency with which these contributions are cited by others. Subtle changes in reasoning, however, can only be detected by analyzing the content and style of the individual's major work. I propose to do that in this chapter. By focusing on Wittgenstein and Whitehead, I implicitly take them to be paradigms of adult development. This is a "great persons" approach to human psychology and a few comments on this methodology are in order.

A variant of the idiographic case study approach, the "great persons" perspective has a long tradition behind it, ranging from antiquity to more recent work by Erikson, Maslow and Jung. The weakness of this approach is readily apparent: what is true of great persons is often not applicable to anybody else, especially when dealing with special talents or genius. But this limitation, paradoxically, is also a virtue: the study of great persons can illuminate human *potential*, delineating what *can* happen, and not what *commonly* occurs. A great person approach thus reveals *ideal* rather than *average* adult development. This is important in the study of aging for several reasons. First, in contrast to children's development, which is marked by fairly universal events, adult development involves increasing variability and idiosyncracy. If the main concern about children is "What is normal?" the question for adults, faced with more options, is: "What shall I be?" Great persons help answer that question by offering ideals of maturity; and such ideals are sorely needed in a society that equates aging with decline. Secondly, culture and environment influence adult development, perhaps more than with children. But great persons are those who break free from prevailing traditions and *set* the conventions for succeeding generations. A great persons approach, then, offers a picture of human potential, less hampered by social constraints.

I shall start my discussion with Wittgenstein, because the changes in his thinking are dramatically clear, and then proceed to Whitehead. With both men my aim is not to provide a complete psychobiography, but rather to offer an account of adult cognitive development. I will accordingly focus on work they wrote for publication, taking those papers to be examples of their best thinking.[1] I shall conclude this chapter by reviewing recent research in adult cognition, and discussing the methodological implications of a developmental shift from quantitative to qualitative modes of reasoning.

Wittgenstein

Some background is helpful in understanding Wittgenstein's remarkable intellectual career (Rhees, 1984; Malcolm, 1967). Born in Austria in 1889,

Wittgenstein's earliest work was in engineering, and he had a particular interest in aeronautics. He enrolled at the University of Manchester as a research engineering student and while there, designed a jet engine. Wittgenstein subsequently became interested in mathematics, and at the age of twenty-three went to study under Bertrand Russell in Cambridge. He left the university a year later, and from 1913-1914, lived in a small hut in Norway, working on various topics in logic and philosophy. When World War I broke out, Wittgenstein enlisted and served with distinction in the Austrian artillery. Like Descartes, who began his famous *Meditations* while serving in the army, Wittgenstein completed his first philosophical work during war: indeed, he took the manuscript with him when captured as a military prisoner. Later published as the *Tractatus Logico-Philosophicus*, Wittgenstein's first philosophical work explored the nature of language and was immediately hailed as a major accomplishment. The *Tractatus* amply reveals Wittgenstein's youthful thinking to be 1) precise, 2) reductive, 3) abstract, 4) cognitive and 5) declarative. Quotes from Wittgenstein's work are perhaps the best way to communicate his youthful mode of reasoning. Fortunately, a detailed understanding of his philosophy is not necessary to appreciate his style of thought.

"Everything that can be thought at all can be thought clearly," Wittgenstein insisted. "Everthing that can be put into words can be put clearly" (4.116)[2] *Precision* was his ideal, and Wittgenstein impatiently rejected ambiguities. These goals were attainable, Wittgenstein felt, by adopting highly *reductive* methodologies. Such an approach would reveal the basic, clear-cut structure of both language and the world. "Every statement about complexes can be resolved into a statement about their constituents and into the propositions that describe the complexes completely" (2.0201). No matter how complicated a sentence was, Wittgenstein argued, it could be broken down into more manageable units, and a complete characterization provided. The same, he insisted, applied to the world and its objects (2.021ff). "The world divides into facts" (1.2), he wrote, and "Each item can be the case or not the case while everything else remains the same" (1.21, see also 2.062, 4.023). Hence, we can isolate facts, and study them, one by one, without fear of ambiguities, or complicating interactions. By reducing language and the world to its basic elements, we attain precise and absolute knowledge of both. The analogy to quantitative scientific reasoning, with its emphasis on reduction and precision is quite evident here.

Of course, Wittgenstein recognized that many aspects of human experience cannot be made clear and definite—he was not blind to the realm of values, intuition and mystical issues. He simply excluded those areas from inquiry. Basically, he argued that we either can or cannot talk about an issue. If we can talk about it, we can be precise and reductive. If we cannot talk about it, then there is no problem to discuss. "When the answer cannot be put into words, neither can the question be put into words. The riddle does not exist. If a question can be framed at all, it is also *possible* to answer it" (6.5). More baldly Wittegenstein asserted, "We feel that even when all *possible* scientific questions have been answered, the problems of life remain completely untouched. Of course, there are then no questions left and this itself is the answer" (6.52). "The solution of the problem of life is seen in the vanishing of the problem" (6.521). He essentially *reduced* all problems to verbal expressions.

The thrust of Wittgenstein's thinking is clearly *abstract*, seeking *a priori* knowledge. By analyzing the nature of language, he sought "the essence of all description and thus the essence of the world" (5.4711). He believed that language governs our concepts, and thus fixes our understanding of nature. Empirical facts were of less interest to him: "We can describe the world completely by means of fully generalized propositions," Wittgenstein wrote, "i.e. without first correlating any name with a particular object" (5.526). Wittgenstein's model was mathematics with its universal, abstract truths (4.5, 5.471, 5.4711, 6.1232), and he organized the *Tractatus* in the fashion of a mathematical argument. Indeed, the examples he uses to dramatize his points are extremely abstract and often involve dense logical and mathematical notation—illustrations only a mathematician or logician could enjoy.

The dominating interest in the *Tractatus* is *cognitive* and descriptive and this contrasts sharply, as we shall see, with his later work. Indeed, the youthful Wittgenstein argues that the fundamental nature of language is descriptive. "A proposition is a picture of reality," he wrote. "A proposition is a model of reality as we imagine it" (4.01; also 4.016). Essentially, Wittgenstein held that names correspond to objects, and the organization of names into sentences corresponds to the organization of objects in the world, the way the arrangement of shapes in a portrait reproduces the appearance of the objects portrayed.

Throughout the *Tractatus*, Wittgenstein's style can best be described as confident and *declarative*. He makes sweeping statements, almost in an *ex cathedra* manner. He accordingly does not discuss possible objections from readers nor attempt to answer them in advance. Youthful idealism, ambition and self-confidence infuse Wittgenstein's early work.

The qualities of Wittgenstein's early thought, I argue, are the defining features of quantitative scientific reasoning. (Indeed, this is one reason for analyzing Wittgenstein's early thinking—it sheds much light on the nature of scientific reasoning). The importance of precision, abstraction, reduction and description in science is undoubtedly self-evident, but the connection between Wittgenstein's philosophical reasoning and *quantitative* thought requires explanation. Science, no less than the youthful Wittgenstein, seeks to define basic units of analysis, independent of the contexts in which those units occur. Hence physicists define atoms and subatomic particles, irrespective of whether the atom comes from a rock or a rooster. In just the same way, Wittgenstein sought the logical atoms of meaning, independent of what particular words or sentences were said. Abstracting physical or logical units from their contexts makes them equivalent to each other. Their idiosyncratic features are ignored. Hence they can be tallied up, counted and treated statistically: numbers, after all, are units abstracted from all context (Chinen, 1987b, 1986a). While science goes on to treat its data quantitatively, Wittgenstein did not, but his basic abstract, reductive approach implies a quantitative perspective.[3]

Despite the wide admiration that the *Tractatus* earned him, Wittgenstein soon gave up philosophy, left the intellectual ferment of Cambridge and became an elementary school teacher in rural Austria. Although he inherited a considerable fortune from his father, Wittgenstein gave it away to family and charity. During this time, he tried a variety of vocations: he contemplated entering a monastery, designed his sister's mansion and participated from time to time in the Vienna Circle of philosophers, which was then promulgating scientific positivism. In 1929, at the age of forty, Wittgenstein returned to Cambridge, and received his doctorate on the strength of the *Tractatus*. He was appointed a Fellow of Trinity College, but at the age of forty-seven, he retired to a hut in Norway once more. There he began working on what later became the *Philosophical Investigations*. Wittgenstein then returned to Cambridge and in 1939 was appointed to the prestigious chair in philosophy previously held by the eminent, late G. E. Moore. When World War II broke out, however, Wittgenstein left the university and served as an orderly in a hospital. Afterward he returned to Cambridge, but soon resigned his chair, and went to live in rural Ireland. He completed the *Philosophical Investigations* there in 1948 and died a few years later, at the age of sixty-two, felled by cancer at the height of a remarkable career.

Like the *Tractatus*, the *Philosophical Investigations* is widely regarded as a seminal contribution to philosophy. Both works focus on the nature of language, but the two diverge dramatically in substance and style.

In contrast to the precise, reductive, abstract, cognitive and declarative tone of the *Tractatus*, the *Philosophical Investigations* is 1) concrete, 2) tolerant of ambiguity, 3) contextual, 4) pragmatic and 5) dialectical. Again, direct quotes are the best way to appreciate his new style of thinking, and a detailed understanding of Wittgenstein's philosophy is not necessary for this purpose.

First of all, the mature Wittgenstein rejects the abstract *a priori* approach so characteristic of the *Tractatus* (#97, #100, #101).[4] "The more narrowly we examine actual language, the sharper becomes the conflict between it and our requirement," Wittgenstein wrote, referring to his youthful ideal of precision and clarity. "For the crystalline purity of logic was, of course, not a *result of investigation* it was a requirement. The conflict becomes intolerable; the requirement is now in danger of becoming empty.—We have got on to slippery ice where there is no friction and so in a sense the conditions are ideal, but also, just because of that, we are unable to walk. We want to walk: so we need *friction*. Back to the rough ground!" (#107). That "rough ground" is simply everyday life, and Wittgenstein spends most of his time in the *Philosophical Investigations* reflecting on concrete problems from ordinary experience. Indeed, the genius of this mature work lies in the many subtle and perceptive insights Wittgenstein reveals in ordinary events. The shift from the abstract, mathematical and logical examples of the *Tractatus* to *concrete* problem-solving is dramatic.

In grappling with everyday experiences, Wittgenstein recognizes the importance and unavoidable nature of *ambiguity*. He gives up trying to make precise, logical definitions, as he attempted in the *Tractatus*, and settles instead for the more indefinite notion of "family resemblances" (#66, #67; also #71, #79). He notes, for instance, that no single definition of a game includes all possible varieties: Olympic games differ from tiddlywinks, or playing with the cat. But together games constitute an extended family, with varying degrees of similarity to each other—the way brothers look more alike than cousins. The mature Wittgenstein thus acknowledged ambiguous distinctions, and in-between cases: "What is most difficult here is to put this indefiniteness, correctly and unfalsified, into words" (#227e). Instead of excluding vague or inarticulate meanings, Wittgenstein now embraced them. "Given the two ideas 'fat' and 'lean', would you be rather inclined to say that Wednesday was fat and Tuesday lean, or vice versa? (I incline decisively toward the former.)" (#216e). The wry humor of this quotation, I should also note, is another new element in the *Philosophical Investigations*, and contrasts with the serious, inspired tone of the *Tractatus*[5].

In contrast to his youthful reductionism, which focused on fundamental units of logic and reality, independent from anything else, the mature Wittgenstein emphasizes the importance of *context*. He rejects the notion—so central to the *Tractatus*—that a word or sentence can have a logical meaning in itself, independent of anything else (#155, #188e): "The question is: 'In what sort of context does it occur?'" (#188e). Here Wittgenstein introduced his seminal concept of a "language game," arguing that words and sentences have meaning only for a group of people who follow a system of rules, like any other game. And language games, in turn, are situated within "forms of life" (#23)—patterns of behavior, like tradition and convention. Consequently, the meaning of language is relative to particular situations. Wittgenstein emphasized repeatedly that a major determinant of meaning is the purpose with which language is used, and he noted that even the concepts of precision and certainty vary, depending upon the situation (#243). "No *single* ideal of exactness has been laid down; we do not know what we should be supposed to imagine under this head" (#88).

If the youthful Wittgenstein felt that logical analysis offered *the* complete account of language, the mature philosopher recognized the limits of any single description, including his own: "We want to establish an order in our knowledge of the use of language: an order with a particular end in view; one out of many possible orders; not *the* order" (#131, also #133, #199e, #200e). He scaled back his youthful ambitions considerably: "In giving all these examples, I am not aiming at some kind of completeness, some classification of psychological concepts. They are only meant to enable the reader to shift for himself when he encounters conceptual difficulties" (#206e).

Pragmatic considerations clearly come to dominate the thought of the mature Wittgenstein. If description and cognition were the chief concerns of the *Tractatus, practical use and action* is that of the *Philosophical Investigations*. Wittgenstein, for instance, came to reject the view that description is the essence of language—the central thesis of the *Tractatus*. He asserted instead that language has many uses. "What we call '*descriptions*' are instruments for particular uses. Think of a machine-drawing, a cross-section, an elevation with measurements, which an engineer has before him. Thinking of a description as a word-picture of the facts has something misleading about it: one tends to think only of such pictures as hang on our walls: which seem simply to portray how a thing looks, what it is like. (These pictures are as it were idle.)" (#291; also #23, #304). Indeed, Wittgenstein emphasized the instrumental function of language over its cognitive and descriptive elements (#43): "Think of the tools in a tool-box; there is a hammer, pliers, a saw, a screw-driver, a rule, a glue-pot, glue nails and screw—The functions of words are as diverse as the functions of these objects. (And in both cases there are similarities)" (#11). Indeed, in the *Philosophical Investigations*, Wittgenstein does not attempt to *describe* what language is, so much as *demonstrate* what it does. He does not, for instance, *talk* about the abstract limits of language, as he does in the *Tractatus* (5.6, 4.121, 4.126). Instead, he *shows* what language can or cannot do, with detailed discussions of concrete examples. Action rather than description characterizes the style of the *Philosophical Investigations*.

Even more generally, the later Wittgenstein argued that understanding can involve action quite apart from language. "I may recognize a genuine loving look, distinguishing it from a pretended one. ... But I may be quite incapable of describing the difference. And this is not because the languages I know have no words for it. For why not introduce new words?" (228e). This kind of practical understanding exceeds the capacity of language to capture, but is an everyday experience. In reflecting on relationships with people, like friends, Wittgenstein wrote: "My attitude towards him is an attitude towards a soul. I am not of the *opinion* that he has a soul" (#178e). That is, the individual acts in a certain way and does not merely utter words (#174, #177, #201).

The confident, declarative and almost pontifical tone of the *Tractatus*, becomes conversational and inquisitive—dialectical—in the *Philosophical Investigations*. The mature Wittgenstein makes no sweeping statements, but rather raises questions. The general format of the *Philosophical Investiga-tions* is something like this: is such and such true? Well, not quite, because of this example from daily life. Well, then, is so and so true? Again, not quite, because of this other example. . . .

The dialectical spirit of Wittgenstein's later thought is summed up in his famous argument against introspective knowledge. In contrast to most phi-losophers of his day, who insisted that introspection upon private experience delivered absolutely certain knowledge, Wittgenstein argued that a solitary individual could never know whether he was right or wrong. An individual might invent rules for himself, but never be certain whether he followed them correctly or not. Only interactions with other people permit us to correct our mistakes (#268). "Do not ask youself," he wrote, "'How does it work with *me*'—Ask 'What do I know about someone else?' " (#206e). More dramatically, he advised, "Do not try to analyze your own inner experience" (#204e). A dialectical thrust is evident here, but practiced, rather than simply preached.

Wittgenstein's mature thinking, then, is concrete, contextual, relativistic, pragmatic and dialectical. It corresponds less with traditional scientific thought, than certain varieties of the "human sciences," as I shall elaborate further on.

Alfred North Whitehead

Although an influential figure in twentieth-century thought, there have been few biographies of Whetehead, much less psychological analyses (Lowe, 1985). He was an intensely private individual, kept few personal notes, and had his wife destroy those after his death (Lowe, 1962, 1985; cf. Whitehead, 1941). While his emotional life can therefore only be inferred, his cognitive development is directly accessible: he was a productive writer, and his publi-cations reveal the development of his thinking.[6]

Whitehead's intellectual odyssey can be divided into three phases—first, involving science and mathematics, second, involving education and the phi-losophy of science and finally, involving metaphysics and theology. He began his career as a mathematician, and was elected to the Royal Society for his work. The titles of this period are instructive. "On the Motion of Viscous Incom-pressible Fluids" was completed at twenty-five years of age, and *A Treatise of Universal Algebra* at thirty-seven. In the latter, Whitehead proposed a formal conceptualization of addition and multiplication that would hold for all alge-bras. The work is precise, abstract, reductive and *a priori*, and is very much similar in spirit to Wittgenstein's *Tractatus*. Whitehead also published "On Mathematical Concepts of the Material World" when he was thirty-seven. In this second work, Whitehead presented a description of space and time based on mathematical vectors, rather than discrete points. The latter, of course, is the traditional Euclidean, Cartesian and Newtonian view of space. Whitehead was inspired in these mathematical-scientific projects by Maxwell's recent work on electricity (Lowe, 1985), which seemed to prove that mathematics was an *a priori* key to physics, and thus to all of nature.

Whitehead was intensely interested in religious and ethical questions in his youth. His father was a minister as was one of his brothers. Whitehead himself was a member of "the Apostles" group at Cambridge—an elite intellectual group which often debated religious and ethical issues. While an undergraduate, however, Whitehead explicitly put aside his religious interests, and turned to mathematics and logic. Like Wittgenstein, Whitehead suspended the ambiguous and elusive realm of religion and ethics, in order to pursue rigorous, logical studies.

After joining the faculty of Trinity College, Whitehead collaborated with Bertrand Russell on the *Principia Mathematica*. Together they analyzed mathematics into a finite number of basic logical concepts and rules. The work, published when Whitehead was forty-nine years of age, is still considered a *tour de force* of logical analysis. It is abstract, *a priori*, precise and reductive.

In 1914, Whitehead left his mathematics post in Cambridge and moved to London. The change was somewhat risky because Whitehead had no new position in London. Although biographical material is scanty, Whitehead appears to have been going through a mid-life transition. Whitehead was soon appointed professor of mathematics at the Imperial College, and later became dean there. Active on numerous Royal Commissions concerning British education, Whitehead published several essays in the field. "The Principles of Mathematics in Relation to Elementary Teaching" appeared when he was fifty-one, "The Aims of Education," when he was fifty-five, and "Technical Education and Its Relation to Science and Literature," the following year.

Whitehead's philosophy of education reflects a major shift from his mathematical-scientific period. Where he sought abstract, *a priori* universal knowledge in his early work, at mid-life Whitehead came to stress the importance of *concrete particulars*: "We shall ruin mathematical education if we use it merely to impress general truths. The general ideas are the means of connecting particular results. After all, it is the concrete special cases which are important" (1917, p. 47).

The older Whitehead, like the older Wittgenstein, rejected the ideal of precision and abstraction. Whitehead now affirmed the importance of context, and the unavoidable presence of *ambiguity*. This change can be seen particularly clearly in Whitehead's philosophy of science. He argued that the traditional scientific concept of objective, quantifiable entities is simply an abstract fiction (Whitehead, 1919, 1920; Lawrence, 1968; Lowe, 1962). "I insist," Whitehead wrote, "on the radically untidy, ill-adjusted character of the fields of actual experience from which science starts. This fact is concealed by the influence of language, molded by science, which foists on us exact concepts as though they represented the immediate deliverances of experience. The result is that we imagine that we have immediate experience of a world of perfectly defined objects implicated in perfectly defined events ... the neat, trim, tidy, exact world which is the goal of scientific thought" (Whitehead, 1917, p. 110).

In particular, Whitehead rejected the notion of an independent entity that could be defined and studied by itself—a central postulate of reductive science. Whitehead proposed an alternative view, which he called the "method of extensive abstraction" (1917, 1919). Precisely defined entities, he argued, are constructed from a sophisticated process of abstraction. A point, for instance, involves a process of delineating a volume of area, and then imagining that volume becoming progressively smaller and smaller, *ad infinitum*. The limit of this progression is the abstract mathematical ideal of a dimensionless point.

In essence, Whitehead emphasized the importance of *context* and *action* in defining an object or an event: a point is defined in terms of its surrounding space, and the action of imagining smaller and smaller volumes. A quotation taken from a slightly later period in his life dramatizes Whitehead's new contextual perspective: "The question is not True? or False? but When? and Where?" (1929). Whitehead's new relativistic stance is quite clear here, and contrasts with his youthful endeavor to find universal abstract truths.

Whitehead also came to emphasize *action* over pure, abstract intellectual reflection. A practical, performative attitude emerges in his writing at mid-life, just as we saw with Wittgenstein. "The insistence in the Platonic culture on disinterested intellectual appreciation is a pshychological error. ... This essential intervention of action in science is often overlooked" (1917, p. 37).

In short, Whitehead shifted from a precise, abstract, *a priori*, reductive and declarative mode of reasoning in his youth, to a concrete, pragmatic, contextual and relativistic spirit at mid-life. Wittgenstein made the same transition, and it is interesting to note that both men were involved in teaching and education at the time of their shifts: Wittgenstein taught elementary school children in Austria, and Whitehead was dean at the Imperial College in London.

In 1924, at the age of sixty-three, Whitehead was appointed a professor of philosophy at Harvard. Instead of retiring from active life, he began his final phase, writing philosophical and theological essays. His initial work includes *Science and the Modern World*, given as the Lowell Lectures at Harvard when Whitehead wax sixty-four, and *Religion in the Making*, from a year later. In this final period, Whitehead shifted from a focus on concrete practical applications, to a metaphysical emphasis on meaning and consciousness. He became one of the few twentieth-century philosophers to attempt a comprehensive metaphysical account of the world, integrating recent developments in science with traditional humanistic and religious concepts. Wittgenstein did not demonstrate a similar development, but as noted earlier, he died prematurely of cancer, at the age of sixty-two. Whitehead started his metaphysical writing after sixty-four.

In contrast to many scientists and philosophers who turn to metaphysics late in life, Whitehead's contributions have had a significant influence in contemporary theology. His later work, then, must be taken seriously, and cannot be dismissed as cognitive decline, or personal pontification. What is particularly interesting is that Whitehead's later writings reveal a distinctive third mode of reasoning, which might be described as unitary, cosmological and intuitive.

An important theme in Whitehead's metaphysics, for instance, is what Lowe characterizes as a panpsychic outlook (Lowe, 1962), the view that all things have some kind of sentience, so that man and nature, mind and body, are really one (Lawrence, 1968). Indeed, Whitehead attributed a basic sort of sentience to inorganic objects like molecules, and argued that conscious experience is merely a special case of a primordial sentience present in all things. He accordingly considered the traditional distinction between "mind" and "matter" to be an abstraction derived from a more basic, unified species of sentience, which Whitehead called "perceptivity": "... the most individual actual entity is a definite act of perceptivity. So matter and mind ... must be relatively abstract" (Whitehead, 1926, p. 95). The universe is unitary, and dichotomies are imposed upon it by abstraction.

Whitehead also emphasized how values are intrinsic to nature and not merely projected there by individuals: " 'Value' is the word I use for the intrinsic reality of an event" (Whitehead, 1925, p. 136). So the mature Whitehead embraces all the things he had excluded from his youthful work—questions of value, meaning and as we shall see, God. He integrates consciousness with material phenomena, in a new unitary mode of thinking.

Whitehead later elaborated these views in *Process and Reality*, published when he was sixty-eight years of age, although they were more accessibly presented in *Adventures of Ideas*, published when Whitehead was seventy-two, and *Modes of Thought*, at seventy-seven. God appears prominently in his work at this time, along with questions about ultimate meanings, and the origin of the world. We might therefore call this type of thinking "cosmological,"[7] especially to contrast it with the pragmatic reasoning of Whitehead's middle years.

A central concept in Whitehead's third period of thought was the notion of process: "It is true that nothing is finally understood until its reference to process has been made evident" (Whitehead, 1938, p. 46). Whitehead's concept of process was modeled on the notion of a vector, which had fascinated him in his youth. His concept, though, now took on mystical connotations.

Process is the fundamental feature of all reality, he argued, involving a dynamic movement from a finite or particular thing, to infinite, unknown horizons: "In process the finite possibilities of the universe travel towards their infinitude of realization" (1938, p. 54).

Whitehead argued that we are normally not aware of process, and focus instead on particular objects. Those objects are abstractions, however, extracted from a vast, underlying sentient process in the world. Process, in a sense, elaborates or articulates particular objects, which constitute secondary realities. God, Whitehead added, is the origin and guarantor of the cosmologic process: ". . . that ultimate unity of direction in the universe" (Whitehead, 1938, p. 49). In turning toward indefinite processes, rather than concrete objects, or abstract precision, Whitehead's final mode of thinking may be called "intuitive": it does not depend upon sensual observations, or on intellectual analysis, but rather on a basic kind of "prehension" or primordial sentience.

Stylistically, Whitehead retained something of a declarative tone in his later writings. Unlike Wittgenstein, Whitehead did not shift toward a conversational style. Whitehead, however, did begin writing more popular works in maturity, in contrast to the dense, abstract reasoning of his early mathematical publications. Interestingly, Whitehead began to include more and more vivid metaphors and analogies in his mature writing, turning to real human life for illustrations of his points, rather than abstract arguments. Whitehead's remarkable career thus demonstrates two important points: first it corroborates the general pattern we saw with Wittgenstein—the move from abstract, *a priori*, reductive, precise reasoning, so typical of quantitative science, to pragmatic, concrete, contextual, relativistic and dialectical thought. But Whitehead also goes on to illustrate a distinct third mode of understanding, which I shall discuss briefly further on.

From Quantity to Quality: A Developmental Perspective

The remarkable intellectual careers of Wittgenstein and Whitehead offer a dramatic paradigm of adult cognitive development. To be sure, many caveats are in order. Both Wittgenstein and Whitehead are men, and the cognitive development of women may follow a different course. Both men were also roughly contemporaries, and the parallels between them may reflect their influence on each other. This, in fact, is relatively unlikely. Although both philosophers worked in Cambridge, they overlapped for only a short period, 1912-1913. Indeed, the two developed their philosophies very much out of phase with each other, suggesting they came to their insights independently: as Whitehead shifted to a concrete, pragmatic approach, Wittgenstein elaborated the precise, abstract perspective of the *Tractatus*; when Wittgenstein later wrote the *Philosophical Investigations,* with its concrete pragmatic approach to language, Whitehead had already plunged into metaphysics.

The parallels between the two thinkers may also arise from cohort effects since they both lived around the turn of the century, so an analysis of individuals at different times in history, and from different cultures would be in order. Both Wittgenstein and Whitehead, however, rejected prevailing philosophical traditions in developing their own distinctive viewpoints, so they cannot be considered simply creatures of their times.

Most importantly, recent research in adult cognitive development suggests that the pattern Wittgenstein and Whitehead exemplify is a general one. Compared to young adults and adolescents, mature individuals use less abstract reasoning and more pragmatic problem-solving (Blanchard-Fields, 1986; Cavanaugh, et. al. 1985; Fischer, Hand, Russell, 1984; Labouvie-Vief, 1984; Labouvie-Vief & Chandler, 1978; Labouvie-Vief, Adams, Hakim-Larson, Hayden, DeVoe, 1985; Sinnott 1975, 1981, 1984 a, b). The change occurs in diverse fields, including social interaction and moral reasoning (Gibbs, 1979; Vasudev & Hummel, 1987; Leadbetter, 1986; Murphy, Gilligan, 1980). Dichotomous, either/or thinking gives way to an acceptance of ambiguity, and an attempt to integrate alternative views, rather than choosing between them (Blanchard-Fields, 1986; Dittmann-Kohli, Baltes 1986; Kohlberg, 1984; Kramer, 1983; Perry, 1970). Conviction and certainty, those two hallmarks of youthful thinking, yield to reflective relativism (Chandler, 1987; Perry, 1970; King and Kitchener, 1985, 1981; Chinen, 1986 b; Blanchard-Fields, 1986) and a dialectical stance emerges (Basseches, 1984; Kramer, Woodruff, 1986). The resulting pragmatic mode of thinking corresponds to intuitive notions about mature wisdom, compared to youthful cleverness (Berg & Sternberg, 1985; Berg, 1986).

The shift from abstract, reductive reasoning in youth, to pragmatic problem-solving at mid-life has several important psychological causes. For one, formal operations—the nub of abstract thought—first arise in adolescence. As with any new toy, the young individual delights in using this novel ability, and applies it everywhere. A preference for abstract, *a priori* thought results. Second, the complexities of real life are often overwhelming to adolescents. Emotions are newly intensified by sexuality and must be mastered, as well as the bewildering social and vocational worlds. By temporarily excluding feelings, the individual learns to think logically, in a clear and reliable way. Hence, reductive reasoning, which excludes ethical, religious and emotional issues, is a temporary expedient. The individual focuses on "objective" facts, isolated from confusing contexts. Rigorous rationality is delicate when it first sprouts, and must be protected from rank undergrowth.

As the young adult moves from a sheltered school setting to the work world, he or she makes commitments to career and family. Lofty ideals and pure knowledge then run headlong into pressing practical realities (Van Kaam, 1979; Levinson et. al., 1978; Havighurst, 1972). *A priori* plans and convictions must be squared with the brute effects of chance events (Bandura, 1982). Adaptation, rather than abstraction takes precedence. Experience with real people and mastery of particular domains of expertise supplement mere "book learning": pure *reflection* thus becomes practical *judgment* (Blanchard-Fields, 1986; Roodin, Rybash, Hoyer, 1986; Dittmann-Kohli, Baltes, 1986; Hoyer, 1985; Berg, 1986; Rebok, et. al., 1986; Walker, 1986). Engaged in multiple endeavors, from family to work, the individual can no longer think only of him- or herself, but must consider a whole network of relationships. The idealism and discipline of youth become the obligation and compromise of mid-life. Quantitative, abstract description is forced to become pragmatic, grounded judgment.

If this shift is a feature of adult development, why do not more prominent scientists illustrate the pattern? Two factors are important here. First, as Wittgenstein and Whitehead themselves demonstrate, the shift to pragmatic thinking is associated with teaching, whether in elementary school or university settings. Their youthful pursuit of pure knowledge evolved into an endeavor to pass on that knowledge and make it useful to the next generation. Most scholars and scientists follow just this course: mentoring and administrative responsibilities become increasingly important at mid-life and both are generative endeavors which take time away from research and writing. Thus the shift to pragmatic thinking may not be reflected in written records.

Second, abandoning quantitative thinking for qualitative modes requires great flexibility and courage, especially when the former is rewarded richly and the latter, poorly. Both Wittgenstein and Whitehead were unusually adaptable individuals. Wittgenstein, of course, changed careers several times, moving from engineer to mathematician, thence to soldier, philosopher, elementary school teacher and back to philosophy. More telling, he gave up his prestigious chair in philosophy, at the height of his career, to develop his mature thought more fully—something few academics would do. Whitehead, for his part, moved to London in the middle of his career, with no definite job prospects and then many years later—at a time when most individuals look forward to a comfortable retirement—he went to Boston, to work in metaphysics—a field much maligned at the time. This kind of willingness to change is critical for psychological growth in the second half of life (McLeish, 1976; Peck, 1968; Thurnher, 1975; Jaquish & Ripple, 1984; Perosa & Perosa, 1985).

If a growing body of evidence points to a transition from quantitative reasoning to pragmatic judgment at mid-life, the shift to an intuitive, unitary mode of thinking, which the later Whitehead exemplifies, has been studied much less. But recent discussions in the literature provide intriguing evidence for such a development. Jung (1925, 1929, 1930) was one of the first to hypothesize the change, noting a turn toward inner experience, and away from practical rational considerations in the second half of life. Neugarten (1966) confirmed this "interiority," while others have observed an increase in "magical" thinking among older adults (Neugarten & Gutmann, 1958; Kuhlen, 1968; Sheehan, et. al., 1981; Chiriboga, 1975; Berezin, 1961). Previously thought to be regression, more recent work suggests that this "magical" thinking represents an integration of previously excluded emotional experience (Labouvie-Vief, 1986a; DeVoe, 1986; Hakim-Larson & Schoeberlein, 1986; Labouvie-Vief, 1986b). A more "mythic" mode of thought reappears, along with more vivid internal imagery (Giray, 1985). Associated with these developments is a deepened ability to understand metaphors (Bowsell, 1979; Labouvie-Vief, Campbell, Weaverdyck, Tanenhaus, M., 1980), an affirmation of intuitive understanding over discursive rationality (Chinen, et. al., 1985), and a tendency to see the world in holistic terms (Koplowitz, 1984; Funk, 1985; Cook, 1985). These changes coincide with an increased interest in transcendent, cosmological questions rather than pragmatic, worldly problems (Gutmann, 1977; Van Kaam, 1979; Kakar, 1979; Radhakrishnan & Moore, 1957; Chinen, 1985, 1984a, 1984b; Munsterberg, 1983). In short, after years of pragmatic problem solving, the obligations and compromises of mid-life give way to an intuitive, transcendent and holistic mode of reasoning, exemplified by Whitehead's metaphysical work.

Methodological Implications

Beside dramatizing adult cognitive development, the evolution of Whitehead's and Wittgenstein's thinking highlights several important points about the relationship between quantitative and qualitative methodologies. First of all, the latter includes the former. This can be seen clearly in the careers of Wittgenstein and Whitehead. Neither man repudiated his youthful writing; instead they regarded their early work to be special cases of their later thought. The young Wittgenstein, for example, made description the central function of language. The later Wittgenstein regarded description to be only one of many functions. Where precision and exactness were goals of the early Wittgenstein, the older philosopher recognized that those concepts arose from and were defined by specific contexts. Whitehead, similarly, came to regard mathematical and scientific work as highly focused and specialized ways of thinking, useful for certain purposes. He began, for instance, with a mathematical notion of "extensive abstraction," based on the concept of a vector. He later generalized this basic idea until it became the cosmological principle of "process": the mathematical notion is actually an abstraction of "process." Wittgenstein's and Whitehead's work, then, suggest that quantitative thinking is focused, and specialized. Indeed, rigorous scientific thinking is exactly that and research is possible precisely because larger issues are excluded—from the physical climate outside the laboratory to the social climate surrounding the experimenters. By contrast, pragmatic judgment deals with the surrounding context and all the ambiguous elements. It therefore inevitably gives less definitive answers.

A caveat is important here. Qualitative reasoning includes many different kinds of thought so that pragmatic judgment must be distinguished from other varieties of humanistic reasoning. Literary and phenomenological modes of understanding, for example, seek empathic recreations of human experience as an end-in-itself (Dilthey, 1976). Pragmatic judgment does not: empathy is important if it helps solve a human problem. Pragmatic reasoning is also "grounded," i.e. tied to specific examples, and particular issues—a point particularly clear in Wittgenstein's *Philosophical Investigations*. This contrasts with "global" qualitative thinking, seen in some forms of ethics, much philosophy and most political discussions: general principles of human existence and meaning are debated, without being anchored to specific situations. Such global reasoning is typical of adolescents. Indeed, part of the prevailing prejudice against the "human sciences" may come from an attempt to suppress this emotional mode of understanding. Such temporary suppression, as noted before, can help foster the development of rigorous reasoning. What the examples of Wittgenstein and Whitehead demonstrate is that the opposition between quantitative and qualitative modes of reasoning is partially resolved at mid-life, when the two are supplanted by an eclectic, pragmatic mode of reasoning.

The latter is what professionals use in their work (Knorr, 1979; Schon, 1983; Chinen, et. al., 1985; Chinen, 1987a, b, 1986b): physician, engineer and teacher all know abstract principles of specialized sciences—physiology to physics, or psychology. And they all uphold lofty ideals, whether concerned about healing the sick, conquering nature or illuminating minds. But the unique skill of a practitioner comes in applying abstract knowledge and humanistic concerns to particular problems—a sick patient, a river to be crossed, a student having trouble with a subject. Pragmatic judgment unites the subjective and objective dimensions, in a concrete situation.

The pragmatic mode cuts across disciplines, too. For example, rigorous textual analysis—legal readings, for instance, in contrast to personal literary enjoyment of a poem—requires the application of abstract hermeneutic principles adapted to specific situations (Gadamer, 1984; Ricoer, 1978; Habermas, 1973, 1983). Ethical problem-solving also requires the pragmatic approach (MacIntyre, 1984). Indeed, I suggest that pragmatic judgment is a basic mode of reasoning (Chinen, 1987b, 1986a) and it underlies what is currently described as "action research," "grounded theory" or "practical hermeneutics" (Bernstein, 1983; Gadamer, 1984; Ricoeur, 1978; Habermas, 1973, 1983; Rorty,

1982; Rabinow & Sullivan, 1979). This mode of understanding has not been defined as precisely and logically as that of natural science, but there are several compelling reasons for this "deficiency." First of all, pragmatic reasoning is inherently ambiguous, since it addresses the elusive factors that quantitative thought automatically excludes. As a methodology, therefore, it cannot be as precisely defined as the scientific approach, which, in any event, is less completely characterized than readily admitted (Habermas, 1973, 1983; Knorr, 1979). Second, formal inquiry into the pragmatic mode is relatively new, compared to that of natural science. Further investigations are needed, and may be encouraged by demographic factors: the current generation of academic leaders, many of whom started their careers at the same time shortly after World War II, are now around the age when Wittgenstein and Whitehead shifted from abstract to pragmatic reasoning.

Third, the very concept of methodology reflects an abstract mode of reasoning: methodology seeks *the* definitive approach, applicable to all subject matter, from the atom to chimpanzees and human civilizations. Methodology attempts to refine a few tools (currently statistics and the hypothetico-deductive method) that can be used everywhere, irrespective of contexts, or divergent purposes. Pragmatic reasoning has no such illusions, acknowledging instead the overwhelming complexity of the world, and the influence of "local factors," unique to particular situations. Universal methodology is not the goal—rather a collection of useful techniques, and precedents. Pragmatics concerns itself with *heuristics*, not methodology.

The pragmatic mode is consequently more difficult to teach. There is no general recipe, like that sought in quantitative work. Pragmatic judgment is learned by slogging through specific problems, in a case-by-case manner—a messy, time-consuming, and highly labor-intensive endeavor. Apprenticeship, like the physician's internship or the graduate student's research, must enrich book learning. Education is therefore a life-long process that does not end with certification, as if the scholar himself was a methodology, which once shaped, can be applied to any and all problems, like a well-honed tool.

The importance of Whitehead and Wittgenstein to methodological discussions can be summed up fairly simply: their careers illustrate the difference between the scientific and pragmatic modes of reasoning, and the validity of each—in the proper contexts. It is not a question of whether quantitative or qualitative methods are better than the other, although this is how the issue is usually cast. To paraphrase the mature Whitehead, the question is: for what purpose, where and when, is one particular approach better than the other?

This work was supported in part by the Robert Wood Johnson Foundation Clinical Scholars Program.

Notes

1. Whitehead was a prolific writer so that my analysis of his work involves only samples of writing from his major periods. I thus rely upon secondary sources for corroboration. Wittgenstein wrote only two books for publication, so that secondary sources are not needed. Although some of Wittgenstein's private notes and those taken by students in his lectures have been published, I focus only on Wittgenstein's two books.

2. References are to the numbering used in the *Tractatus Logico Philosophicus*, translated by D. F. Pears, B. F. McGuinness. (Atlantic Highlands, NJ: Humanities Press, 1974).

3. The *a priori* nature of Wittgenstein's philosophy may seem unscientific. But the youthful Wittgenstein did not reject empirical evidence, he merely made abstract theory primary—valuing universal, general laws, over particular examples. And this is precisely what science seeks, with the "hypothetico-deductive" method: observations are important only as they confirm or disprove general theories.

4. References are to sections in *Philosophical Investigations*, (3rd edition), translated by G. E. Anscombe. (NY: MacMillan Co., 1968).

5. Interestingly enough, the appearance of humor may be a subtle characteristic of mid-life maturity (Peck, 1968; Vaillant, Bond, Vaillant, 1986; Vaillant, 1977; Chinen, 1986).

6. Whitehead, born in 1861, actually belongs to the generation before Wittgenstein. The reason for discussing Whitehead second is that he wrote prolifically, so that the course of his intellectual career is more complex to unravel than Wittgenstein's.

7. By "cosmological" I mean something more general than the usual technical definition of the term. I refer to any thinking about ultimate questions, whether cast in theological, metaphysical or scientific terms. This general concept is useful for Whitehead, because his later work ranged over all three areas.

References

Bandura, A. (1982). The psychology of chance encounters and life paths. *American Psychologist* 37: 747-755.

Basseches, M. A. (1984). Dialectical thinking as a metasystematic form of cognitive organization. In M. L. Commons, F. A. Richards, C. Armon (eds.) *Beyond formal operations: Late adolescent and adult development*. New York: Praeger.

Berezin, M. (1961). Some intrapsychic aspects of aging. In N. E. Zinberg, I. Kaufman, (eds.) *Normal psychology of the aging process*. New York: International Universities Press. 93-117.

Berg, C. (1986). The role of social competence in contextual theories of adult intellectual development. *Educational Gerontology* 12: 313-325.

Bernstein, R. J. (1983). *Beyond objectivism and relativism: Science, hermeneutics and praxis.* Philadelphia: University of Pennsylvania.

Blanchard-Fields, F. (1986). Attributional processes in adult development. *Educational Gerontology* 12: 291-300.

Boswell, D. A. (1979). Metaphoric processing in the mature years. *Human Development* 22: 373-384.

Botwinick, J. (1977). Intellectual abilities. In J. E. Birren, K. W. Schaie, (eds.) *Handbook of the psychology of aging.* New York: Van Nostrand Reinhold.

Buhler, C. (1968). The general structure of the human life cycle. C. Buhler, F. Massarik, (eds.) *The course of human life: a study of goals in the humanistic perspective.* New York: Springer.

Cavanaugh, J., and D. Kramer, J. Sinnott, C. Camp, J. Markley. (1985). On missing links and such: Interfaces between cognitive research and everyday problem-solving. *Human Development* 28: 146-168.

Chandler, M. (1987). The Othello effect: Essay on the emergence and eclipse of skeptical doubt. *Human Development* 30: 13-159.

Chinen, A. B. (1987a). Symbolic modes: A semiotic perspective on clinical object relations. *Psychoanalysis and contemporary thought.* 10:373-406.

Chinen, A. B. (1987b). Modes of understanding and mindfulness in clinical medicine. *Theoretical Medicine.* 9:45-72.

Chinen, A. B. (1986a). Scientific, humanistic and practical modes of understanding: a semiotic analysis from psychotherapy. Paper presented to the Annual Meeting of the Semiotic Society of America, San Francisco, California.

Chinen, A. B. (1986b). Adult development, self-contexting and psychotherapy with older adults. *Psychotherapy* 23: 411-416.

Chinen, A. B. (1985). Elder tales: Fairy tales and transpersonal development in later life. *Journal of Transpersonal Psychology* 77: 99-122.

Chinen, A. B. (1984a). Modal logic: A new paradigm of development and late-life potential. *Human Development* 27: 42-56.

Chinen, A. B. (1984b). Eastern wisdom, western aging. Paper presented to the Annual Meeting of the Gerontological Society of America, San Antonio, Texas.

Chinen, A. B. and A. Spielvogel, D. Farrell. (1985). The phenomenology of clinical intuition. *Psychological Perspectives* 16: 186-197.

Chiriboga, D. and M. Thurnher. (1975). Concept of self. In M. F. Lowenthal, M. Thurnher, D. Chiriboga. *Four stages of life.* San Francisco: Jossey Bass, 62-83.

Cook, S. R. (1985). Stage 5, 5/6, and 6 in Loevinger's ego developmental sequence: an analysis. Paper presented to the Second Symposium on Post-Formal Operations, Harvard University, 1985.

Dennis, W. (1966). Creative productivity between the ages of 20 and 80 years. *Journal of Gerontology* 21: 108.

DeVoe, M. (1986). The language of emotions over the life course. Paper presented at the Annual Meeting of the Gerontological Society..

Dilthey, W. H. (1976) *Selected Writings*. P. Rickman (ed.) Cambridge: Cambridge University Press.

Feibleman, J. K. (1975). *The stages of human life*. The Hague: Nijhoff.

Fischer, K. W. and H. H. Hand, S. Russell. (1984). The development of abstractions in adolescence and adulthood. In M. L. Commons, F. A. Richards, C. Armon (eds.) *Beyond formal operations*.

Frenkel, E. (1936). Studies in biographical psychology. *Character and Personality* 5: 1-34.

Funk, J. (1985). Postformal cognition and musical composition. Paper presented at the Second Post-Formal Operations Conference, Harvard University.

Gadamer, H. G. (1984). *Reason in the age of science*. Cambridge: MIT Press.

Gibbs, J. C. (1979). Kohlberg's moral stage as theory: A Piagetian revision. *Human Development* 22: 89-112.

Giray, E. F. (1985). A life span approach to the study of eidetic imagery. *Journal of Mental Imagery* 9: 21-32.

Guardini, R. (1957). The stages of life and philosophy. *Philosophy Today* 1: 78-79.

Gutmann, D. (1977). The cross-cultural perspective: notes on a comparative psychology of aging. In J. Birren, W. Schaie (eds.) *Handbook of the psychology of aging*. New York: Van Nostrand Reinhold.

Gutmann, D. (1964). An exploration of ego configurations in middle and later life. In B. L. Neugarten (ed.) *Personality in middle and late life: Empirical studies*. New York: Atherton Press, 114-148.

Habermas, J. (1973). *Theory and practice*. Boston: Beacon.

Habermas, J. (1983). Interpretive social science vs. hermeneuticism. In N. Haan, R. N. Bellah, P. Rabinow, W. M. Sullivan (eds.) *Social science as moral inquiry*. New York: Columbia University Press.

Hakim-Larson, J.; Schoeberlein, S., (1986). Strategies of self-regulation. Paper presented at the Annual Meeting of the Gerontological Society.

Havighurst, R. (1972). *Developmental tasks and education*. New York: Van Nostrand.

Jaquish, G. and R. Ripple. (1984). A life span developmental cross-cultural study of divergent thinking abilities. *International Journal of Aging and Human Development* 20: 1-10.

Jung, C. (1930/1960). In *Collected works volume 8.* Princeton: Princeton University Press.

Jung, C. (1929/1967). The secret of the golden flower. In *Collected works volume 13.* Princeton: Princeton University Press.

Jung, C. (1925/1967). Marriage as a psychological relationship. In *Collected works volume 17.* Princeton: Princeton University Press.

Kakar, S. (1979). Setting the stage: The traditional Hindu view and the psychology of Erik H. Erikson. In S. Kakar (ed.) *Identity and adulthood.* Delhi: Oxford University Press.

Kitchener, K. and P. King. (1985). The reflective judgment model: Ten years of research. Paper presented at the Second Post-Formal Operations Conference, Harvard University.

Kitchener, K. S. and P. M. King. (1981). Reflective judgment: Concepts of justification and their relation to age and education. *Journal of Applied Developmental Psychology* 2: 89-116.

Knorr, K. (1979). Tinkering toward success: Prelude to a theory of scientific practice. *Theory and Society* 8: 347-370.

Kohlberg, L. (1984). *The psychology of moral development.* San Francisco: Harper and Row.

Koplowitz, H. (1984). A projection beyond Piaget's formal-operations stage: A general system stage and a unitary stage. In M. L. Commons, F. A. Richards, C. Armon (eds.) *Beyond formal operations.*

Kramer, D., (1983). Post-formal operations? A need for further conceptualizations. Human Development 29: 280-290.

Kramer, D. A. and D. S. Woodruff. (1986). Relativistic and dialectical thought in three adult age-groups. *Human Development* 29: 280-290.

Kuhlen, R. (1968). Developmental changes in motivation during the adult years. In Bernice Neugarten (ed.) *Middle age and aging: A reader in social psychology.* Chicago: University of Chicago, 115-136.

Labouvie-Vief, G. (1984). Logic and self-regulation from youth to maturity: A model. In M. L. Commons, F. A. Richards, C. Armon (eds.) *Beyond formal operations.*

Labouvie-Vief, G. (1986a). Developmental dimensions of adult adaptation: Perspectives on mind, self and emotion. Symposium presented at the Annual Meeting of the Gerontological Society, Chicago, IL.

Labouvie-Vief, G. (1986b). Natural epistemologies and dimensions of adult development. Paper presented at the Annual Meeting of the Gerontological Society, Chicago, IL.

Labouvie-Vief, G. and M. Chandler. (1978). Cognitive development and life-span developmental theory: Idealistic versus contextual perspectives. In P. Baltes (ed.) *Life-span development and behavior, vol. 1*. New York: Academic Press.

Labouvie—Vief, G. and S. O. Campbell, S. L. Weaverdyck, M. Tanenhaus. (1980). Metaphoric processing in young and old adults. Unpublished manuscript.

Labouvie-Vief, G. and C. Adams, J. Hakim-Larson, M. Hayden, M. DeVoe. (1985). Logical problem solving and meta-logical knowledge from preadolescence to adulthood. In Press.

Lawrence, N. (1968). *Whitehead's philosophical development: a critical history of the background of process and reality*. New York: Greenwood.

Leadbeater, B. (1986). The resolution of relativism in adult thinking: Subjective, objective, or conceptual? *Human Development* 29: 291-300.

Levinson, D. J. and C. Darrow, E. Klein, M. Levinson, B. McKee. (1978). *The seasons of a man's life*. New York: Ballantine.

Lewis, C. I. (1943/1969). Modes of meaning. In T. Olshewsky (ed.) *Problems in the philosophy of language*. New York: Holt, Rinehart, Winston.

Linn, M. and H. Siegel. (1984). Postformal reasoning: A philosophical model. In M. L. Commons, F. A. Richards, C. Armon (eds.) *Beyond formal operations*.

Lowe, V. (1962). *Understanding Whitehead*. Baltimore: Johns Hopkins Press.

Lowe, V. (1985). *Understanding Whitehead: The man and his work*. Baltimore: Johns Hopkins Press.

Macintyre, A. (1984). *After virtue: A study in moral theory*. Notre Dame: University of Notre Dame Press.

McLeish, J. A. B. (1976). *The Ulyssean adult: Creativity in the middle years*. New York: McGraw-Hill.

Maitland, D. J. (1981). *Against the grain: Coming through the midlife crisis*. New York: Pilgrim Press.

Malcolm, N. (1967). Ludwig Wittgenstein. In *The encyclopedia of philosophy*. New York: Macmillan.

Munsterberg, H. (1983). *The crown of life: Artistic creativity in old age*. New York: Harcourt Brace Jovanovich.

Murphy, J. M. and C. Gilligan. (1980). Moral development in late adolescence and adulthood: A critique and reconstruction of Kohlberg's theory. *Human Development* 23: 77-104.

Neugarten, B. L. (1964). *Personality in middle and late life: A set of empirical studies*. New York: Atherton Press.

Neugarten, B. and D. Gutmann. (1958). Age-sex roles and personality in middle age: A thematic apperception study. *Psychological Monographs: General and Applied* 17: 2-34.

Neugarten, B. (1966). Adult personality: A developmental view. *Human Development* 9: 61-73.

Oser, F. F. and K. H. Riech. (1987). The challenge of competing explanations: The development of thinking in terms of complementarity of 'theories'. *Human Development* 30: 178-186.

Peck, R. (1968). Psychological developments in the second half of life. In B. Neugarten, (ed.) *Middle age and aging: A reader in social psychology*. Chicago: University of Chicago Press.

Perosa, S. and L. Perosa. (1984). The mid-career crisis in relation to Super's career and Erikson's adult development theory. *International Journal of Aging and Human Development* 20: 53-68.

Perry, W. (1970). *Forms of intellectual and ethical development in the college years*. New York: Academic Press.

Rabinow, P. and W. M. Sullivan. (1979). The interpretive turn: Emergence of an approach. In P. Rabinow, W. M. Sullivan (eds.) *Interpretive social science: A reader*. Berkeley: University of California Press.

Radhakrishanan, S. and C. E. Moore. (eds.) (1957). *A sourcebook in Indian philosophy*. Princeton: Princeton University Press.

Rebok, G. W. and L. R. Offema, P. Wirtz, C. Montaglione. (1986). Work and intellectual aging: The psychological concomitants of social-organizational conditions. *Educational Gerontology* 12: 359-374.

Rhees, R. (ed.) (1984). *Recollections of Wittgenstein*. Oxford: Oxford University Press.

Richards, F. and M. Commons. (1984). Systematic, metasystematic, and cross-paradigmatic reasoning: A case for stages of reasoning beyond formal operations. In M. L. Commons, F. A. Richards, C. Armon (eds.) *Beyond formal operations*.

Ricoeur, P. (1978). *The philosophy of Paul Ricoeur: An anthology of his works*. C. E. Reagan, D. Stewart (eds.) Boston: Beacon.

Riegel, K. (1976). Dialectical operations: The final period of cognitive development. *Human Development* 16: 346-370.

Roodin, P. A. and J. W. Rybash, W. J. Hoyer. (1986). Qualitative dimensions of social cognition in adulthood. *Educational Gerontology* 12: 301-311.

Rorty, R. (1982). *The consequences of pragmatism*. Minnesota: University of Minnesota Press.

Rosen, J. and B. Neugarten. (1964). Ego functions in the middle and later years: A thematic apperception study. In B. L. Neugarten (ed.) *Personality in middle and late life: Empirical studies*. New York: Atherton Press, 90-101.

Schon, D. (1983). *The reflective practitioner: How professionals think in action.* New York: Basic Books.

Sheehan, N. W. and Diane E. Papalia-Finlay, F. H. Hooper. (1981). The nature of the life concept across the life-span. *International Journal of Aging and Human Development* 12: 1-13.

Simonton, D. K. (1985). Quality, quantity, and age: The careers of ten distinguished psychologists. *International Journal of Aging and Human Development* 21: 241-254.

Sinnott, J. D. (1975). Everyday thinking and Piagetiation operativity in adults. *Human Development* 18: 430-443.

Sinnott, J. D. (1981). The theory of relativity: A metatheory for development. *Human Development* 24: 293-311.

Sinnott, J. D. (1984a). Postformal reasoning: The relativistic stage. In M. L. Commons, F. A. Richards, C. Armon (eds.) *Beyond formal operations.*

Sinnott, J. D. (1984b). A model for solution of ill-structured problems: Implications for everyday and abstract problem solving. Presented to the 1984 Annual Meeting of the Gerontological Society of America, San Antonio.

Thurnher, M. (1975). Continuities and discontinuities in value orientation. In M. Fiske-Lownethal, et. al. *Four stages of life.* San Francisco: Jossey Bass, 176-200.

Vaillant, G. (1977). *Adaptation to life: How the best and the brightest came of age.* New York: Little, Brown.

Vaillant, G. E. and M. Bond, C. Vaillant. (1986). An empirically validated hierarchy of defense mechanisms. *Archives of General Psychiatry* 43: 786-794.

Van Kaam, A. (1979). *The transcendent self.* New Jersey: Dimension.

Vasudev, J. and R. Hummel. (1987). Moral stage sequence and principled reasoning in an Indian sample. *Human Development* 30: 105-118.

Walker, L. J. (1986). Experiential and cognitive sources of moral development in adulthood. *Human Development* 29: 113-124.

Whitehead, A. N. (1941). Autobiographical notes. In *The philosophy of Alfred North Whitehead.* P. A. Schilpp (ed.) New York: Tudor.

Whitehead, A. N. (1917). *The organization of thought: educational and scientific.* London: Williams and Norgate..

Whitehead, A. N. (1919). *An enquiry concerning the principles of natural knowledge.* Cambridge: Cambridge University Press.

Whitehead, A. N. (1920). *The concept of nature.* Cambridge: Cambridge University Press.

Whitehead, A. N. (1925). *Science and the modern world.* New York: Macmillan.

Whitehead, A. N. (1926). *Religion in the making.* New York: Macmillan.

Whitehead, A. N. (1938). *Modes of thought.* New York: Macmillan.

Whitmont, E. C. (1969). *The symbolic quest: Basic concepts of analytical psychology.* Princeton: Princeton University Press.

Wood, P. (1983). Inquiring systems and problem structure: Implications for cognitive development. *Human Development* 26: 249-265.

Wittgenstein, L. (1922/1974). *Tractatus logico philosophicus.* Tr. D. F. Pears, B. F. McGuinness. 1974. Atlantic Highlands, NJ: Humanities Press.

Wittgenstein, L. (1953/1968). *Philosophical investigations.* (3rd edition) tr. G. E. Anscombe. NY: Macmillan Co.

Participant Observation

Chapter 5

Talking About Menopause: A Dialogic Analysis[1]

MARY GERGEN

The focal points of this chapter are two: to illustrate how dialogic methods of analysis have created perspectives on various areas of psychology; and more specifically to detail how dialogic methods illustrate the form and functions of a discussion group, which was centered on issues related to menopause. The central concern of the editor, Eugene Thomas, and myself, is to present issues of aging through methods that are congenial with the "human sciences approach." Meeting these goals in this one paper will produce an intersection of high density traffic. Let's hope we can emerge without a scratch.

What aspect of aging are you addressing?

I am interested in middle age, particularly the lives of women between youth and old age. Psychology has little to say about middle age, generally, and even less about the adulthood of women. Once the excitement of marriage and childbearing are over, the next stop for women in terms of development is old age. The only intervening pause in the journey is for menopause, which is usually ascribed as the beginning of the last lap. As a woman in her forties, I had a negative reaction to this perspective, and I wanted to contribute something to help rectify this situation. I am concerned that women who are reaching the end of their childbearing years do not assimilate the vision of themselves that the social sciences offer. This chapter is an initial effort born of my desires for changing the status quo. It is not, by any means, a thoroughgoing counter-attack against conventional wisdom, but only an initial sally.

But first could you say something about what dialogic methods mean to you in the context of this chapter?

Dialogic methods are based on the basic metaphor of the conversation, in which dialogue is the major (but not the only) ingredient. Dialogue emphasizes the interaction of two or more speakers, who are listeners as well. Just one who speaks and one who listens is not a dialogue. Nor is it a satisfactory dialogue if both are talking, and no one is really listening. This conception of a dialogue includes the notion that the product of the conversation is a shared creation, one that could not have existed without the particular contributions of each party to it. This means that no one created it, nor could it be reproduced by replacing one party with another. Within the definition of the dialogue is also the implicit understanding that the interaction is contextualized. It takes place within a particular place within a particular time. Its meaning is connected to this tissue of intersecting events. It is dangerous to withdraw a portion for study. Our analyses are always and inevitably disruptions. Yet there is often a hopeful spirit underlying this conception of dialogue, a basic belief that the outcome of a dialogue must produce some type of rapport among the actors; one expects that dialogue might create the process by which increased understanding, joint action, mutual enhancement of outcomes or some other valued goal is produced.

Dialogic methods are a diverse set of practices that have in common the use of dialogue as a centerpiece of the analysis, for example, in a study of a group. You will see what I mean as I go on, I hope.

Dialogic methods might be used in a variety of disciplines then. Could you be more specific about how they are used?

The first way that I am using a dialogic method (which you may have noticed) is in the way I am writing this paper. I am imagining you out there, engaging me in a conversation about dialogic methods and how I have used them. Although I sometimes suspect that you find this way of organizing somewhat peculiar, I think it does help you to more easily find the questions of interest to you, and it gives me a greater sense of doing something interesting. No one likes to write into a vacuum, and I am no exception. As I write I feel more as though I am in a dialogue with you. I am also using this form to remind you of the centrality of dialogue to my analysis. I like to practice what I preach, so I am trying to use dialogue to explain how useful dialogue is.

This is not to say that dialogic analysis requires a dialogue for presentational purposes. However in the present case it is useful as a sensitizing device for us both. I am also using this dialogic style as a means of taking my feminist philosophy seriously. Dialogic methods question traditional forms of presentation (which can be subtly or overtly sexist and oppressive). I cannot fully escape from the patriarchal linguistic traditions that allow for communication, but I can soften the barriers between the writer and the reader, and the analyzer and the analyzed. While I do see important parallels between presentation and form of analysis, I do not want to dwell overly long on this use of the dialogic method.

Can you describe some situations in which dialogue is "authentically" used?

I want to distinguish three ways of using dialogic methods, in what I am calling an "authentic" way, and which are not typically used by social psychologists. These are the ones I want to apply in the analysis of the group discussion on menopause. There are differences among them, but they are much more similar to one another than to traditional social psychological methods.

First, *dialogues have long been used as means for interpreting* the intentions, emotions, motivations, attitudes and relational ties of persons, fictional and real. In this case, the dialogue is regarded as the outward representation of unseen, inner forces. Social scientists who are not operating within an experimental methodology frequently use an interpretive framework for understanding their subjects. The conversations and other interactions within an encounter are used as signifiers for the internal world of the signified. To use these words from the French linguistic tradition will remind some readers of the problems incurred in attempting interpretation. How is it possible to find a clear relationship between the levels of signifier and signified, words and underlying meanings? The classical problem in a nutshell is, of course, how can we decipher what a person means by her/his words? The issues stemming from the work of deconstructionist writers such as Derrida (1978) leave us feeling unsteady when we try to assert the validity of our interpretations of any situation.

Despite such limits to validity, many social scientists, in an interpretive vein, analyze dialogues as oral and written texts to discern the ways in which scientists go about their work, for example. Analyses by Mitroff (1974), Latour and Woolgar (1979), and Gilbert and Mulkay (1984) demonstrate the function of dialogue in constructing the realities of the natural sciences. In this way dialogic study is used to undermine the concept of objective knowledge. Often in the course of their work such analysts attribute to their respondents cognitive processes inferred from their actions. Intentionally or not, the dialogue is a key to the invisible, internal psychological world of the scientists under study.

One of the attributes of many such hermeneutical endeavors is its self-reflexivity. Unlike the paradigmatic experimental social psychologist, many analysts using this method admit more freely to their own biases and recognize their own cultural blinders (Woolgar, 1987). As Roy Wagner (1975) has described the actions of ethnographers, they participate in the subject culture not as natives, but as those simultaneously enveloped in their own world of meaning as well as that of the people under study. Investigators, such as James Clifford (1983), claim that their accounts are joint productions of respondents and themselves. By implication the analysts seem to concur that their accounts are not settled once and for all. From this perspective people are not always seen to have discoverable fixed attitudes, goals, beliefs or motives, but are seen as constantly shifting as the nature of their interchange varies.

While many researchers thus use dialogues as indicators of other realities, *dialogue can also become a topic of inquiry in itself.* A recent book by Jonathan Potter and Margaret Wetherell called *Discourse and Social Psychology* (1987) advocates this position. They emphasize the performative nature of language, that is, people use language in order to do things. Therefore language patterns may change as the need to do things changes. For example, a woman may state that she has no interest in talking about menopause in one portion of a discussion, and then say that she really values discussions of this sort in another. Such performatives cannot be understood outside of the pattern of action in which they are embedded. Thus to understand language performance requires a focus on human interchange or dialogue. In this case discourse is not an epiphenomena of another realm (the mind). Rather it is a phenomenon in itself. From this perspective one is invited to analyze the ways in which linguistic "moves" within a dialogue can have an impact on subsequent actions of the participants. This effort is different from using a linguistic move to demonstrate the speaker's underlying attitudes.

Perhaps an example might help clarify the distinction between these two ways of using dialogic methods to understand interpersonal relations.

This distinction is difficult to maintain, I think. Let me try an example. I will draw from the dialogue of my group meeting. (Later I will introduce you more formally to the group. Please be patient.)[2]

During the early part of the discussion the participants avoided mentioning any of the presumed psychological side-effects of menopause. However, in one portion of the discussion the following occurred: Mary: "I wonder if periods themselves make you feel younger?" (General comments from the group ensued.)

Marla: (Talking about how all the women she knows who are through menopause are happy about being post-menopausal.) "There's one person now who we talked about, her periods are very irregular and she's feeling unstable. Now maybe these other people who I talked to who feel so good now, didn't feel so good before. (Loud general talking, agreement.) They're not talking about how they felt before."

Looking at this scene from a discourse analysis frame, we might say that in the linguistic "move" described above, Marla brings up a possible negative consequence of menopause: being emotionally unstable during the transition to menopause. One might interpret this as a "move" to produce solidarity of the group as non-menopausal women vs. menopausal ones. This is done by indirectly probing the group about their understanding of the situation she brings up. Are the "older girls" trying to deceive the younger ones by not letting them in on the secret of the transition? Are they putting on a happy face now, but refusing to acknowledge the suffering that they have gone through? Are they suffering now, but unwilling to tell the younger women? The effect of Marla's statement might be interpreted as creating a form of bonding among these pre-menopausal women. Support for this interpretation comes from Suzanne's remarks that follow. Suzanne describes what she sees as the inevitable feeling of loss that comes of knowing you can never have children again.

Suzanne: ". . . when you say goodbye to a part of your life there has to be some little thing you feel, to be honest." Suzanne's comment "to be honest" reinforces the need for this group to recognize that the older women may be deceptive in their dealings with the youngers.

This analysis concentrates on how the language produced within the group is used to manage group activity. This type of analysis follows the Potter and Wetherall discourse analysis approach (1987).

Alternatively, this example might be described in the interpretive mode, wherein dialogic methods are used as a means of interpreting underlying meanings. The remark "Now maybe these other people who I talked to who feel so good now, didn't feel so good before . . ." could be regarded as Marla's expression of her own fear of becoming emotionally unstable. Suzanne's comments about losing the ability to bear children could also be construed as an underlying personal concern.

You mentioned earlier that there were three ways in which dialogical methods might be used "authentically." The first was the interpretation of the performative use of language and the second the interpretation of individual motives. What is the third?

The third use of dialogic methods is to induce some form of change among the participants. I derive this view from my feminist orientation. One of the feminist perspectives that I have accepted is that knowledge construction is a social act. The meanings of things are a group product (Clifford, 1983; Crapanzano, 1980). Groups of people create the validation for what is considered known, and they do this through communal interactions (Favret-Saadia, 1977). Even though certain ideas may be synthesized by given individuals, the currency of any idea must be given value by the community surrounding it. In this process changes occur that are the result of the dialogue within which the ideas are set (Gadamer, 1976; Wortham, 1987). Giving ownership to ideas, that is seeing ideas as private property, is symptomatic of patriarchy, in which everything, including the sea, is "owned."

Feminists often call into question this concept of ownership (Owens, 1983). In recognition of the changing nature of ideas as a result of mutual interchange, this project was construed as an effort to change women's ideas of menopause. I saw my vision of female adulthood as the seed around which the dialogic change might occur.

I would like to know what you hoped to accomplish with this project?

My involvement with this project was an outgrowth of a desire to create a method for studying lives that would not violate ideals of research that I had written about under the rubric of a feminist metatheory and methodology (Gergen, 1988). I asked myself what would happen if I were to do a research project following my own critiques. This led me to establish that the project would have to be *intersubjective, participatory and emancipatory.*

It sounds like a noble endeavor, but how did you translate these phrases into practice? How was the research "intersubjective," for example?

First, I decided that I would recognize in all phases of the study the interdependence and mutual involvment of the subjects and me. This is a major contradiction of the rules of a so-called objective science. While the cardinal principle of positivistic science is that the scientist and the subject of inquiry must have a neutral relationship so that the scientist may make dispassionate observations from a position of independence, I saw this as a self-deceptive and unrealizable standard. In contrast, I accepted the inevitability of relatedness and decided to maximize the possibilities for relating that prior acquaintance allows. I took this decision to accept relatedness to the point of deciding to invite as my subjects a small group of friends. In addition I decided to call myself a subject as well. I filled out forms, paid myself a subject fee and signed a receipt. (So if nothing else, I got $15 and a free lunch from the occasion.) This does get rather tricky, doesn't it?

Also in violation of the usual standards of normal science, where the events under study are cut away, as much as possible, from entangling outside influences, my goal was to avoid decontextualizing the research. Other feminist critics and I have discussed problems of decontextualization elsewhere (cf, Gergen, 1988; Minton, 1986; Parlee, 1979; Vaughter, 1976). Instead I tried to allow for an event to occur that was quite conventional: a luncheon among friendly acquaintances who know each other primarily from playing tennis together. I invited my friends to come to my home. We sat at a table on my porch, first having a group discussion and then lunch. While we had never been together at my house in just this configuration, we had all been at tennis club luncheons before. Having a tape recorder on the table and being invited to discuss menopause and the life styles of women between forty and sixty was not a typical event at a tennis lunch, but it was not out of the question that this group of eight women would find themselves discussing women's issues and personal concerns at such gatherings.

In general, how would you characterize your group?

Besides being tennis players, we are all college graduates, and Suzanne and I have advanced degrees. We ranged in age from forty-one to forty-eight. All of us were pre-menopausal, although Terry had had a hysterectomy in her late thirties. At the time of the dialogue we all were married, living with husbands in our own homes, with children who were mostly teenagers or young adults. Suzanne and I were the only full-time "career" people, although Bonnie has her own small craft business at home. Others had worked, were working part time or looking for new work opportunities. Debra was in the U.S. with her husband and children from Australia.

Earlier you mentioned that you wanted the research to be participatory. What do you mean by this, and in what ways did you try to achieve this goal? And while the reader has the floor, isn't it a contradiction in terms to talk about achieving participation, something like saying, "I made us all share our opinions"?

The goal of participatory research is to eliminate, insofar as possible, any hierarchical or authoritarian aspects. Such a goal must be considered an ideal to be approximated rather that a practical reality. Once I had decided that I wanted to arrange this project, I had taken one step down the road to authority. When I chose the problem, the method, the participants, the fees, the time, the space and the structure of the occasion, I had taken many giant steps toward authority. A more fully participatory project would be less unilateral in these facets of development, and, if I had it to do over again, I would involve myself more deeply in structuring a participatory approach. While I would emphasize the desirability, even the necessity of a participatory approach, I am also opposed to the position that denies the right of a social scientist to explore issues that are not identified as problems by the affected population and glosses over the different levels of expertise among participants.

Within the group discussion itself, I strove for a balanced, egalitarian discussion. I tried to facilitate the free expression of ideas, and I limited by discussion comments to introductory remarks, and to expressing my ideas about mid-life development after the discussion was well underway.

What about the emancipatory goal? How was that achieved?

The emancipatory facet of the research defies the customary positivist version of science that requires a neutral or "value-free" approach to a problem. This criteria has been so thoroughly mauled by a decade of critics that review seems unnecessary. My view of valuational research has several components that do require attention, as they are more stringent than that of simply admitting in the last paragraph of a research article that all researchers are mortal, and thus are subject to quaint and conventional value biases of some unspecified nature.

Emancipatory research, as I define it, agrees with Shulamit Reinharz's (1985) view (among others, but I do admire her work especially) that researchers not only should declare their "values" relevant to a particular domain, but should openly foster them in their work. My criteria for emancipatory feminist research are: 1. to advance my research goals; 2. to create an effective opportunity for change for those who are involved in the research endeavor; and 3. to be personally open to change as a result of the commingling of influences emanating from the interplay of participants.

My sympathies are engaged by this type of approach because instead of the usual vague promises to "help mankind," the researcher is committed to the more immediate well-being of the co-participants. The sharpest contrast I see between this feminist approach and all others is that the uni-directionality of influence effects is negated. Influence is seen as transactional. The researcher is as vulnerable to change as are the other participants. This may lead to a dynamic, open-ended, egalitarian and possibly chaotic research process. These terms highlight the discrepancies between this approach and the conventional research arrangement, where the last thing one would want is the potential for chaos.

So why did you decide to concentrate on middle-aged women? The method you describe could be applied to many areas.

True. So far I've concentrated on the methodological considerations, the "how," of this endeavor. Now I'd like to talk about the "why," which is perhaps more central to me and this book than the "how." I'd like to convey to you some of the background of this project by sharing some personal reactions. (This action is part of the feminist mode of this chapter, as I see it; it comes from the belief that research ideas often derive from private concerns, not as deductive inferences logically calculated from some pure theory.)

I was forty-five years old when I began this project. The next decade marker was fifty. If one looks at the psychological or sociological literature for a description of this period in a woman's life, one immediately is struck by the nearly unbroken silence. Between forty and sixty women appear to be almost missing from life. The only event of any consequence in terms of life-span development is menopause. It represents a time of a woman's life in which loss, longing, abandonment and decline prevail. I report these things not as a matter of fact, but as a distillation of the "wisdom" that may be found in social science texts, scholarly reference books, medical journals and the media more generally. The accepted facts about women are that they will lose their primary biological function of childbearing, their physical attractiveness (which is a source of esteem and power for most adults) and their vocational function as mothers when their children grow up, (leaving them with their well-publicized "empty nests"). While men may not receive much more attention in the forty to sixty range, they are seldom described in such dour tones as women are. If, for example, we look at Freud's descriptions of a thirty-year-old woman versus a thirty-year-old man, in his thirty-third lecture, we see an even earlier indication of the different outcomes of the genders/sexes, with women viewed as rigidly finalized and men as youthfully resilient (Freud, 1939).

I looked around at my own life, at those of my friends and colleagues and at women in public life. Jane Fonda was older than I, as was Joan Collins. Many well-known women had not donned the sackcloth and ashes and given-up on life once they were forty. Some women, like Barbara Walters, for instance, had not only grown in stature, but in beauty as well. Certain contemporary perceptions of middle-aged women, thus, struck me as at great variance with the tales of gloom fostered by the "science industry." Yet, psychological wisdom is reflexive in a culture. What textbooks, medical columns in newspapers and popular psychological tracts say matters. Thus, women who might normally be enjoying their new freedoms, liberated from "the curse" and their children, might question themselves, looking for the signs of depression, loss, aimlessness, illness and aging that are predicted for them. And normally, if one looks long enough and hard enough, compelling evidence will be forthcoming.[3] My major aim in the research project was to use the dialogic format to create a rebuttal to the bleak notion of what it is to be a "middle-aged" woman in America.

I understand your motives, both self-interested and, on your terms, altruistic. While it is admirable to try to change women's images of "middle-age," you can't deny that women do go through physiological changes. Menopause is a fact of life, and possibly a medical issue, isn't it? How do you propose to deal with these facts?

I need to mention one more component in the research package. I've discussed my feminist metatheory and methodological considerations, and I've described my motivational impetus to the project. But I have neglected to mention a missing element, one related to the theoretical component of the research. This is my acceptance of a social constructionist framework. (See K. Gergen, 1985 for an overview of this perspective in psychology.) From this standpoint, nothing stands by itself as a social fact. Rather, a social constructionist would describe menopause as a social fact with the attributes and associations necessitated by cultural conventions. Note, that similar social event, the climaterium, is also gaining currency as a biological event in the lives of men, but so far it has not made the top of the medical charts. It is faltering in significance, perhaps, because it does not serve men's social needs to emphasize an end to their potency. On the other hand, the climaterium may not be totally useless as a "biological event" for men because it might help to explain a poor sexual performance.

What I am focussing on, however, is the extent to which a biological event is singled out, popularized and significated according to other important social meanings in the culture. Menstruation and menopause are both important constructs in most societies because they are used to signal the delimits of a significant social function: becoming pregnant. (Why societies care who can and cannot become pregnant is a very deep question of religious and economic, as well as social, significance, and is beyond the scope of this paper.)

How did you propose to use the social constructionist framework in your research?

My plan was to begin a discussion group focussed on the issue of menopause and its significance in women's lives. I assumed that the participants already would be influenced by the popular culture to accept the social construction of menopause as an indicator of the loss of youth, of beauty and of functional roles. I was not certain however of their individual experiences with menopause. (My own personal history was that at that time I had had one "hot flash" and one ten-minute discussion with my closest childhood friend, who told me that she had begun taking hormones.)

My over-arching plan was that within the flow of the discussion I would try to set out my views concerning the social construction of biological events, such as menopause, and to suggest that the attendant "loss" effect that had been propounded in educational materials and the media was essentially anti-woman. While this seems to be a plan fraught with arrogant overtones of big sister superiority, I did consider deeply the dialectic aspect of the discussion. I did not see myself as involved in a linear action of the participants taking in what I said, and suddenly becoming disciples of my words. (Besides, since we were peers on the court they were not interested in suddenly viewing me as an authority figure for them.) I did, however, want to move them from an acceptance of what I call "the medical model of menopause," that is an undesirable, but inevitable failing of the body leading to a general decline and psychological malaise, to a more positive image of adult women, in general, and themselves, particularly.

Well, what were the outcomes of the research?

As I confessed earlier, I combined traditional social psychological methods, using pre- and post-measures of attitude change, with other analyses. I wanted to isolate the possible effects of the discussion on individual attitudes toward menopausal issues as indicated by paper and pencil measures. When the participants arrived at my home they were separated and given a small battery of surveys to complete. Then after the session they were given a similar packet to take home with them to fill out the following day and mail back to me. One such questionnaire, Opinions about Menopause, was retested. This instrument was designed to tap agreement with traditional medical and psychiatric views about menopause. For example: "Menopause is basically a medical problem"; and, "Women usually get emotionally more unstable after menopause." The participants could indicate agreement or disagreement on a 7-point scale. A second retested scale was called Images of Woman. This one was designed to assess changes in self-image at twenty, thirty-five and as projected to age fifty. (Menopause is usually in process by age fifty.) Using a semantic differential format they rated themselves on twenty paired adjectives at each of the three ages. I anticipated that the impact of the discussion group would decrease group agreement with the medical model of menopause, and increase the positivity of ratings of self-image at fifty.

It seems that this might be a good place to report what you found using traditional methods.

There is something so clean and well-defined about the facts one obtains from adding numbers, plotting graphs and handling statistics. There was "hard" evidence that participants became less committed to the medical model after the discussion, but with eight discussants, the statistical analyses for significant differences were hardly worth attempting. After the discussion, participants more strongly disagreed with the statements, Most women "would rather continue to menstruate than not," "feel negative about their loss of fertility," "keep menopause a secret, as something shameful," "become less attractive after menopause," "get emotionally more unstable after menopause" and "are less interested in sex." These represented a majority of the questions asked, and I think indicates that the anti-women medical model views were rejected by the women as strongly or more so after the discussion group than before.

In terms of the self-image scale, I discovered a ceiling effect problem. My guests turned out to be very positive in how they rated their self-images at the outset, and there was not much room for improvement after the discussion. Beforehand they saw themselves as very competent and satisfied people at twenty and at fifty years of age. Interestingly many indicated that they were less satisfied with life at thirty-five. (The discussion brought out comments about how hard life was then, especially with satisfying the demands of their mothering roles.) After the meeting, the only areas of noticeable enhancement in self-image were in the traits of **stability** and **strength**. They tended to see themselves as becoming increasingly stable and strong at fifty. Of course these increases provided support for my expectation that the nature of the discourse would have the effect of changing the image of the older woman to a more positive view.

The traditional methods seemed to lead in positive directions, but were not very sensitive, it seems, to the changes that you perceived on a more intuitive level. But what about analysis of the dialogue itself? Is there anything to be learned from the pattern of interchange—specifically how dialogic methods can help us understand issues of life-span development among middle-aged women?

I cannot analyze the entire text of the discussion in detail here. Like a gold mine, it could provide endless materials, depending on the theoretical framework you chose. A Marxist, for example, might have a field day gleaning support for the view that these women represent capitalism in its dying flourish. I would like to simply try to stick to the path of showing how the dialogue served as the means by which the group maintained itself, confronted the task I brought to the group and resolved the tension between the members' own normal social interactions with each other and the expectations I had for them as discussants. As an overview, I perceived the discussion as dividing into three stages: *denial and resistance; cohesion and containment; and review and restoration.*

The first stage of the discussion focussed on the denial of the topic. Menopause was shameful or boring to speak about and/or irrelevant to them. (While I was one of the group in some sense, as the organizer of the experience, I was also part of the "problem" the group had to confront. Thus, I feel more comfortable using the third person pronouns to describe the seven other members of the group.) The group began with a dilemma to confront: How do they maintain their usual friendly and casual interdependence in the context of a "psychological experiment" about a taboo topic of discussion? In the second stage, more details related to menopause were revealed, and the goup groped for a means of developing cohesiveness while confronting the topic. I think this stage displayed an anxious negativity surrounding talk about menopause and also aging. Menopause was something that happened to others. Personal details began to be revealed, and the discussion began to be more intense. Fears that lay behind the mask of mystery and silence about menopause were noted. In the third stage, review and restoration, the group began to review the evidence and, with some security about the solidarity of the group, restore their original confidence in themselves and their group ties. They found their solution in a manner that took some of my ideas into account, yet was original. They were able to build a group fantasy in which they contrasted the relatively comfortable life they envisioned for themselves at fifty to their earlier tribulations as struggling housewife and mother. They began to fantasize about the joys of living with their "empty nests." Expressions of worry about husbands and their ability to make the transition were exposed. Finally, the discussants had built for themselves a solution to the challenge of age: they were going to beat the system. As relatively well-to-do, well-educated and active women, they were going to avail themselves of the best in information, health care and personal services that would extend their youth indefinitely. In so doing, of course, they would redefine the social construction of what it means to be "fifty."

Through the creation of a dialogue they managed to create a cohesive group, daring through small steps of self-disclosure to go deeper into the murky issue of menopause. Finding a level of trust and sharing there, they risked further disclosures. Finally they had gone as far as they felt comfortable, as a group of eight; they proposed more intimate conversations with close friends as a forum for opening dialogues on deeper insecurities and fears.

You describe the first state of the discussion as one of denial and resistance. Why do you perceive it as such?

My interpretation that the discussants begin by denying the significance of menopause in their lives comes from the initial remarks of the participants.

Bonnie: I thought one of your questions was interesting, that it's [menopause] something to be ashamed of . . . and I think that . . . not that it's something to be ashamed of. I don't know of anybody that has even spoken to me about it.
Debra: It's an age branding, isn't it?
Bonnie: Yes, I mean in this age of youth you certainly aren't going to go around and admit that you are involved in this process. . . .

It seems to me that Bonnie's remarks are designed to ask if this is a permissive atmosphere in which this possibly shameful topic can be discussed. I have asked them to talk about something that might reveal their possible weakness or shame. Bonnie seems to be testing whether the social support is there. Debra, of course, zeroes in on one significant aspect of the concern, being branded as old. The group then begins to declare that they were too young to concern themselves personally with the topic. They position themselves to me as cooperative, but disinterested participants.

The original stance of the group seems to be that they will cooperate with me in being a part of this "experiment," but they want to make it clear that this is not their idea, and the topic is not of their choice or interest. The function of the dialogue serves to separate each of them from issues of menopause, and perhaps thereby not risk their status within the group.

The group begins to mention where they have heard or seen something about menopause.

Sandy: I'm forty-one and I don't really ... listen, its not something you're going to sit around and discuss unless you have to. I mean I wouldn't think of it as a particularly interesting topic of conversation. ...

Suzanne: [Mentions a friend who is fifty-six and seems to be still menstruating.] We don't discuss intimate things like that. Not that we don't discuss it, but as she [Sandy] said, it's not all that fascinating; we're going to get another ten years."

(Very strong laughter follows.)

Marla: ... I don't really think about it because it's too far away. I don't have to think about it YET. (Marla is the oldest person in the group at 48.)

The denial tactics are shifted somewhat when Debra, one of the youngest and most attractive group members, "admits" that she is beginning the process. Debra: Well, I think I'm going through it right now. I'm forty-one. (She describes her symptoms.) And my mother was exactly the same. It doesn't worry me in the slightest.

Debra takes a daring plunge into the dialogue with this admission. I think she is able to do this because she is extremely popular within the group, young and known for speaking her mind. Her comments are a dare to all the older group members to be more forthright. Debra follows the line of denial [i.e. menopause is not a problem] held at the moment. Then strangely, it seems to me, she suddenly corrects herself.

Debra: That's incorrect. It does bother me. I will go to a doctor, just to be sure. ... It's just that thing in the back of the mind ... you want it checked.

Do you see Debra's remark as the transition between the denial and resistance stage and the second stage you describe as cohesion and containment?

Yes, although things do not run so smoothly in actual conversations, the tendency is to swing into recitations of gloom. Debra's comments seem to pave the way for the group to speak more freely about menopause. They are testing the waters of trust, and carefully keeping the dialogue focussed primarily on others.

Marla: The most concerned I ever was, really and truthfully, about menopause, was when I was a freshman in college and my roommate's mother was going through menopause at that time, and she went off her rocker. She was boiling dishrags for dinner. Hadn't slept with her husband in who knows how long.

[Group responds with ohs, ahs.]

Marla: This girl was telling me these tales. . . . God, at that point I was wondering if everyone did that sort of thing. . . .

Suzanne: I think there is a lot of association to things we expect to be there: of getting older, of getting forgetful. . . .

Bonnie: [Talking of her mother] In the back of my head, I thought, 'Oh, she must be going through menopause, she's really crabby, why does she have to be like this?' . . .

The group then shifts the topic to menstruation, and what a bother that is. As menstruation is an experience that breeds solidarity among the group, it is a safe topic to develop within the dialogue. By complaining about the trials of menstruating they build a platform from which menopause may be discussed more personally. They also can agree: If menstruation is a negative event then getting it over with should be a positive one.

While group cohesiveness and trust are building, one group member seems to stress the others with her willingness to bring up negative topics. Eventually the group walls off many of her comments, almost as if she did not speak. Her situation is different from other group members in that she has had a hysterectomy, and has only one ovary.

Terry: Everybody I talked to said that if you don't have hormones you do age. . . . They've talked about the wrinkles, and the way the one girl said, the vagina.

[Group murmurs agreement sounds.]

Terry: The dryness of the vagina, that's how the doctor could tell she had aged. It was lack of hormones. . . . Oh, and the other thing was osteoporosis from the lack of hormones. So all this scared me, and I thought . . . I think I'll go to the doctor. I think I'll get hormones. Among my friends that are going through menopause, that's a big discussion.

The group after serious, measured discourse finally laughs and jokes after Terry mentions the hot flashes one friend has been experiencing.

It seemed that the group could not tolerate any more problematic symptoms from Terry, and looked for an opportunity to "lighten up." Suddenly Debra began clowning around.

Debra: The favorite joke around the club now, (she holds her hands at her waist and makes gestures about pulling up her breasts), if you're not doing this. . . . (Laughter and remarks from the group blot out sentence.)

Debra: They joke about old age. When you get older, they start to hang. . . . I guess as you get older there's a close relation between tragedy and comedy.

Suzanne: Things are so tragic you have to laugh.

In this segment of the discussion the ills associated with menopause are being laid out on the table. Suzanne's last remark highlights a group coping strategy, using humor to mask concern when the dialogue gets too depressing. In this sense I call the strategy of the group one of containment. They probe the questions put forth, often by me, but they don't let the conversation get too grim before they confine it, mostly with humor.

Following Suzanne's remark, Sandy begins to weave a second aspect of the eventual solution to the problem of how to live with menopause: She emphasizes how much better off the group is now than older women once were. Sandy: We just look so much better than past generations. (Group agrees vigorously.) I mean ... we are such a healthy generation. ... I think it is just tremendous. I see more less trim people in their twenties. ... I think that's really sloppy. I think why do you look like that when there's no reason for it? You know you can really do something with yourself. Now look at this group. ... I think we are a good-looking healthy generation, and I don't think that menopause is going to affect us like it did past generations. Because we feel better. (Group agrees.) We're healthier, we feel better, and we're going to be able to play through it, tennis, golf, whatever.
Pat: If you stay home and brood, then I think you're going to make more of it than maybe is there.

The group has reached a state in which they feel comfortable owning the fact that they are coming into the menopausal zone of life. They have reached concurrence that menopause would be easier on them because of their physical care. Sandy's metaphor that we will play through it seems very apt. Her comments stress the idea that despite the minor inconveniences of menopause, the active, healthy life styles we lead will stave off problems. The worst thing to be done would be to sit home and worry about it. I want to pursue other avenues of concern besides physical symptoms and conditioning with them. I again stress the fabric of trust and cohesiveness the group has achieved.
Mary: ... What about the emotional side to menopause? Some think [menopause symbolizes that] you've come to the end of a life style.
Sandy: I think most people when they go through menopause are also going through having their kids leave. Maybe it has nothing to do with menopause ... maybe it has to do with everyone going here and going there.
Marla: Another thing that concerns me is ... how bitchy we've become. ... It's got to be connected with menopause. There has to be some kind of result on our mental well-being because of the physical changes in menopause ... while we're going through it, its got to do something mentally to us, I would think. Make us more sensitive, more unstable.
Suzanne: How could I get much more? (Group laughs.)

Sandy has exposed the "empty nest" question, and Marla has responded with a personal concern of being more emotionally unstable and negative. These are two pertinent concerns often associated with aging women. Suzanne humorously deflects the argument that women get unstable emotionally when they reach menopause by admitting that she has always been extremely "emotional." Sandy again comes up with a method of solving emotional problems concurrent with this age. She has raised one of the threatening problems, and she often takes the responsibility for solving them.

Sandy: I think that if you can talk it out . . . the older I get the more I appreciate my girlfriends . . . and rely on them so much. I have a terrific relationship with my husband, . . . but boy, there's nothing like a good girlfriend to sit and chat and cry with and laugh with, and let your hair down, it makes things much easier. If you keep things inside of you they tend to grow, and be more serious than maybe they are.

I think Sandy's comments cut both ways in this moment in the dialogue. She is telling the group that it is good, even necessary to talk to women friends about these issues. And at times there may be things to worry and cry about. Yet at the same time she does implicitly draw a line between this group and a one-on-one talk with a good friend. She may be telling me and the other members that this group is not that type of context. She will not cry and worry with us.

Pat: I know that's true. When I think about my friends, we're all about the same age, and I know we're all going to hit it together.

(Group breaks into chatter, laughter.)

Suzanne: I think this generation talks a lot more than our mothers did. . . . I think they thought it was something to be ashamed of.

Suzanne's comments suggest that it is OK for this group to talk about menopause, and it is not only something for very close friends to share. The ability to admit to negative feelings, and to be able to share these feelings with friends is resolved within this portion of the dialogue. The group continues to explore the negative aspects surrounding menopause. Periodically threads of optimism are strung among the gloom. Throughout much of the discussion, I bring up problems that have traditionally been associated with menopause: sexual abandonment, loss of love and aging. The group parries my concerns using various strategies described above. They manage to maintain the group facade and their own sense of self-esteem, but with greater self-disclosure.

The group members also defend against any challenges to their status as attractive, vital women.

Suzanne: (Speaking of going through menopause) . . . It's not like you're walking through the airport, and you put your stuff through and you come out and you're another person . . . (voices all rise in agreement) . . . and you can look at someone and say AHHA! (Laughter is hysterical.) you've gone through menopause, haven't you?

While the group seems to agree that others cannot tell from the outside if you have gone through menopause, internal factors may indicate your change. Interestingly Suzanne, who had just strongly argued that you cannot tell if menopause has occurred, is the one to mention a negative indicator, and then to counter it almost in the same breath.

Suzanne: I've had people say to me . . . that you sort of dry up, that your juices aren't as flowing. (She speaks of the differences between young and old animals and people, and mentions that young people may avoid older people because they do not have this vital quality.) I think there is a "juices flowing" kind of thing here. But I know plenty of gals who are past menopause who are full of it, and I find that very encouraging.

While Suzanne seems to have brought up a negative commentary on menopausal women, she seems reluctant to hold this position for long.

Earlier you characterized the last portion of the discussion as a period of review and restoration. What did you mean by this description?

As the discussion is shaped, the various socially accepted "goblins" of menopause have been brought out for viewing, and have been discussed. Within the review and restoration segment, the group, with its boundaries intact and its viability established, concentrates on resolving how to best proceed with the problem of facing menopause. I use the terms review and restoration to indicate that material that had been discussed is reintroduced and negative elements are recast more positively.

Marty: When I think now of the women I know who have been through menopause, not one of them is not happy about it. They are all happy about having gone through it. Having their period finished. They've given me a very positive feeling about it. I haven't heard any complaints.

Sandy: I'm much more confident now . . . and I don't know why to tell you the truth. I feel like I could conquer the world. And I'm simply biding my time right now, and my future is all ahead of me.

Debra: . . . we were living in Sydney; he asked me how I'd feel if we didn't stay there very long. It really hit me. Now when he says we are moving, I say great. I have much more confidence in myself. The difference really hit me. I don't know if that's a sign of aging or what.

Not everyone feels so rosy, but within the context of the group it is allowed.

Pat: I have difficulty projecting myself into the future. . . . Len is fairly . . ., What's the word I want to use? Give me a polite word (Laughter)—Independent. Very macho-oriented. The woman does this, the man does that. . . . When I see older people, . . . wives have become mothers to these men. . . . I think, oh God, I don't want to end up like that. Old married couple fighting with each other.

You mentioned that you tried to present a view of how women might envision themselves in a more positive way after menopause. You planned to introduce them to the view that menopause was a social construction. What happened as a result?

In the last portion of the discussion, I did try to summarize my view that menopause is a social construction, given meaning and value by the culture to all of us. It is a meaning that often conveys a strong negative message to women about their social value. I hoped that women would not accept this definition and that they would form new images of adult women beyond their childbearing and rearing days. I wanted our discussion group to lend itself to this goal.

How was this idea received by the group?

It was not a brilliant success, in the way I had envisioned it, but other consequences occurred as a result of the dialogue that were gratifying. First of all I discovered that my participants were fairly entrenched in a "naive realism" epistemology. They were not very interested in thinking about biological events as social constructions. They were not willing to easily give up on the "reality" of menopause. In this sense I failed to accomplish my goal.

Did you learn something by engaging in this participatory framework of research that you might have missed otherwise?

Glad you asked. Yes. As a member of the group, I was looked upon as an equal participant by the others most of the time. And, in terms of life experiences with menopause, it was the case. What I realized as we talked was that among us we had developed an alternative solution to reconceptualizing the event as a non-event, which I had gone into the research desiring. The outcome was that we might overcome the limits of the event through superior weapons of exercise, diet, health practices and the social support of our friends.

Through this analysis I "discovered" that by organizing the event and creating the means to attempt certain goals, I separated myself from the group in significant ways. Many of the group's comments, I believe, were directed at the group problem of handling my intrusion as a psychologist into a very loosely knit group of friendly tennis players.

Did you find the operations of the group satisfying, given your intersubjective, emancipatory, feminist research goals?

Yes, and I would state it like this: These women seemed to grow in trust and confidence about themselves and their futures through their participation in this dialogue. Each one was in a better condition to expand her social role as a mature woman after this research encounter than before. As one of my goals was to benefit my actual subjects, rather than make some vague promissory note about benefits to "mankind" in the next decade, I was satisfied in that respect.

The dialogue also helped form a viable group, one that could function to work out the issue of what to say about the topic of menopause within this setting. At least within this protective shell of group membership statements were made that supported my notion of what image women should have of their menopausal lives.

From a social constructionist perspective, I also feel some joy about the success of the endeavor. As I have already mentioned, I failed to "teach" the notion of social constructionism to the participants, yet, they seemed to create a solution to the problem, as I saw it, by actually planning to transform the image of the older woman through action, rather than thought. While none of them was willing to deny the reality of menopause as a biological event, they were eager as individuals to act and feel about themselves in a manner that challenges the characteristics associated with the older-woman image. Through their behaviors they would remake what it means to be "fifty." It will be the work of others in the society to readjust the image to the people.

What happens next? Do you envision any specific projects related to this work?

During the discussion, members of the group suggested that it would be helpful if women who were actually going through menopause, and who had gone through it, could be part of the group. Each of the participants seemed to take on a profound naiveté in the face of this inquiry, and they thought more valid information could be garnered from respondents with more direct experience. I agree that this would provide an interesting perspective. My choice of pre-menopausal women was, in part, an effort to influence images before a commitment to a changed status had occurred. Perhaps older women would be less persuasible even than younger ones. I would be interested in pursuing the line of inquiry that suggests that menopause is not a central event in most women's lives.

What about the dialogic method? Do you see its utility expanded beyond this project for you?

I feel some commitment to this method, for reasons I've mentioned. I think it is hard to avoid practicing it once one has gotten involved with it. I am interested in using something of this type to explore the personal narratives of young girls, especially those who are very likely to become pregnant. I wonder if such an approach might have an emancipatory effect on the girls, and also I wonder what changes might occur in me as a result.

I hope those who read through this chapter might also be encouraged to experiment with the dialogic methods themselves. Especially those who do interviewing work might easily reconceptualize and adapt what they do within the dialogic framework. This approach has already been well documented by Elliot Mishler (1986).

Lastly I am curious about the group members. Over two years have passed since your group met. What has happened to them?

Amazing things have happened. Good taste and brevity prevent me from giving a complete recital of these lives. I did speak to Suzanne recently about this project. She said she wished we'd do it again, since now it would be so much more relevant. I also asked Bonnie what she recalled of this gathering. She said she remembered what a good time everyone had. I suppose there are worse ways to remember being involved in a psychology investigation.

Notes

1. This research was supported by a grant from the Penn State University Faculty Scholarship Fund.

2. Except for my own, the names of the discussants have been changed.

3. I am not the only investigator who has suspected that menopause has been construed as a detrimental factor in women's lives. A study comparing attitudes about menopause indicated that women did not view menopause as negatively as members of the medical professions (Cowan et al., 1985). Bernice Neugarten reported that among 100 women, ages 45-55, menstrual cycle was an unimportant predictor of psychological well-being: only 4 percent thought menopause was an important worry and 96 percent were able to mention positive aspects of menopause. Yet, an underlying ambivalence toward menopause was indicated, as most women rated themselves more favorably than "women in menopause" (Neugarten, 1973)

Cross-cultural studies also indicate that among menopausal women, depression, the principle psychological syndrome related to menopause, is only found in cultures where women's status decreases after menopause (Bart, 1971). Menopausal depression seems to be the result of cultural demands for women to restrict themselves to the maternal role (Becker, 1964). Depression is not simple a matter of hormones, or their lack, but rather of lack of alternative life options.

References

Bart, P. (1971). Depression in middle-aged women. In V. Gornick & B. K. Moran (eds.) *Women in sexist society*. New York: Basic Books.

Becker, E. (1964). *The revolution in psychiatry*. Glencoe, IL: Free Press.

Clifford, J. (1983). On ethnographic authority. *Representations* 2: 132-143.

Crapanzano, V. (1980). *Tuhami: Portrait of a Moroccan*. Chicago: University of Chicago Press.

Cowan, G. L. W. Warren and J. L. Young. (1985). Medical perceptions of menopausal symptoms. *Psychology of Women Quarterly* 9: 3-14.

Danziger, K. (1985). The methodological imperative in psychology. *Philosophy of the Social Sciences* 15: 1-13.

Derrida, J. (1978). *Writing and difference*. tr. Alan Bass. Chicago: University of Chicago Press.

Favret Saadia, J. (1977). *Deadly words: Witchcraft in the Bocage*. Cambridge, England: Cambridge University Press.

Freud, S. (1939). *New introductory lectures of psychoanalysis*. New York: Norton.

Gadamer, H. G. (1976). *Philosophical hermeneutics*. tr. D. E. Linge. Berkeley: University of California Press.

Gergen, K. J. (1985). The social constructionist movement in modern psychology. *American Psychologist* 40: 266-275.

Gergen, M. (1988). Toward a feminist methodology. In M. Gergen (ed.) *Feminist thought and the structure of knowledge*. New York: New York University Press.

Gilbert, G. N. and M. Mulkay. (1984). *Opening Pandora's box: A sociological analysis of scientists' discourse*. Cambridge: Cambridge University Press.

Latour, B. and S. Woolgar. (1979). *Laboratory life: The social construction of scientific facts*. Beverly Hills, CA: Sage.

Minton, H. L. (1986). Emancipatory social psychology as a paradigm for the study of minority groups. In K. S. Larsen (ed.) *Dialectics and ideology in psychology*. Norwood, NJ: ABLEX.

Mishler, E. (1986). *Research interviewing: Context and narrative*. Cambridge: Harvard University Press.

Mitroff, I. (1974). *The subjective side of science*. Amsterdam: Elsevier.

Neugarten, B. L. (1973). A new look at menopause. In C. Tavris (ed.) *The female experience*. Del Mar, CA: CRM.

Neugarten, B. L. et al. (eds.) (1964). *Personality in middle and late life*. New York: Atherton.

Owens, C. (1983). The discourse of others: Feminists and postmodernism. In H. Foster (ed.) *The anti-aesthetic: Essays on postmodern culture*. Port Townsend, WA: Bay Press.

Parlee, M. B. (1979). Psychology and women. *Signs: Journal of Women in Culture and Society* 5: 121-133.

Potter, J. and M. Wetherell. (1987). *Discourse and social psychology: Beyond attitudes and behaviour.* London: Sage.

Reinharz, S. (1985). Feminist distrust: Problems of context and content in sociological work. In D. Berg & K. Smith (eds.) *Exploring clinical methods of social research.* Beverley Hills, CA: Sage.

Vaughter, R. (1976). Psychology. Review essay. *Signs: Journal of Women in Culture and Society* 2: 120-146.

Wagner, R. (1975). *The invention of culture.* Englewood Cliffs, NJ: Prentice Hall.

Woolgar, S. (ed.) (1987). *Knowledge and reflexivity.* London: Sage..

Wortham, S. (1986). Dialogue: Two Conceptions. Unpublished manuscript. University of Chicago.

Chapter 6

The Domestic Meaning
of Institutionalization

JABER F. GUBRIUM

Turn to any ad for a nursing home in the telephone yellow pages and you're likely to find it described as having a homelike atmosphere. The message is that, despite being an institution, it can provide domestic tranquility, a home-away-from-home for a loved one. The message, of course, is also about placement, informing those concerned that because the institution, too, can provide "loving care"—another familiar phrase—families needn't be overburdened by an impaired elder or distressed by the placement decision.

One might guess from this that a major theme of the placement decision for the family would be the domestic meaning of institutionalization, referring to whether a facility or a household, respectively, can be, or is any longer, a home. On the one hand, in assessing the quality of care in nursing homes in general, and for specific facilities in particular, one would expect families to be expressly concerned with whether a nursing home is homelike and provides the loving care a family might offer. On the other hand, the domestic well-being of the family as a whole would seem to be significant too, centering on the question of whether, in the chronic and distressful circumstance of a member's progressive impairment, an overburdened household can be a home to anyone. As a placement theme, the domestic meaning of institutionalization would seem to hinge on both concerns, the interpretation of domesticity in relation to household, home, and institution.

Yet, if we peruse the related scholarly literature, we find remarkably little research dealing with the theme. Research on the quality of care in nursing homes centers larely on environmental and staffing characteristics, ignoring the issue of quality as it relates to the domestic concerns of the family for the patient. As Johnson and Grant (1985, p. 111) summarize, evaluation criteria are typically based on resident characteristics and their care satisfaction, the assessment of the physical and social environment, or the professionalization of the staff and care provision. Interestingly, following Johnson and Grant's summary, a familiar checklist appears specifying what to look for in a nursing home in making placement decisions (pp. 120-121). It is headed "What a family needs to know." Ostensibly, signs of quality can be identified from facility characteristics alone, such as its staff configuration and the appearance of cleanliness.

The caregiver-burden literature, in contrast, is more explicitly focussed on the family as a component of the care and institutional placement equation, but it also leaves aside the issue of domesticity. Little attention is paid to caregivers' regard for the domesticity of their own households resulting from the stresses on the family of the burdens of care. Rather, this literature's target question is how the patient's impairment affects caregiver stress and, in turn, figures in the placement decision. Gwyther and George (1986) conclude that the growing number of studies in this area seems to show (1) that the caregiver's felt burden depends on the caregiver's relationship with the patient, on how differences such as sex, age, and living arrangement affect stress and decision-making, and (2) the relative insignificance of the patient's symptoms and behavior for understanding caregiver functioning. Concerning the latter, there is reason to believe, for example, that institutional placement is better predicted by factors such as the degree of support the caregiver receives from other family members. By and large unstudied is the process of how an overburdened caregiver takes stock of the home he or she provides for the impaired family member in relation to what the household has become for the caregiver and other family members.

There are, in effect, two homes at issue regarding the domestic meaning of institutionalization—the caring household and the institution—both of which are points of interpretation in placement decisions. Nursing home advertising seems to tell us as much; existing research appears to have skirted the issue.

Based on a continuing field study of the Alzheimer's disease experience (Gubrium, 1986a), this chapter empirically addresses the theme and issue. Data are presented to illustrate how quality of institutional care, on the one hand, and the changing domesticity of the household, on the other, figure in the placement decision. It is argued that, among other interpretive concerns (Gubrium, 1986a, 1986b, 1987), placement takes on its meaning in relation to two domestic considerations: the questions of what is a good nursing home and when a caring household is no longer home. The two are, of course, contingent, but for the purpose of addressing the domestic meaning of institutionalization against the two bodies of literature, their data will be presented separately. Furthermore, it is argued that both concerns are subject to the constant interpretation and specification of experience in relation to a public culture of responses. The public culture is composed of shared understandings evident in and about the disease's popular and professional literatures, broadcast media and the everyday discourse of those concerned (Gubrium, 1986a, chap. 4).

The Study

Participant observation and focussed interviews provided access to caregivers' considerations of the domestic meaning of institutionalization. As part of a larger study of the descriptive organization of senility, support groups for the caregivers of Alzheimer's disease patients were observed in two cities over a three year period. One of the support groups was sponsored by a day hospital for Alzheimer's disease patients. The Alzheimer's Disease and Related Disorders Association (ADRDA) also sponsors support groups for caregivers in cooperation with its many chapters across the nation. ADRDA support groups were observed in both cities. In one city, participating adult children and spouses were separated into different groups; in the other city, family caregivers met together. Throughout the fieldwork, caregivers periodically were interviewed both in their own homes and in respite care settings. All references to persons and places in this and other reports are pseudonyms.

Maximum variation was sought in the composition of the groups and participants. Some support groups were facilitated by members, others by service providers. Some were didactic, while others aimed at self-help. Both male and female caregivers participated, related in different ways to the patients in their care. Caregivers had a broad range of educational and occupational backgrounds. Because Alzheimer's disease victims tend to be elderly, the risk varying with age, the family caregivers themselves were mainly middle-aged or elderly. The Alzheimer's disease literature suggested that the social composition of the support groups studied reflected the participating caregiver population at large.

Social composition aside, it was not so much the representativeness of the groups and participants that made the field data useful as it was the data's contribution to understanding the domestic meaning of institutionalization as a process. The aim of the study from which these data were drawn was not to generalize onto a population from a sample of caregivers and support groups, but to empirically comment on existing models of the disease and the disease experience. Reflecting that aim, the target of this chapter is current conceptualizations of quality of care in institutions and the prevailing understanding of the placement decision. The aim in general is guided by strategic, not representative, sampling.

What is a Good Nursing Home?

Among the caregivers and support groups studied, answers to the question "What is a good nursing home?" did include consideration of standard, checklist-like criteria found in the literature. Caregivers frequently fretted about cleanliness, what they took to be an institutional reputation for patient inactivity, the lack of skilled nursing staff, among other common worries. But in considering placement, the issue of the nursing home's domesticity was never far away. The very theme highlighted in nursing home ads—about a homelike atmosphere—regularly captured their attention and mediated their related deliberations and testimony. Quality of care was never just a matter of the presence or absence of quality characteristics, but quality in relation to what an institution's public image typically was not, namely, not home.

While participants tended to resent taking up what some referred to as "all the talk about nursing homes," there were occasions when particular homes or kinds of homes were compared and contrasted. The question of whether they provided homelike atmospheres and loving care had two facets: whether a facility's amenities would serve merely to house the patient or be a home, and whether the patient would be in the company of strangers or "family." Both facets were points of the placement consideration.

Housing versus Home

Let us turn to caregivers' deliberations over the first facet and examine its practical meaning for those concerned. Based on common what-to-look-for checklists and quality of care criteria in general, we might hazard to guess that a good home would be signalled by the presence of amenities such as wholesome food, cleanliness, privacy and proper furnishings, with mere housing (some say warehousing) resulting from their absence. Field data suggest otherwise.

Consider Bertha Hughes's testimony in a session of her support group that was almost totally devoted to her particular "worries" about placing her seventy-eight-year-old demented husband in a nursing home. To participants, Bertha's was a familiar story. Bertha regularly punctuated her comments with worried expressions about her husband's continual decline, his need for personal attention and her inability to satisfactorily provide for his love of the outdoors. She frequently pointed out that if Lester, the husband, needed anything out of life, it was to be in the yard or somewhere else out of the house. As Bertha remarked at one point in the session:

> I've looked into a lot of them [nursing homes], and I just don't like what I see, except maybe for one of them. [Offers comparative details] I hate to even bring it up, really. I don't like to think about putting Les in one of those places. It just worries me to death to think of him all cooped up in a nursing home. He's a big guy and you know how he loves the outdoors. He just loves the yard, anywhere but in the house. I don't have to tell you how I have to spend all my time taking him out.

Several participants responded. As usual, they begged her not to worry, although they added that they understood how worrisome the problem was. They also tried to help her to see what some called the "good side" of nursing homes, even though, again, each admitted that any home would be a worry to anyone. Thelma, whose husband had already been placed in a nursing home, explained:

> Mike [her husband] is in a nursing home that I'd consider one of the better ones around. It's over on Bellman Avenue. You know the one with the fancy windows on the front. It's clean. I was really surprised to find how friendly the people are. Well . . . it's not quite home, I know. But it's a place for him. I just couldn't handle him anymore.

This turned the group to the consideration of quality of care in general. Each spoke of nursing homes with which they were personally acquainted. The poor and good qualities were detailed. Where one home was considered good because it was clean, another was said to offer acceptable care because the staff was friendly. At one point, the conversation dwelled on urine smells and what they signalled about quality care. One participant stated flatly that if he walked into "one of those places" and smelled urine, he'd know "right away" that it was poorly run, even though, he admitted, he never really had been in a nursing home. Another participant remarked that what she looked for were the activities, adding that she had seen too many people "just sitting around in wheelchairs" in nursing homes and that meant that the staff was sitting on its "duff." In contrast to urine smells, this participant, like some others, read good care from visible activity.

Support group participants had had various experiences with nursing homes. That much was clear from their conversation. Some had never been in one, but were vicariously acquainted with them through others' experiences. A few already had placed a family member in a nursing home. Others were in the throes of actively seeking admission. Still others stated flatly that they would never consider a nursing home. Regardless of their individual differences, their talk and assessments of the quality of care in nursing homes in general mirrored the familiar what-to-look-for checklists as well as criteria commonly found in the literature on quality of care. In the context of answering the *general* question "What is a good nursing home?" responses were typical of popular understandings. Indeed, if the various concerns over quality of care in their general discussions were listed, they would, point for point, approximate what one might find in the literature. In this context, the participants reproduced a veritable public culture of answers to the question.

Bertha was soon to reenter the conversation and return to her concerns for her husband, Lester. She mentioned how helpful all of the comments had been and that, even though she had not made up her mind, she would take everything that was said into account when it was time. But, then, interestingly, she added:

> I couldn't stand to put anyone in a place that was dirty either. Lester has never been fussy but he does like that fresh, outdoor kind of smell. That's why I dry all his clothes out on the clothesline. To me, the clothes smell funny when I bring them in. But him ... he likes that. To him, it's clean. I put everything else in the dryer. See that's the problem with those places [nursing homes]. How am I going to manage to make him feel clean if they're going to do his clothes and then lose half of them?

As Bertha elaborated her sentiments about placement and cleanliness, it became evident that what she meant by cleanliness was at considerable odds with what others meant, as others, too, soon found themselves to be with each other.

As participants elaborated individual interpretations, some even grew visibly irritated at how "picky" others could be in their preferences. Sam, for example, pointedly asked Bertha if it wasn't "silly" to be concerned with outdoor smells when there was so much else to worry about in a nursing home. He went on to warn Bertha:

> Pardon me for saying so, Bertie, but if you think outdoor smells is where it's at, you better think again. You're not going to get that in a nursing home, except maybe street smells coming through the window. [Laughter all around] My sister's in a nursing home and still knows me, God bless her, but it's the soiled clothes you've got to look for and the spoiled food in their hair. Now that's dirty! Thanks God, Claremont [his sister's nursing home] is not like that. As long as they keep her [his sister] clean, it's a good home by me.

Responding to Sam's comments, another participant stated that it would be "a cold day in hell" before she would keep her husband totally clean even in their very own home. For her, cleanliness meant managing to keep the patient acceptably clean for most of the time. As she noted, it was "natural for some of that to happen anywhere," adding, though, that she nonetheless wasn't about to put her husband in a nursing home, no matter what.

From one support group to another, talk of the amenities of good institutional care indicated that there was agreement only in principle regarding what was homelike. As long as consideration of the question "What is a good nursing home?" remained at a general level, centered on seemingly recognizable factors such as cleanliness and activity, all agreed that any nursing home where the conditions were absent was merely housing patients and residents, not providing a good home for them. This meant, of course, that such a "home" was not fit for their stricken family members, let alone anyone in need of long-term care. At this level, in their agreement, the domestic meaning of institutionalization was tied to a shared public culture of understanding about what constituted a homelike atmosphere.

Careful attention to shifts in the specificity of considerations showed that agreements in principle belied wide differences of opinion. When testimony and discussion centered on select criteria in relation to what was "like home" for *particular* patients, what had been nearly universal agreement in general could have been agreement about the disagreeable. For example, while all agreed that activity was important, what some were agreeing to turned out to be, upon specification, what others were totally opposed to, or "couldn't imagine," for their loved one.

Support group proceedings showed that the domestic meaning of institutionalization regarding the question "What is a good nursing home?" was interpretively more complex than suggested by existing conceptions of quality of care. General references and considerations reflected the implicit message of nursing home ads, which, in turn, were part of a public culture of goodness criteria. Particular references and considerations were individualized interpretations tied to specific home experiences and patient biographies, which, in extended discussions, virtually turned the consensus of the general into the uniqueness of each case. When deliberations and exchanges focussed on individual cases—on what was a good nursing home for one family, one member, or another—participants could became rather exasperated with specifications that had more generally enjoyed their consensus and common cause. Answers to the question "What is a good nursing home?" were a source of consensus and camaraderie when they reflected the public culture; they could be comparatively irritating otherwise.

The native responses to the question evident in support group proceedings suggested that the nursing home as an institution could be homelike, but that its domestic meaning was specified by experiences diversely located in individual circumstances. As such, the facet of the question concerning whether an institution just houses or can be a home was answerable only to a degree, reflecting its public culture. Otherwise it was articulated case by case.

Strangers versus Family

The other facet of the question "What is a good nursing home?" pertains to its familial character. Ideally, a home is inhabited by those who behave like family, even though they might not be formally kindred; a house, as popular usage has it, is not necessarily a home in this regard. This, too, was uppermost in the minds, and talk, of participants. This facet of the question dealt more with what was personally done for, or on behalf of, the patient, not what the facility offered in the way of services. What is not cosmetic is not easy to detect by means of what-to-look-for checklists. One overburdened spouse called them "the little things." Others referred to them as "things you can't put your finger on," "TLC" (tender loving care), "feeling wanted," among a host of ways to describe the hallmarks of genuine family life.

A what-to-look-for checklist or research criteria for quality care would suggest that the domestic meaning of an institution could be deciphered by a matching procedure. To learn whether a candidate home offered that desirable condition found in facility ads—"loving care"—one would simply check off, on a list of criteria, what was or was not apparent upon an inspection of the facility. For example, in a visit to a nursing home, one might check to see if the home's administrator had a state license; there was provision for special therapies, meaningful activities and physician services; and the environment was uncluttered and odor-free. Some consumer organizations even rank the quality of nursing homes based on the matching procedure; homes meeting most creteria are placed at the top of the list, others lower.

Support group proceedings show that the logic of the matching procedure is an overrationalized representation of how caregivers figure the question of whether a home can be family-like. Like the other facet of the question "What is a good nursing home?" generally accepted criteria for loving care are mediated by applications to individual cases. As participants' testimony and discussions indicate, there may be total agreement about what makes a facility homelike, yet considerable agonizing over whether service providers can "really" be like family and not just a "bunch of strangers" caring for a loved one. A phrase often used is "going through the motions," meaning the provision of care with no spirit of devotion—which a "real" family presumably would offer.

Beyond the complications of specific application, the overrationalized representation of checklists and formal criteria contrasts with an appreciation of the incommunicable in these matters. It was evident that the core meaning of "loving" and "family-like," as they applied to what was done for patients, was, as the phrase "things you can't put your finger on" suggests, incommensurable (cf. Gubrium, 1988).

In a home interview, Kenneth Kaiser, the seventy-seven-year-old former participant in a support group, whose demented wife, Selma, was now in a nursing home, grappled with this facet of the question in wondering about the "things you can't see and point your finger at" that were being done for Selma in her facility. While Kenneth's comments came from someone who had already placed a family member in a nursing home, they reflected the concerns and comments of those considering placement as well as those responding to others in the process of doing so. While a decision might have lead to actual placement, it was clear that it did not necessarily end consideration of the meaning of loving care (Lynott, 1983). At one point in his testimony, Kenneth asked:

You know, sometimes I wonder what it's like for her in there [the nursing home]. Don't get me wrong, it's clean. She's taken to activities everyday and that. I mean they keep her pretty busy. [Elaborates] It's funny because sometimes I can't even find her because they've got her involved in so many things. It's more than I could ever do for her at home. I know she doesn't really understand what's going on some of the time, but she can surprise you sometimes, too. Those girls [staff members] have the patience of a saint. But, like I said, you wonder sometimes about those things you can't see, that you just can't point your finger at.

It was evident that Kenneth thought his wife's nursing home was, as he later put it, "top notch." He used the phrase to describe many of its services: a top notch staff, a top notch administrator, top notch activities and so on. As he continued to describe the facility, a veritable checklist of "top notch" characteristics came forth. Yet, it was evident, too, that there was, for each top notch condition, something that he just couldn't "point a finger at." As he noted:

Like I said earlier about the little things. I remember what Katherine [a support group participant] said one time. You remember her from the support group, the one who had such a hard time imagining what it would be like for her husband to be in a nursing home, the gal that used to break down and cry all the time—poor kid. I don't show it, but that kind of thing goes through everyone's mind. I know when Selma was with me here in the apartment, we were very loving . . . up to end. Whatever she said to me—and some of it was pretty bad stuff even when I knew she knew it—something there let's you get past it. It's not something a stranger would put up with. That's what worries me a lot. You never know, do you? Don't get me wrong, all that stuff I said before about the place [nursing home], well, like I said, it's top notch. Well, you know what I mean.

Time and again, the same indefinite concern was expressed by others in the support groups. While some could readily infer signs of loving care in familiar terms of checklists, there was a decided openendedness. It was not so much indecisiveness, for loving care was taken into account in actually making placement or nonplacement decisions. Rather, there was repeated reference to a feature of caring that seemed to be, for lack of words to describe it, something "you just can't point your finger at." It was something that families, at least in principle, were believed to have, but was lacking among strangers, that incommunicable something done on behalf of anyone who was family, just because they were family (cf. Gubrium and Buckholdt, 1982). The implication, of course, was that "being family" was something expected, not necessarily done. By the same token, nonkindred could also be family and it was precisely its application to nursing home staff that was not decipherable from formal criteria or cosmetic evidence of quality care. Against the incommunicable, studies that model and measure the domestic meaning of institutionalization are experientially inauthentic.

When is a House No Longer Home?

The other home at issue regarding the domestic meaning of institutionalization is the caring household. There is a familiar expression that is partly suggestive of an answer to the question "When is a house no longer a home?" The expression is "it's time," referring to the point in time when home care becomes a disservice to all concerned, no longer justifiable, and institutional placement to be sought. One of the criteria for judging when it's time is the impact of the impairment and its related caregiving burden on the family. It has been said that at some point in the caregiving process, family members begin to realize that they, especially caregivers, are the "second victims" of the disease and that their own and the family's welfare as a whole is as much at stake as the patient's. When a house is no longer a home to anyone and the family risks disintegration, it's time.

This is fine in theory, in accordance with what is maintained in the received wisdom of the disease's public culture. The idea is that families, and support groups themselves, go through stages of acceptance, from full devotion to cure and home care at the start, to realization of the caregiver's and family's separate needs and the necessity of making the placement decision (Gubrium, 1986a). In practice, the points at which these stages are reached are far from clearcut. Indeed, a continuing focus of caregivers' related concern is the turning points. Theory and practice are endlessly counterpoised in considerations of the caring household for the domestic meaning of institutionalization.

The caregiving-burden literature casts the family as a factor in a care equation. A significant finding is that support from the family is at least as important a factor in caregiver stress as the actual impairment (cf. Zarit, Orr, and Zarit, 1985). Field data suggest, however, that the family and domesticity are not just factors, but focal issues interpreted in relation to the many ingredients of the caregiving process and the placement decision. Support does not just enter into the caregiving experience as a condition bearing on caregiver stress; it is continually addressed for its meaning against family functioning as a whole.

The Varied Meanings of Support

Let us first consider variations in the meaning of support. Afterward, we turn to how the interpretations affect answers to the question "When is a house no longer home?"

According to the burden-of-care literature, the supportive family forestalls institutionalization. It has been said, for example, that daily visits by relatives to the caregiving household moderate stress (Zarit, Reever, and Bach-Peterson, 1980). This finding, it appears, is only justifiable in the circumstance that visiting positively affects support. Compare the following descriptions for the meanings assigned to family visits. The variety was typical in the proceedings studied.

Having heard the usual number of stories of caregiving experiences and their impact on the family, Fred, the seventy-two-year-old caregiver and husband of Sybil, his demented wife, also spoke of how his wife's illness had affected his adult children. As some others did, Fred interpreted the children's help positively:

> Cookie's [one daughter] just a gem. You couldn't have a better kid. She comes over every day and looks in on her mother. You should see it. [Conveys Cookie's help in detail] Like I said, that girl can do a million things at once. And she never complains. And my sons, well, they're a real help too. A day doesn't pass that I don't get at least a phone call from them. "How's it going?" "How're you feeling, Pa?" [Describes his son, Ollie's, weekend help with home maintenance]
>
> Sometimes I wonder if I deserve them. They never complain. [Repeats some of his children's supportive activities] I know that it's a real burden on me and I can imagine how it's affecting them on the inside. I think Sybil's not recognizing Cookie is especially hard on her. She cries sometimes when Sybil asks her who she is.

Fred's comments launched the group into an extended discussion of the meaning of family support. The proceedings showed that, while Fred's situation was much envied and resembled some of the others' family experience, it was by no means universal. For some, "support" was at best something to be avoided. All knew of Beverly's situation caring for her stricken mother at home along with being a homemaker for her working husband, sons and daughter. Beverly's own sisters lived nearby and had families of their own, but they called Beverly daily and visited with her at least twice weekly. The sisters often took their mother home to give Beverly some relief from the burden of caregiving for an increasingly demented patient.

As far as daily and weekly contacts with her sisters were concerned, Beverly, too, stated that she couldn't ask for better support. Indeed, in this regard, according to Beverly, the sisters were unparalleled. But the support was complicated, even becoming overshadowed, by hatefulness. Beverly explained:

> Talk about help, well, you all know my sisters. There's not a day goes by that they don't poke their noses in the door. And they're just not fair weather

friends, either. I mean they really are supportive. I can't count how many times Cynthia [one of the sisters] has made dinner for us and brought it over to the house. She knows how hard it is fixing three and four dinners a day because everyone's got a different schedule. I mean it could drive you nuts.

The other side of it is that they're [the sisters] starting to drive me nuts. [Referring to her endurance in caring for her mother] So far, so good. It hasn't been all that bad, with their help and everyone sharing. At least I can say they're [the sisters] around, not like some of the others that you never see [other caregivers' family members]. But my sisters have gotten into this nursing home mindset lately and it's driving me bananas. Why should I put Mother in a nursing home? I really feel ashamed to say so, but it's getting to be that I don't want them [the sisters] around me anymore. Everyday, it's "Mother would be better off in a nursing home. Mother this and Mother that." What am I supposed to do? It's getting to be that just as soon as one of them walks into that door, we start to argue about it. You've heard of hateful families, well, I'm start-ing to hate being at home when they come around. I hate to admit it, but some-times I ask Penny [her daughter] to stay home from school when I know they're coming and give an excuse that I had to run an errand for Matt [her husband].

The situation was a difficult one. While all agreed that Beverly had the best family support, it was evident to them, too, that the family was becoming increasing split over the issue of institutional placement. While some acknowl-edged that the support forestalled the point at which it was time to seek placement, they realized as well that the increasingly prevalent meaning of the sisters' visits was eclipsing its supportive function. As participants rumi-nated over Beverly's situation, their testimony showed that they were aware that support was not a clearcut matter of visitation, complements or material contributions. Indeed, as the facilitator reflected on the complications, she asked, "Am I hearing what you're all saying is that support depends on what you have to, like, pay for it?"

The question launched the proceedings into a discussion of what one of the participants described as "both sides" of the matter, meaning, in the lan-guage of exchange introduced by the facilitator, the costs and benefits of support. In response to this, even Fred, who had earlier lauded his children's support, expressed concern for how the burden of care might be affecting all of their lives, in particular, as he put it, "how it all was making us a bit edgy with each other and keeping me from being a real father and grandfather to them." Fred believed that his children's visits should be happy ones, but explained that he "knew" that there was tension there and that family mem-bers sometimes did snap at each other. Nonetheless, according to Fred, the benefit of "pulling together and working at it as a team" outweighed their costs.

Proceedings across the support groups studied, as well as participants' individual testimony, showed that the expression "both sides" was a shorthand for the many and varied meanings of support. The language of costs and benefits was not so much a metric for evaluating support as it was used by those concerned to convey support's complex "give and take." Some even put it in moral terms, suggesting that in these matters, one had to take the good with the bad. As a caregiver pointed out, "Nothing, not even relatives, are all black or white."

Variation in meaning flowed with interpersonal comparisons and the interpretations that emerged in their common consideration. Where a caregiver had assessed his support as total or in some way otherwise positive, at the behest of another caregiver's outwardly similar but differently interpreted experience, the original caregiver might "discover" that there was another version of his situation. The varied meanings of support in individual cases were never isolated but were construed and ramified through others' experiences, tying support to ongoing deliberations of what it *could* mean. As such, support was not so much an existing condition, describable as a factor in a caregiving equation, as it was a topic of consideration in taking stock of the domestic meaning of institutionalization.

Support, House and Home

The varied meanings of support were part and parcel of the question of when is a house no longer a home. Caregivers asked themselves and each other if they were just living, day to day, for the sake of the patient, being Alzheimer's disease's virtual "second victim," with no life of their own. As far as family and general household were concerned, this drew attention to the issue of whether the household was just a place to care for the victim or was a loving, caring home. Answers were appreciated against what was known or believed about the homelike provision of the nursing home and admittedly bore significantly on the placement decision.

Those already convinced of the possible need for institutionalization were prepared to compare an eventual destiny for their patient with what, as it was commonly put, "it was doing to your family," the "it" referring to both the disease and the burden of care. Those who had not yet seriously considered placement were challenged by the same comparison. Reflecting a feature of the disease's public culture, facilitators tended to work with a developmental view of the matter (Gubrium, 1986a, 1987). They took the caregiving experience as progressing naturally from a stage of firm devotion to home care where the household was believed to be the victim's home, to a stage of eventual acceptance of the nursing home as the only reasonable way of managing a demented patient. Yet, being convinced or challenged was not a good indicator of one's longevity as a participant in the support groups, for there were veteran participants who, according to some opinion, insisted on remaining in the stage of total home care, just as there were novices who moved fairly quickly to the presumed realization that one knows, sooner or later, that an Alzheimer's burden cannot harbor a home life for anyone in the long run.

What seemed to be firm family support for the caregiver could be suspect. Take Pearl Dorn's experience. Compared to others in her support group, her family was attentive and giving. As Pearl had conveyed time and again, both her own sister and her sister-in-law helped in caring for Don, Pearl's demented husband. The sister and sister-in-law were reported to be an exemplary support system. As Pearl frequently noted, "except for the constant physical burdens of caring for him [Don], I'd have to say that the family is warm and loving." According to Pearl, she attended the support group for three reasons: to get tips on how to care for her husband and cope with an Alzheimer's disease victim, to help others in the same situation, and to "get away from it all once in a while." None of the reasons cited reflected a family crisis. Pearl stood for what the caregiving home and extended family support system could be, but, according to some, rarely was.

References to Pearl's kindred and family life were constant sources of comparison for participants, serving as standards for taking stock of their own burden and its impact on the home. It was not unusual for a caregiver to speak of what the burden of care was doing to his or her home life and to use what was commonly known of Pearl's home situation to make a point in contrast. By the same token, those who communicated positive descriptions took Pearl's situation to be an exemplar of what their home situation resembled. As a source of comparison and personal evaluation, Pearl's situation did not leave the support group when she no longer attended; as with so many other cases, hers was part of group folklore regarding the impact of the disease on house and home, sustained by the collective memory of those who had known and interacted with her.

Pearl's seemingly exemplary caregiving situation at home, of course, did not go unchallenged. No one's experience did, just as no one's experience was without sympathy and consideration. In the context of the disease's household travails, Pearl's family's endurance was less lauded than possibly foolhardy: for some, it was a study in disbelief. Joanne Feldon, the caregiver for her eighty-one-year-old demented husband, typified the disbelief and challenge. In one group session, in Pearl's presence, Joanne had commented:

> I find it hard to believe that you [Pearl] don't sometimes think about it all, I mean what it's all done to your family over the years. [Joanne then detailed the kinds of impact the burden could have on family life.] I mean it must have had some effect. No thirty-six-hour job I know of doesn't take its toll. It gets to be that a person doesn't have any time for herself, let alone the family. I, myself, just don't have time for my children or my grandchildren. And

> believe you me, I'd just love to be grandmom before those kids grow up. You all know what it means; I don't have to tell you. It can mean that you just give up all hope of having a normal family life. You're just a custodian, a thirty-six-hour custodian. And, Pearl, that's not what I call a home life, help or no help. I have to say that I've been thinking about a nursing home for Ted [her husband].

Pearl responded in what seemed to have become her customary fashion, accepting the challenge and reaffirming what she had repeatedly conveyed to the group about house and home. Joanne maintained a dubious attitude, later adding that, in time, Pearl would see it differently, elaborating on what many took to be the natural history of the experience. Pearl never accepted the natural history as applicable to her. When she eventually left the group, what remained of the knowledge of her attitude and experience, while becoming an exemplary part of the group's folklore serving individual comparison, also was taken by some as an exception to the normal course of events in the disease's home-and-family chronology.

Denial

The challenge of the question "When is a house no longer home?" also could be diagnostic. Whether those who, like Pearl, did not accept the natural history of the home-and-family chronology were in fact denying the realities of a household as no longer home, did not prevent others from rhetorically using the idea of denial for diagnosing exceptions to the chronology rule. Joanne, for example, not only cast friendly aspersion on Pearl's claim to be domestically unaffected by the burdens of care, but when Pearl held to her own interpretation, Joanne diagnosed Pearl as denying something better known by those without a related psychological investment. Those who rhetorically used denial to persuade others that Alzheimer's disease does indeed "wreck family life" or in time "destroys the home" no matter what the support, again applied a familiar theme of the disease's public culture, one which facilitators appropriated liberally. As far as the support group itself, the received wisdom concerning group dynamics was that a group which moves from concern with cure and custody, to overcoming the commonplace denial of the household effects of overwhelming burdens of care and placing priority on needs of the family as a whole, is itself well on the way to being a true source of support and self-help.

It should be noted that the use of denial in rhetorical diagnosis was not foolproof. While some participants took the means of persuasion to heart and considered their possible denial regarding the familial truths of their households, others denied that they were denying. A few even scoffed at the condition itself as a legitimate psychological state. Nonetheless, those who spoke the language of denial and effectively persuaded others of its presence as a barrier to the realization that, in the Alzheimer's disease caregiving experience, a house is no longer home to anyone, constructed the individual household facts of a common domestic understanding of institutionalization.

Conclusion

Existing conceptualizations of quality of care in nursing homes, on the one hand, and caregiver functioning, on the other, as they both relate to the placement decision, stand in considerable contrast with the latter's interpretive dynamics. Field data show, first, that while the literature appears to stay clear of what seem to be two obvious experiential points of the placement decision—the homelike atmosphere of the facility and the question of whether the household is any longer home—caregiving family members take into account the domestic meaning of institutionalization in figuring when "it's time."

Second, the comparative homes offered by facility and household to the victims and families of those concerned are subject to interpersonal interpretation and specification. As such, caregiver concern with households, facilities and their relative domesticity, is not an individual experience. Answers to the question of whether a household is any longer home hinge on shifting criteria drawn from the experiences of various caregivers, whose examples present diverse baselines for personal assessment. The measurement of individual caregiver functioning systematically eclipses the social conditions from which "individual" experiences are derived, which, incidentally, is a significant violation of the independence assumption of related statistical description (cf. Gubrium and Lynott, 1987).

Third, field data indicate that there is both general and particular attention paid to the issue of domesticity in home and institutional care. In general—when those concerned attend to the ideas of institutional care, home life and their relative quality—conventional wisdom is reproduced. There is general agreement on factors commonly listed in what-to-look-for lists and focal in quality-of-care studies. But placement decisions are not exclusively general matters. Interpretations of particular individual needs and circumstances are taken into account. Domesticity is a complex array of meanings derived from both public understandings and private interpretation. As such, what-to-look-for lists provide only one kind of guideline for solving what is otherwise the practical task of figuring what is best for all concerned, case by case, comparison by comparison.

Fourth, while there is a good deal of rational calculation in placement decisions, such as the continual comparison and evaluation of the meaning of support and its implication for placement, the data suggest that it is important not to overly rationalize the experience. Quality-of-care research understandably strives to discover *the* ingredients of good care: studies of caregiver functioning aim to specify *the* diverse variables of the caregiving equation. The field data, in contrast, suggest that what the ingredients and variables are cannot be altogether clear. The related interpretive work of those concerned is, itself, a continuous process of clarification, as particular homes, families and facilities are now evaluated against others, on the one hand, and standards of judgment now redefined, on the other. The challenges and provocations of constant comparison and emergent standards tell of the practical work of domestic interpretation as much as the challenges and provocations inform us of the ingredients and variables of the palcement decision. There is, then, an unspecifiable underlife to the placement decision, evident only in attending descriptively to its native and practical character.

Finally, fifth, an important implication of the field data for understanding the domestic meaning of institutionalization is that researchers must not underestimate the extent to which subjects, in their own ways, are aware of care equations, variables, the ingredients of a good home and so on. Being more or less part of a common disease culture, those concerned *use* the public understandings that researchers and others specify as ingredients of their subjects' situations. The latter apply them in circumstances as diverse as the varied caregiving situations they find themselves in. To separate usage and circumstance from the public understandings comprised of variables, chronologies and ingredients is to dehumanize the very human problem that domesticity is for all concerned in the caregiving experience.

References

Gubrium, Jaber F. (1986a). *Oldtimers and Alzheimer's: The descriptive organization of senility*. Greenwich, CT: JAI Press.

Gubrium, Jaber F. (1986b). The social preservation of mind: The Alzheimer's disease experience. *Symbolic Interaction* 9: 37-51.

Gubrium, Jaber F. (1987). Structuring and destructuring the course of illness: The Alzheimer's desease experience. *Sociology of Health and Illness* 9: 1-24.

Gubrium, Jaber F. 1988. Incommunicables and poetic documentation in the Alzheimer's disease experience. *Semiotica* 72:325-253.

Gubrium, Jaber F. and David R. Buckholdt. (1982). Fictive family: Everyday usage, analytic and human service considerations. *American Anthropologist* 84: 878-885.

Gubrium, Jaber F. and Robert J. Lynott. (1987). Measurement and the interpretation of burden in the Alzheimer's disease experience. *Journal of Aging Studies* 1: 265-285.

Gwyther, Lisa P. and Linda K. George. (1986). Introduction to symposium on caregivers for dementia patients: Complex determinants of well-being and burden. *The Gerontologist* 26: 245-247.

Johnson, Colleen L. and Leslie A. Grant. (1985). *The nursing home in American society*. Baltimore: Johns Hopkins University Press..

Lynott, Robert J. (1983). Alzheimer's desease and institutionalization: The ongoing construction of a decision. *Journal of Family Issues* 4: 559-574.

Mace, Nancy L. and Peter V. Rabins. (1981). *The 36-hour day*. Baltimore: Johns Hopkins University Press.

Zarit, Steven H., Nancy K. Orr, and Judy M. Zarit. (1985). *The hidden victims of Alzheimer's disease*. New York: New York University Press.

Zarit, Steven H., Karen E. Reever, and Julie Bach-Peterson. (1980). Relatives of the impaired elderly: Correlates of feelings of burden. *The Gerontologist* 20: 649-655.

The Intensive Case Study

Chapter 7

Temporality and Affect: The Personal Meaning of Well-Being

ROBERT L. RUBINSTEIN

Few present-day social or behavioral scientists would disagree with the view of Allport who wrote in 1953 that,

> The prevailing atmosphere of theory has engendered a kind of contempt for the *psychic surface* of life. The individual's conscious report is rejected as untrustworthy and the contemporary thrust of his motives is disregarded....

Those concerned with gerontological theory, research and practice might be surprised to learn that this quotation (somewhat shortened here) is taken as the opening theme in the search for quantitative measures of psychological well-being described by N. Bradburn in *The Structure of Psychological Well-being* (1968). This significant work discussed the theory behind the construct psychological well-being, now often used to measure the dependent variable or "outcome" in much quantitative gerontological research.

Bradburn agreed with Allport's criticism and took it as the stepping off point for his scholarly exercise. Allport's goal, it seems, was to criticize the reliance on unconscious psychological explanations of behavior. In distinction, Bradburn supported the view that we should take the "self reports" of respondents—their conscious representations—much more seriously.

An irony here is that the focus on "self reports" as indexed through the several well-being scales now widely used in social gerontology is today viewed by many as having the same sorts of structural difficulties against which Allport reacted in the key features of depth psychology. Among these are a theoretical primacy unenlightened by social conditions, and hence uncritical application, and questionable relevance to the everyday lives of individuals.

I argue here that a sense of well-being, a subjective emic measure of how things are, develops from two key phenomena. The first is an individual's on-going consideration and interpretation of where she is now in contrast to where she once was. This idea is related to the notion of W. James and others that aspects of the social self are structured or clarified in relation to groups and people as points of reference. Here, reference points of the self are temporally transposed so that an internally-experienced state-of-being exists in reference to prior experiences or states-of-being over the life course.

The second phenomenon is regulation of a personalized model of well-being. This model consists of several parts. The first is the establishment of an experientially normal or acceptable state-of-being. The second is carrying out the things that need to be done to maintain this subjectively-defined normalcy. Things to be done are individually abstracted from cultural standards of personhood. The last is a theory of how to correct the situation when thing go wrong. Important in this respect, as we shall see below, is whether the management of the problem is done inside or ourside the person.

In exploring some ideas for this paper with colleagues at a multidisciplinary research department in a geriatric center, I suggested, rather naively, that a discussion of the differences between two older people who had the same precise set of responses to a well-being inventory would form the basis of a provocative essay. One colleague noted that no one who commonly employed quantitative measures that featured well-being as an outcome variable had any illusion that people with the same scores were somehow the same in any or all respects. Studies of well-being are the results of the examination of correlations between significant variables, as measured by standard instruments, over large samples. My colleague made an analogy to intelligence tests: nobody assumes that two persons with the same IQ are automatically similar in other ways. Another colleague noted that there was nothing new about my idea; rather, it duplicated nuances of on-going disputes between "nomothetic" and "idiographic" research, a set of conflicts whose existence, much like the Centralia fire, is underlying and unresolved but makes known its existence with outbursts of smoke and fire.

There may be an accurate analogy between IQ tests and well-being measures in at least one respect. There is a growing awareness that measures of well-being may contain some degree of cultural bias. Allen Glicksman (personal communication), in a secondary analysis of data from subjects in two large all-elderly data sets (N = 1612) that utilized the Philadelphia Geriatric Center Morale Scale found that aspects of the psychological well-being of Jewish elderly are significantly poorer than non-Jews, and that this difference is not explained by health status, social relations or socioeconomic status, but probably should be attributed to cultural values and cultural styles of expressive behavior.

Nevertheless, the analogy between IQ tests and well-being measures is perhaps overblown. For example, not only are IQ tests used to sort and discriminate between people, but they may be used to determine important life events, for example whether one gets into a particular school or not. Large service industries have grown up around "educational testing." The effects of measuring well-being of the older person have been somewhat more modest: while some policy decisions are based on a consideration of quantitative measure of well-being, assessments of well-being may also lead to particular clinical interventions or to inclusion in a particular study group.

Yet the notion of well-being has a special place in the minds of most gerontologists and therefore criticizing the construct is difficult because without well-being as a central construct, much of gerontology would lose one important focus. One of the goals of our interdiscipline is to increase the well-being of older people. This is a noble aim. It makes understanding research easier for those whose concerns are primarily in the realm of practice and who see research as somewhat of a luxury. Yet one might argue, as several qualitatively-oriented researchers have done (albeit usually not in print), that despite its goals, the concept of well-being exists as a kind of fetishized commodity in social gerontology. This comes despite some repeated warnings about the potential sterility of "morale" studies (Carp and Nydegger, 1975; Nydegger, 1977) and their critical re-examination (Gubrium and Lynott, 1986). Even a cursory glance at recent professional meeting agenda and gerontological journals and books demonstrates a continuing central focus on the notion of well-being (or psychological well-being or morale or life satisfaction or one of several other terms) and its measurement.

The concept of well-being must therefore be seen as a "key symbol" within the quasi-academic culture of social gerontology. It is a notion that synthesizes the multivocal, diverse referents of "scientific" methodology and research procedure, of practice, of concern for the elderly and, possibly, some ways in which the elderly conceptualize themselves. It acts, too, as a metonymical bridge in which the very narrow and constricted notions of well-being in the scientists' culture "represent" the very rich subjective worlds of older individuals. While the use is literary, it may be metaphor of limited success.

Mishler, in his important recent book, *Research Interviewing* (1986), argues that one false aspect of positivist social science is its stance outside social discourse and as privileged through its practice of scientizing human social life. Following Bakan's (1967) criticisms of the experimental method in psychological research, Mishler argues that in undertaking social science research of the traditional close-ended, stimulus-response type, we engage in a "strategy of concealment" in which "investigators' aims, theories, and findings are hidden from subjects and respondents." He notes that such investigators "undertake their studies in a state of surprise anxiety, worried about whether their subjects will really be naive and whether subjects might do or say something that does not fit the investigator's preconceptions and thus make more difficult their analyses and interpretations" (1986: p. 133). Thus quantitative survey research investigations are built on two assumptions: (1)

that the constructs the investigator has decided are significant are in fact both significant and sophisticated enough to capture the distinctive nature of subjects' opinions, moods, affects, experiences and (2) that the level of social science sophistication, and the terminology and concepts of this is somehow "higher" or "more cerebral," are not part of general discourse and are not possessed nor used by research subjects. The conduct of much standard social science research may be thought of as an attempt to operationalize both assumptions, but both are flawed. Investigators' interest in well-being exists in tandem with an increasing concern with and orientation to dimensions in this concept as part of our general cultural life. Similarly, it is clearly the case that "psychological thinking" has increasingly become a part of our general cultural discourse.

Present-Day Well-Being in Temporal Perspective

The purpose of this chapter is to describe how a conception of well-being distinctive from that employed in social gerontology may be discovered in the way in which two elderly informants discuss their well-being, or the general quality of how they are in life.

One point I make here (after considering the two informant accounts) is that the meaning of well-being is indexical, referring to affects that are situated in the larger life course. Thus the construct of well-being is not only a scientific one, utilized by some investigators as part of the culture of science, but it is also a native one, utilized in distinctive ways by individuals. We are made aware of the variety of representations of personal affect that individuals employ. Key, too in this discussion is the role of narrative in understanding an individual's life. Following Gee (1985), White (1980) and others, I am suggesting that the act of narration is one important means of making sense of experience. Below, we will consider examples in which experiences of important affects are narratively and metaphorically described as trajectories. But the trajectory is only one of a variety of possible frameworks individuals might employ to situate or describe their well-being over time. Others might include points in time, key events, atemporal dominant themes, flavors, color or textures.

Thus it is that the approach taken here differs from that of Gergen and Gergen (1984, 1986, 1987). In their series of papers, they have approached the study of the self from the perspective of narrative ("narratives of the self") and the significance of temporal context. These are important contributions. Yet their approach works from preconceived notions of narrative structure (such as a small group of fixed plot structures) to the stories people tell; in contrast, I attempt here to work from what people actually say to the variety of structures they might contain. An additional difference is that in their assessing a generalized feeling of well-being among a research sample by asking them to draw a time-line of well-being, means were computed for the sample as a whole. While this is an interesting technique that produces worthwhile results, our interest here, rather then in aggregate scores and predetermined structures, is in making a contribution to the study of the individual and in coming to view the as-yet-poorly understood dimensions of personal meaning. I think it is important in doing this to begin as fully as possible with what people say about their own experienced worlds.

A second point I make here is that individuals' native constructs or versions of well-being and their cultural bases have hardly been explored and I offer this paper as a very modest beginning. In it, I present and analyze narrative accounts by two older people of their lives. In these accounts the meaning of present day well-being is significantly informed by its contrast with former states and is interpreted by means of individual guidelines within the context of an individual's sense of personal meaning.

Types of Well-Being

Two general types of well-being may be designated as the personal interpretation of well-being and quantitative well-being.

Quantitative well-being may be thought of as akin to "subjective well-being" measured by Bradburn's scale and numerous other instruments. In an often-cited paper, Larson (1978) has described how subjective well-being is strongly related to health, socioeconomic factors and degree of social interaction, less so to marital status and certain aspects of living arrangements. In contrast, sex, race, age and employment status show no consistent relation to well-being. Negative life situations, especially low income, appear to be related to greater vulnerability to other negative life events. Lawton (1983: p. 65) notes that well-being in older people "may be represented in sectors of behavioral competence, perceived quality of life, psychological well-being and objective environment."

In examining the other type of well-being, that of an interpretive nature, three important concerns emerge.

First, the interpretive process is subjectively comparative in that the present day is compared to the past. This is done on the basis of present-day concerns in the context of each person's scheme of understanding. This idea is akin to that described by Suls and Mullen (1984) that older people often use (past) temporal comparisons, rather than (present-day) social comparisons, to evaluate their abilities. In the cases to be discussed below, the two informants, the pseudonymous Mr. McCue and Mrs. Collins, each presented a discussion of their sense of well-being in terms of a trajectory or life-line.

Each had distinctive systems for interpreting events. Mr. McCue's was more overt, formalize and practiced, tied as it was to a now-internalized set of ideas from Alcholics Anonymous (AA). Mrs. Collins's was not formalized in relation to any shared system of meaning like AA. Rather, it was informed more by personalized interpretations of the meaning of her prior experiences.

Second, evaluation of the present in terms of the past is done on the basis of present-day needs and goals. One important aim of such evaluation may be to maintain a generally positive mood state, or the outward appearance of such, in the face of deleterious change.

Third, in one view of things, the interpretation of well-being may be thought of as a "second-order" phenomenon. By this I mean that the individuals discussed here appear to engage in an active practice of reflection about experiences and their attached moods on the basis of major personal concerns, constructs and meanings. Such reflections may occur both as immediate reaction to events or situations and also as considered, deliberate, mature, patient retroflection in which the phenomena reacted to, as well as immediate reactions, are considered, processed and understood as part of a larger order system in order to "make sense" of things.

Yet there is a danger, too, in conceptualizing interpretation in a way that contrasts "primary" to "second-order" process. In so doing, we are basing our conceptualizing on an underlying dichotomy that is analytically pervasive in Western culture but does not necessarily represent the way things are. This analogy is based on the supposed difference between more primary emotions and the more "cerebral" act of interpretation. *This* dichotomy is, itself, part and parcel of a larger pervasive dichotomy in Western thought, that between "primary needs" and "higher order" culture. This latter (cultural) dichotomy, a form of vulgar functionalism, has been criticized in anthropology, which now sees all orders of cultural life as inherently a part of an overall symbolic system that shapes experiences of all orders of phenomena. Any need to disaggregate these into base and less-base can be seen as a manipulation dictated by our own cultural notions of these phenomena, not by any intrinsic or necessary difference between the two. The dichotomy between emotive and interpretive process, as vulgar psychologism, suggests that feelings are somehow separable from their meaning contexts, a notion that unfortunately seems to be widely shared in mainstream social gerontology research.

Two Cases

I want to turn next to the presentation of detailed cases of the lives of two older people. The first, Mr. McCue, provided a life history testimony in response to a specific open-ended question in a research project about how older Italian, Irish and Jewish widowers reorganized their lives after the death of their spouses. This was one of a series of five interviews with him, lasting about two hours each. In one, we collected a Bradburn inventory, data I never collected from Mrs. Collins, the second informant, who provided an account of her life not directly in response to a single framing question, but rather in the context of an on-going discussion of herself as part of a research project that investigated the environmental experiences of older people and the sense of attachment that some older people develop to their homes.

These cases are presented with two goals in mind. First, they provide an instructive contrasting set from which to examine the meaning of well-being as a temporal construct. Second, as we will discuss in more detail below, they provide material to help us consider native theories of well-being and affect management, germane to the idea that management is internal or external. Such theories exist at the nexus between the experiences of a lifetime; reflection (or "second-order" examination) on these; active construction of meaning; present-day behavioral practices; and an individual's version of cultural ideas on the relationship of thought and behavior to well-being.

Mr. McCue

Mr. Michael McCue, 77, once described himself to me as "an Irish drunk." He began his life-history narrative with the statement, "I was always a good student in grammar school. Not the best maybe, but near the top." This statement of accomplishment prefixed an account of a life that featured a downward trajectory for its first forty-six years.

His narrative began in earnest in high school when he changed schools and his talents and desires were no longer enough to maintain his high grades. He noted, "I graduated in 1925, but just about." He noted, too, that he was a "failure." After graduation, he entered college, lasting three months at one, a year at a second and a semester at a third.

Two key events occurred at that time. He took his first drink at age seventeen, in 1926. "It made me sick," he said of it. A friend told him that he could avoid the sick feeling if he drank some more the next morning. He remained an active alcoholic until he was forty-six.

At about that time, too, he began a relationsip with a woman, from a higher social class, who was engaged to be married to another man who was finishing professional school. He felt that marriage between them was impossible, since his girlfriend's marriage to the professional man was strongly supported by her family. He was in love with her. From time to time, they stayed together at her family's vacation home. He took a series of jobs near there so that he could be close to her. During this period, he was occasionally unemployed, residing, he noted humorously, at the "Hotel Underwood," that is, any place under wooden sidings or walkways or in alleyways. After his girlfriend married, she continued to see him. He noted, "people used to say that her son looks just like me. That broke my heart." It has never been clear to him if the child was his, but he suspects it was. He himself married in his fifties, but had no children of his own.

The affair with the woman involved, he said, a lifelong "guilt complex." Its long-term effects were felt in his need to confront what he felt to be the sin involved, his unrequited love and the pain of it. It was still difficult for him to talk about sixty years later.

Mr. McCue described those events as pivotal yet he did not blame his alcoholism on his unhappy love affair. Instead, he noted that an alcoholic would look to any excuse to drink: "It's a disease. Anything that makes you happy or sad is an excuse to drink."

When his affair ended after a few years, he returned to the Philadelphia area where he got a job unloading railroad boxcars. He drank more heavily and kept his job because he was not closely supervised and was able to drink on the job. He switched to a job at the post office. He asked a friend who worked at the post office and who he described as "an Irishman and a drunk" how he, the friend, managed to drink *and* keep his job. His friend replied, "at the post office, you *have* to be a habitual drunkard." His friend arranged for him to get a job there.

He continued working there until 1942, when he joined the army and was sent to the Pacific. Access to liquor was no problem.

The climax to his alcoholism came in 1953. He continued to work at the post office in jobs in which his lack of sobriety could be managed and was tolerated. He was living in a rooming house in a poor Irish neighborhood. "I don't know how that landlady put up with me. I used to smoke and burn the mattress and the sheets, holes in the carpets. Everything that you read about in the papers, I did, although they died and I'm still living. I guess she tolerated me because I paid my rent with regularity. I was paid every two weeks and I always paid her in advance. For some reason, despite everything, I always paid my debts." The other roomer was an alcoholic; the two used to drink together. "One night I found him dead in his room. When the police came to carry him out, they said to me, 'We'll be back for you later'. I was a walking corpse."

Soon thereafter, his sister and her husband, who were increasingly concerned about him, came to his room and convinced him to enter an alcoholism treatment program at a hospital. "My sister was standing there crying. I kept thinking to myself, 'I'm a jerk'. I said to her, 'All right, I'll go, but I won't stop drinking'. I was concerned because I had just bought a gallon of Sneaky Pete (a kind of liquor) and didn't want it to go to waste. That's how alcoholics think."

"So I entered the hospital. And I don't know how they put up with me there. Then one day the thought came to me—I don't know how it came to me; God must have put it in me—the thought came to me that I'm sick and tired of being a drunk and that I'm sick and tired of being sick and tired. I thought to myself, 'I'll just go back home, finish the gallon, and stop' ".

"Well, I did go back. My sister and her husband took me. I had about two sets of decent clothes, so I went back for them. But she wouldn't let me go up there alone. She said to me, 'You come and live with us'. But she had ten children. She said, 'I don't care if we have to put the kids in the hallway, you're getting a room for yourself.' "

"Well, then, I started going to Masses every day. I didn't put any trust in myself; I had to put all my trust in God. Soon after that, I found AA (Alcholics Anonymous). I had tried that once before; I went but I didn't like it. But now I found a wonderful meeting. The people there helped me and supported me."

The narration of these events by Mr. McCue is a task that seeks to make some sense out of complex and painful events. Implicated in his account is his perception of the role that God has played in his life. It is an understanding he came to only through his involvement in AA and therefore retrospective to his experience of important events. In describing the downwardness of his life, he can now see evidence of how God watched over him, unknown to him, how he managed to survive when others died. Examples of this are his survival of combat; his running into an old friend, who told him how to keep his job after he had submitted his resignation from the post office over a trivial matter; the boss who forbid him to drive trucks any longer, noting, 'Mike, I can't sleep, I'm afraid you'll kill someone or yourself and they'll blame me'; his thoughts about not drinking; and meeting his wife.

At this point, the line of the story turns upwards. He met his wife at an AA meeting and was married in the early 1960s. He noted that his marriage was very happy. After his wife died, her sister told him that when his wife visited her, the sister, she would always say how much she loved him and how happy she'd be to return home to him after the visit. He and his wife purchased a suburban home which was to him the fulfillment of a dream he felt could never be realized. About fifty when he was married, he was amazed that a lot he thought he had missed in life was still available to him. He described the change in himself as gaining a certain perspective on life. When his wife was dying and was sick at home, he said that he felt grateful that he was able to take care of her and also noted, "I was so glad that I was with her when she died." Nevertheless, he was quite depressed in the year following her death. When his wife died, she had a large life insurance policy the existence of which was unknown to him. In the few years since her death, he has enjoyed giving large sums of money to his relatives.

Examined as a whole, his life story is one which juggles the humiliation and shame of alcoholism, guilt and sin and the possibilities of love, acceptance and redemption. While his past is painful, he does not seem to regret it.

Here, the ideas of AA were important to him. Among these are not regretting the past and learning to live with the pain of everyday life. He became able to see, he felt, the workings of God, his "Higher Power" in the AA parlance, in his life, even (retrospectively) in the depths of his illness. He noted, "I used to think to myself, 'God can't possibly forgive me for all the rotten things I did'. But one time I realized what would happen if I was in my mother's house, lying drunk on the floor screaming and the police were coming for me. She'd say to them, 'The poor boy's upset, leave him alone, he didn't mean it' ... That's what she'd say. She was like that; she'd forgive me anything. So when I'd think that God could never forgive me, I'd also think that Mother-love is an infinitesimal speck of how much He loves us, and if my mother forgave me, God certainly would."

One time, in discussing his father, he noted, "And sometime before my father died—he died in '42—when I was in the Army —he said to me, 'Michael, I know you're a hopeless drunk...'—his heart must have been broken, cause I was the oldest son— 'but I want you to promise me one thing, that no matter what happens, you won't miss Mass on Sunday, because if you miss Mass, it means that you lose your faith'. And, you know, even in my worst drunken days, I went. That's how much I owe to my father. And I'd be shaking (from the effects of alcohol) when I went: I'd look forward to winter, so I could wear an overcoat and people couldn't see me shaking."

"I'm ashamed that I never did anything for my father. But I always took his advice. And, I'd go to confession, too. And, you know, that guy I told you about who I found dead, I took him to Mass with me. He said, 'I can't go. I haven't been to church for ten years. I've been married three times'. I told him, 'So what? You're living in a dump with me. Let's go'." Mr. McCue was grateful to do good even when living "on the bum."

Quantitatively, Mr. McCue's well-being was not high. In response to a standard question, he was "pretty happy" these days. In his Bradburn responses, in the past few weeks, he was not particularly excited or interested in something; not so restless he couldn't sit long in a chair; and not "on top of the world." He did feel very lonely or remote from people; pleased about having accomplished something; bored; depressed; and upset because someone had criticized him, in the past few weeks.

But he was a man who had a great capacity to put these feelings into perspective. It was very clear from our interviews that activities, events and feelings of the present day were evaluated in terms of a system of interpretation, distilled from his knowledge of his own history, his religious faith and his involvement with AA. He had a "second-order" ability to evaluate events and his reactions to them; in this sense, he was emotionally mature. Further, his regular activities, those undertaken on a daily basis, were attempts, now almost routinized, to insure the continuation of this practice of reflection (or second-order evaluation). Thus every day of the week he sat through two early Masses at his church. Noting that he was the only one there who seemed to do that, he remarked that this was necessary for him. It not only filled in time, but it also helped give a sense of purpose to his day. Part of his day also consisted of doing errands for some less healthy older residents of his apartment building, stopping at the store, bringing the mail up, chatting just to be friendly. These activities provided the consistency and structure of daily routine that aided reflection and interpretation in operating on mood states. He was attentive, in all our interviews, to note what he felt to be the way in which God had provided for him in his life, not only when he was an active drunk, but also since he came to realize the important role of God in his life. Both significant events and daily minutiae were seen in terms of this larger interpretive scheme with life historical dimensions.

Mrs. Collins

In reviewing notes of conversations with Mrs. Collins, about seventy when we met, it was quite clear that she portrayed her life, globally, as on a downward trajectory, although punctuated by stable and happier periods. One of the first things she said to me after our introduction, was "I've lived my life." The intent of this statement was to indicate a degree of resignation and acceptance that the present was pale and the end was near. Initially, I interviewed her once a week for four months and then met with her more infrequently for a period totaling about a year-and-a-half. Our last meeting occurred after she had moved out of the area.

When I met her, she had been diagnosed as having liver cancer and had been "given" two years to live by her doctors. The cancer was related to her mastectomy, almost two years before the interviews, an event which had made her depressed, with suicidal ideas: "I used to pray that I wouldn't wake up." When I met her, her life had stabilized somewhat. She had tried, but had discontinued, standard cancer treatments because they made her sick and caused her hair to fall out; she was bald and wore a wig. She relied, however, on new medications prescribed by her doctor, on prayer and on herbal remedies sent from the West Coast by her younger son.

She portrayed her life as a series of stable plateaus punctuated by dramatic declines. Her mother came from southern "society." Mrs. Collins had a strong sense of identity with her mother, who had the same first name, who married a similar type of man and who is now one object of Mrs. Collins's daily prayers. Her father was a stockbroker in New York, as were two of her brothers. Her father was also an alcoholic and abusive to her mother. The death of her mother was a pivotal incident in her early life, as were the eerie events surrounding it. A few days before she died, her mother asked Mrs.

Collins, then fifteen, to take a photograph of her in order to complete a partially-used roll of film. Her mother then took the roll to the store for development. Meanwhile, one evening her father came home drunk, and had a dramatic fight with her mother. The mother told the father, "Your words could kill me." She died three days later, of pneumonia. In fact, Mrs. Collins had been planting nasturtiums with her mother that day and her mother apparently contracted a cold "or pleruisy or pneumonia" and died. The children blamed the father for the death. Several days later, Mrs. Collins remembered about the photos and went to the store. The proprietor, who did not know of the death, asked if the woman had died. Mrs. Collins told her that she had and asked her how she knew. The proprietor replied because the women had had five copies of one of the photographs of her made as keepsakes, one for each of the family members. Mrs. Collins believes that her mother must have felt, or known or guessed that her own death was imminent.

After her mother's death, Mrs. Collins's family split up. Her father, ostracized by the younger children, went to live with his married son. Mrs. Collins and her two unmarried brothers took an apartment in New York.

In the ensuing years, both brothers married, and Mrs. Collins came to live with an aunt in Philadelphia. This was another pivotal point. She could have chosen another aunt to live with, one who was childless and wealthy. Several times in our interviews she remarked on how different her life might have been if she had gone to live with the second aunt. In Philadelphia, she obtained a job at a large manufacturing concern, where she met her husband-to-be, then a junior executive.

She noted that she was in love with her husband at first but after a year of marriage, she realized that she shouldn't have married him. She described him as possessing a dual personality. On the one hand, he was "brilliant" and "charming." He loved to play the piano and entertain; he was, for a time, extremely successful in his profession. On the other hand, he had a dark side. He was "terribly insecure." And, he was an alcoholic. Although, at first, his drinking was manageable in the sense that he was able to maintain his job, he was abusive at home. Later, his drinking and abusiveness became more severe.

During the war, Mr. Collins was involved in a number of important war industries. His career was connected to that of a powerful and successful mentor who entered business after the war. During that period, Mr. and Mrs. Collins had two children and lived for a time in Europe, where Mr. Collins built up the European operations for his company. They lived in the grand style there, in large homes with nannies and servants. This was a high point in their life together. The negatives were that he had to be away from home for long stretches of time and that his job involved a great deal of entertaining and therefore drinking. After several years in Europe, there was a company shakeup. Mr. Collins was offered a lateral move, but refused and left the company. They returned to Philadelphia, where they lived with Mr. Collins's mother, while Mr. Collins looked for work. He was unemployed for a year, he drank a great deal and they used up much of the money they had made in Europe. Finally, he was able to secure a job in a related profession. After a time, he was given notice that he address his alcoholism or lose his job. He refused and was fired. He had a break down and was hospitalized. Mrs. Collins noted, "The psychiatrist said, 'Prepare yourself for the fact that he's never coming out'." Nevertheless, he returned home, initially for weekend visits, and finally he was discharged. When his drinking and abusive behavior continued to increase, Mrs. Collins moved out, taking the two children. In a year or so, one son graduated from college and the other from high school.

During this period, Mrs. Collins built a new life for herself. She showed a strength and resourcefulness that surprised her, for she had always felt herself to be dependent on her husband. She changed apartments, after her sons moved away, to one she described as "a fun place," because of her frequent lively parties with her neighbors and friends whom she described as "buddies." She got a job—the first one of her life—had a full social life and dated. She regrets now that she never remarried. When the management of her apartment changed, she moved again and then became involved in an amateur theatre group. When the quality of her new apartment was perceived as deteriorating, she moved again, with a sense of optimism and hope, to a new apartment. Soon after this move, she was diagnosed as having cancer and had a breast removed, followed by continuing treatment for cancer. In the period of recovery from her surgery, she reached the depths of despair. She wished to die. Yet her strength sustained her and when I met her, though she was still very depressed, she went through the motions of living her life.

The Interpretation of Well-Being

Both Mr. McCue and Mrs. Collins displayed the ability to interpret events and their own reactions to them. They were both aware of their own histories as germane to their present-day well-being. And they also both utilized theories about the nature of affect and its management.

The native theories of Mr. McCue and Mrs. Collins related to key devices. The first, no doubt having its basis in Western culture, is the fundamental dichotomy between the inner and outer worlds and therefore the significance of each in regulating the effects of one on the other. The second is that both utilized a powerful metaphor of lifelong well-being, that of the trajectory, or a line over time. The temporal trajectory of well-being is important in both stories, albeit somewhat more explicit in Mr. McCue's account.

The life-long trajectory of Mr. McCue's well-being was downward, then upward. An alcoholic, Mr. McCue's life was increasingly one of unhappiness and destructive and self-abusive behaviors until his recovery from active alcoholism began. His conceptualization of this is as an uncut line over time. Mrs. Collins's trajectory was quite different, in that it was choppier, someties lineal and sometimes piecemeal. She felt events started off well in life, but thereafter each period of relative stability and happiness was followed by a traumatic event leading to unhappiness and some accommodation by her to it. Despite stable periods, even times featuring many positive attributes, the overall trend was portrayed as downhill. Her last and most severe blow had been the diagnosis of breast cancer, followed by a mastectomy, the diagnosis of liver cancer and being told that she had two years to live. She felt herself to be one of the living dead.

Oversimplified, Mr. McCue's native theory of "mood" was that, while negative events occurred and the real purpose of happenings was not knowable to man, a calm inner-self led to the daily ability to put events into perspective. The practice of key behaviors, such as prayer and meditation, on a daily basis were in fact important, but were important insofar as they helped maintain the calm inner-self. Management was basically internal. Depression, such as that experienced in the tremendous pain in the period following his wife's death, was part of life. With the help of God, one could get through, for as he put it, "God never gives us more than we can handle." Further, for Mr. McCue, an important part of keeping things in "perspective" is contrasting where he had been to where he is now.

Mrs. Collins had a "native theory" that was similar to, but distinct from, Mr. McCue's. Beleaguered, depressed and sometimes near despair, during her current chapter in life she had psychically drawn the wagons around her, limiting her social contacts, routinizing her day and use of space and only gradually adding things (such as being interviewed) since her surgery. Her belief, however, was that external behaviors could modify or influence internal states.

Once, when I visited her, we had done some spring cleaning, an activity that she enjoyed tremendously. "I haven't enjoyed something that much in a while," she noted. In discussing its meaning, Mrs. Collins said she was delighted that she had the physical strength and stamina to do it. Its meaning was related, in addition, to her past enjoyment in taking care of her home "when things were good. . . . I used to love being a homemaker, cleaning and straightening," she said. And, the pleasure of this was associated, in her mind, with an idealized sort of marital relationship, the heavily charged cultural symbol of the mutuality and complementarity of home, experienced rarely in the past and never to be experienced again. In this activity, further, it was her hope that her belief in the idea that engaging in activity could lead to an improved mood was now being validated.

She had two conflicting goals in the present period. Often, she just saw herself as waiting out the rest of her life, to the bittersweet end, as she followed the trajectory downwards. But she also made attempts to get back to the higher ground, such as those times she experienced at her "fun apartment" or the secure moral order offered by her upper-class background. Unlike Mr. McCue, for whom inner resources were brought to bear on outer difficulties, Mrs. Collins sought to change her outer behavior in the hope that it would reorganize or unburden her inner life. She operated under the assumption that engaging in specific behaviors would improve her mood. Key in this regard were her efforts to "get out more," to do volunteer work, to go on a vacation with a friend, to use her exercise bicycle or to attend church one evening a week. But usually the buoyancy of these behaviors refused to infect her dark moods for more than a few hours.

Conclusion

Both these informants conducted their lives with underlying theories of how one obtained and maintained well-being. Key to these theories were the relationship between inner and outer selves and the highs and lows of personal history. The ways in which older people manage the relationship between inner and outer states seems to me to be of extraordinary importance and worthy of further study. I assume that many notions about the inner and outer realms and their alignment are culturally-based and shared, though individuals have their own versions of these.

There is a potential here for forging links between research perspectives. For example Lawton (1983) notes that negative and positive affect are important aspects of psychological well-being and found that negative affect is more strongly related to "inner aspects of the person" while positive affect is more strongly related to "external, interactive aspects of the person's world." Yet as has been pointed out here, it continues to be important to consider that the person does not react "instinctively" to events; events and their affects have meanings.

The psychologist Farr (1981; p. 303) has noted that "the conceptions of human nature which prevail in the arts and humanities are much richer in their implications than the models of man currently in use in academic psychology." Here, I have suggested that older individuals' notions of their own psychologies and selves are also rich creations. Little attention has been paid to these in mainstream social gerontology. How can this continue to be?

Notes

1. The data described in this chapter was gathered in two research projects, "The meaning and function of home for the elderly" and "Ethnicity and life reorganization by elderly widowers" both supported by the National Institute of Aging. The support of the institute is gratefully acknowledged.

I would also like to thank my colleagues at the Philadelphia Geriatric Center for many discussions and the free interchange of ideas. In particular, I'd like to thank Allen Glicksman for permission to summarize unpublished findings and for comments on drafts of this paper. A careful reading by Miriam Moss helped clarify a number of points. Also, I'm grateful to Dr. Mark Luborsky for many discussions on some of the topics discussed here which have greatly benefited my thinking about them and for a painstaking reading of an earlier draft of this paper.

I also wish to thank "Mrs. Collins" and "Mr. McCue" for opening their worlds to me. "Mrs. Collins" read and commented on a lengthy draft of an account of her life from which the above summary is taken.

References

Allport, G.W. 1953. The trend in motivational theory. *American Journal of Orthopsychiatry* 23:107-119.

Bakan, D. 1967. *On method: Toward a reconstruction of psychological investigation.* San Francisco: Jossey-Bass.

Bradburn, N.M. 1968. *The structure of psychological well-being.* Chicago: Aldine.

Carp, F.M. and C.N. Nydegger, 1975. Recent gerontological developments in psychology and the social sciences. *The Gerontologist* 15:368-370.

Farr, R.M. 1981. On the nature of human nature and the science of behavior. In P. Heelas and Andrew Lock, (eds.), *Indigenous psychologies: The anthropology of the self.* London: Academic Press.

Gee, J.P. 1985. The narrativization of experience in the oral style. *Journal of Education,* 167: 9-35.

Gergen, K.J. and M.M. Gergen. 1986. Narrative form and the construction of psychological science. In T.R. Sarbin, (ed.) *Narrative psychology: The storied nature of human conduct.* New York: Praeger.

Gergen, K.J. and M.M. Gergen. 1987. The self in temporal perspective. In R. Abeles (ed.) *Life-span perspectives and social psychology.* Hillsdale, NJ: Lawrence Erlbaum Associates.

Gergen, M.M. and K.J. Gergen. 1984. The social construction of narrative accounts. In K.J. Gergen and M.M. Gergen (eds.) *Historical social psychology.* Hillsdale, NJ: Lawrence Erlbaum Associates.

Gubrium, J. and R.J. Lynott. 1986. Rethinking life satisfaction. In B.B. Hess (ed.) *Growing old in America.* (third edition). New Brunswick, NJ: Transaction Books.

Larson, R. 1978. Thirty years of research on the subjective well-being of older Americans. *Journal of Gerontology* 33: 109-125.

Lawton, M.P. 1983. The varieties of well-being. *Experimental Aging Research* 9: 65-72.

Mishler, E.G. 1986 *Research interviewing: Context and narrative.* Cambridge: Harvard University Press.

Nydegger, C.N. 1977. Introduction. In C.N. Nydegger (ed.) *Measuring morale: A guide to effective assessment* Washington, DC: Gerontological Society, Special Publication, Number 3.

Suls, J. and B. Mullen, 1984. Social and temporal bases of self-evaluation in the elderly: Theory and evidence. *International Journal of Aging and Human Development* 18: 11-120.

White, H. 1980. The value of narrativity in the representation of reality. *Critical Inquiry* 7: 5-28.

Chapter 8

Qualitative Research with Older Creative Adults

KAROL SYLCOX FERGUSON

Creativity is often associated with the various ideas, inventions, perform-ances or products of famous people, such as Edison, Einstein and Mozart. Even among those who have studied creativity and are familiar with the lives of people who have been creative, creativity is often thought of in a narrow sense of the term, i.e., as artistic creativity only. For many people, an art class one period each week, if that, was either the sole or major time during which they were encouraged to "be creative."

Creativity is also associated with productivity and youth. There may be several reasons for this association. Youth is the time of most people's lives when they are in good health, have much energy, and are more inclined to take risks, since the concerns of family and other responsibilities have not yet entered their lives. It is believed that such circumstances are conducive to productivity.

Although creativity has been researched extensively, little has been done to learn about the creativity of older people from their points of view. This chapter concerns a study of creative people aged sixty-five and older which was conducted to learn what they think about creativity. The oral history approach was the method chosen to collect the data; case histories were cho-sen as one means to present data.

Research Strategy

Twenty creative individuals aged sixty-five or older were sought for this study. All referrals were received from professionals working directly with elderly individuals, such as directors of nursing homes and senior citizens' centers. All subjects were nominated by these professionals as being actively creative individuals. Each subject's creative products and any pertinent docu-ments about him/her that were available were examined prior to each formal interview. Subjects were asked fifteen questions about four general areas or rubrics related to their creative development: self, schooling and education, friends and family and health.

Table 1

Area(s) of Creativity

Subject #	Sex	Age	Area(s) of Creativity
1	M	88	leadership; strong concern for others and for fairness; creative problem-solving
2	F	71	creative writing; teaching; risk-taking and openness to experience
3	F	76	water-color painting; photography
4	M	71	verbal precocity; creative use of language
5	M	84	poetry
6	F	101	creative pattern-making; crocheting; cooking
7	M	70	painting
8	M	84	artistic creativity; teaching; illustrating; writing; painting
9	F	82	water-color painting; creative writing
10	F	88	creative cooking; needlepoint; tatting; knitting; embroidering
11	M	74	nationally-recognized illustrating and slogan-writing; painting
12	F	76	creative writing; puppet-making; sculpturing; weaving
13	M	73	painting; sculpturing; writing; weaving
14	F	65	doll-making; quilting; clothing design; textile conservation
15	F	77	painting; sculpturing; toy-making; book-binding; sewing; weaving
16	F	80	writing; designing; flower/herb/spice expert
17	F	68	writing; researching; program developing
18	M	74	carpentry; toy-making; needlepoint; rug-making
19	M	73	theater directing; composing music; writing; teaching
20	F	69	creative leadership; program developing

There were nine male and eleven female subjects. Their areas of creativity were varied and included leadership, handicrafts, such as toy-making, needle-point, tatting, and crocheting; and fine arts, such as photography, water-color and oil painting.

Subjects ranged in age from sixty-five years to almost 102 years of age. The mean age was seventy-seven years. Interviews ranged from one and three-quarters to nine hours in length; the average length was four hours. Interviews were tape-recorded, and the researcher transcribed, verbatim, the seventy-three hours of taped interviews. The transcriptions yielded 370 pages of data, an average of 18.5 pages of handwritten transcribed protocol per subject. In addition, there were eight pages of handwritten field notes per subject. Transcriptions and field notes were written in a modified shorthand. Had they been written in longhand and/or typewritten, there would have been at least twice the number of pages of data.

To assure that the researcher was familiar with all data before analyzing it, the data were read in their entirety four times. In order to make the data manageable, they were reduced. Data reductions involved four major steps: 1) reducing information from the transcripts (eliminating elaborations from responses), 2) condensing and collapsing any individual's repetitive responses, 3) reducing the length of specific responses and 4) reducing the number of categories of responses. In order to maintain an accurate perspective about the numbers of people who had similar responses, and in order to present the data graphically, summaries of the data were quantified. Numbers of responses were converted into percentages which were arranged in lists. This proved to be most helpful, for a few subjects were so emphatic in their responses that the researcher easily could have been left with the impression that more subjects felt a certain way or had a similar response than the number who actually did. By being able to glance at a summary of the responses to a given question, the researcher was able to correct wrong impressions and know what the actual numbers were.

After the reductions were completed and percentages listed, the findings were presented in three forms. The first form was a narrative which included every subject's response to each of the fifteen interview questions. This presentation covered all major findings, including all responses which clustered (i.e., responses which were similar and fell into the same category) and all individualistic responses (i.e., responses made by only one subject). It also provided findings which included responses made by subjects which appeared in two seemingly contradictory clusters. For example, some subjects found that their families were both helpful to them in their creative development and hindrances to that development. This presentation also allowed for subjects' emphases in their responses to be noted and for the noteworthy responses to be quoted.

Table 2
Narrative Clusters of Responses to the Question
"What does creativity mean?"

Responses to this question clustered into eleven areas and generated several definitions of creativity. Subjects also mentioned several characteristics of creative people.

Clusters	Percent with this response
1. There is or can be creativity in teaching and/or the aged teacher is creative and develops creativity in his/her students	10%
2. People are "born" creative	10%
3. Creative people are open-minded and exhibit a freedom of thought	10%
4. Luck is an element of creativity	10%
5. My creativity/creations benefit(s) others	10%
6. Problem-solving is an aspect of creativity	10%
7. Creativity involves creative thinking	15%
8. Creative people are resourceful	15%
9. Risk is an element of creativity	15%
10. Curiosity is an element of creativity	15%
11. Creativity can result in or be productivity	15%

In the narrative presentation of findings, clusters of responses are noted. Themes, i.e., the same or very similar responses made by at least two subjects, are grouped. The narrative form also contains information about responses which did not cluster, i.e., individualistic responses, responses which were not duplicated by other subjects. The narrative form also presents any pertinent quotes of subjects' responses which either exemplify typical responses made by the subjects or present unique responses.

The second form was comprised of tables and figures, and focused on identical or similar responses made by at least two subjects to any given interview question (i.e., responses which clustered). This form, a graphic one, lists the clusters, primarily, and only particularly noteworthy individualistic responses. This form of data presentation recapitulates the prose presentation of the findings and focuses upon the major findings, i.e., similar responses made by two or more subjects.

Table 3
Responses to Question: How Were Creative Activities Encouraged/Discouraged by Teachers/Employers?

N	1 Encouraged by teachers generally	2 Encouraged by specific teachers	3 Discouraged by specific teachers	4 Not encouraged by teachers and/or school	5 Job involved this creativity	6 Encouraged by employers generally	7 Encouraged by specific employers	8 Not encouraged by employers	9 Discouraged by co-workers
1		X							
2	X		X				X		
3	X					X			
4		X							
5		X	X						
6	X								
7				X					
8		X	X						
9	X					X			
10	X				X				
11	X								
12	X		X			X			
13				X					
14	X						X		
15		X	X						
16	X		X						
17	X			X					
18		X			X				
19								X	
20	X						X		X
	11 (55%)	5 (25%)	6 (30%)	4 (20%)	2 (10%)	3 (15%)	2 (10%)	2 (10%)	1 (5%)

Case Histories

The third form of presenting the data was through case histories. A case history was written for each subject. Each case history was written with the entire interview in mind, i.e., with consideration for both the formal and informal aspects of the interview. From the narrative presentation of the findings, appropriate quotations were taken and used to write the case histories. Information from the field notes was used in writing the case histories, but the subjects' responses to the interview questions provided the bulk of the baseline data for the case histories. Each case history was organized around the following six areas of information:

1. subject's age and sex,
2. subject's creativity,
3. subject's life's work,
4. subject's current interests,
5. subject's education and
6. subject's family.

These six areas included the four formal variables in the study (self, schooling and education, friends and family and health) and other variables or topics which each subject's responses to the fifteen interview questions concerned. Additional topics were addressed by some individuals, but only those topics which were addressed by all subjects were covered in the case histories in order to make them uniform in structure. Combined, the twenty case histories were forty-eight double-spaced, typewritten pages long.

Three case histories written in the manner described have been selected for inclusion in this chapter. From them, one can see how a great deal of data can be concisely written and made easily understood. The case histories were of varying lengths because some subjects were more talkative and elaborated upon their responses more than others. The names of the subjects have been changed to maintain their anonymity.

The case histories include examples of several characteristics of creative people: verbal precocity and play with words; ability to build upon others' ideas; resourcefulness; ability to view the world with wonder, to respond to experiences as if each of them were a totally new or foreign experience; openness to experience, including use of "flashes" of creative insight leading to the solution of a problem and/or the creation of a product and perseverance. A prevailing belief arising from a few subjects is that it is the individual and his/her creativity which is important, not the age at which he/she creates.

Subject #5: Mr. Mayer

Mr. Mayer was eighty-three years old at the time of the interview. The researcher was referred to the subject because of the subject's creative poetry writing. He refers to himself as a poet-philosopher. His greatest joy is in composing poetry. He worked in the garment industry as a cutter and as a salesman; later in his life, he worked for Pratt and Whitney Aircraft Corporation. Now he composes poetry and shares his work with his neighbors and friends, but seeks a wider audience and wants to publish a book of his poems. He composes his poems verbally and later records them in writing. He composes rhymed verses in iambic pentameter, and can recite many of the hundreds of poems he has composed. He immensely enjoys the different creative processes involved in his work, and is eager to talk with others about them. He is fascinated by the subconscious, intuitive aspects of his composition which he does not understand and cannot control, but recognizes and appreciates.

For half of the years he has lived, he did not use his verbal or writing abilities. He was considered to be a trouble-maker when he was in school because of his continual playing with words, and his jobs after his schooling did not call for the use of his notable wit, retention or recall. It was not until he was forty-two years old that he rediscovered his abilities. He was asked by a co-worker to complete two lines of a limerick. From that instance forward, Mr. Mayer delighted in his ability to compose rhymed verse, and in the joy and comfort his poems gave to others. Mr. Mayer did not further his formal education, but has read many classic works on such topics as philosophy and nature.

At the age of thirty-three, he married. He has one son and two grandchildren. He does not know where they now live and does not hear from them. His friends, many of whom are "extended family members," help him.

This subject has great difficulty in writing prose, but of his rhymed poetry writing, he said:

> When I'm through writing the first line down, another one pops right into my head. If I reach for something and it doesn't work, I throw it out and I get another one and it just seems to come so *naturally*, so *easily*. I feel very lucky that I have the ability to *do* a thing like that. It comes so *natural* to me. I only write in one meter, iambic pentameter. It seems that everything I write comes out poetically. I can't write a good letter because it throws me off; but a poem, I find a solution, a memory, and bring something out. I took my talent for granted and for years and years I never used it to my advantage.

Mr. Mayer wishes that he had been encouraged to use his verbal abilities in a career in which they would have appropriately been used, but he does not dwell on what could or should have been. He refuses to be negative and instead emphasizes strengths in himself and others. He does not complain about his misfortunes or any life events known to be particularly stressful to one in his position. For example, at the time the researcher met with him for the interview, he had just lost his driver's license because of his failing eye-sight, motor reflexes and lack of physical strength. The loss of one's driver's license (and hence his mobility and, to a great degree, his independence) is a very stressful life event. Mr. Mayer's refusal to focus on the negative aspects of his age was not a denial of his aging; he specified and was accepting of the reasons why he should no longer drive.

Of all of the subjects, Mr. Mayer was the only one who would not, despite the researcher's probing, respond directly to the question, "Has ageism been a concern regarding your creative development?"

Subject #6: Mrs. Whipple

Mrs. Whipple was 101 years old at the time of the interview. The researcher was referred to the subject because of her creative pattern-making and pro-lific production of crocheted clothes. She has crocheted hundreds of clothing items. Mrs. Whipple is also a creative cook.

Mrs. Whipple was born and raised on a large farm in Indiana. She was a housewife throughout her life and now lives with and helps her surviving offspring, a daughter aged sixty-five, and her daughter's family and friends. She cooks the family evening meal and bakes breads, pies and cookies "from scratch." She uses no prepared package mixes and she makes all of the pat-terns for the clothes she crochets. She donates many of her products to her church for fund-raising events.

Mrs. Whipple was an excellent student throughout her schooling experi-ences. Although she did not have formal education beyond high school, she is an avid reader and prefers reading to watching television. She completed high school, even though her father died and she had to help her mother run the family farm during the economic depression of the latter part of the nine-teenth century.

She came to live with her daughter ten years ago; before that, she maintained her own home. She is very modest and has an exceptionally good memory. She exhibits much attention to detail in her speaking and in her work. She is highly motivated and willing to try new experiences. Although she never drank alcoholic beverages for most of her life, since she moved into her daughter's home a decade ago, she participates in the family's occa-sional after-dinner enjoyment of a glass of sherry. At the age of ninety-nine, she visited the local senior citizens' center. She was invited to return for future visits, but declined, saying that she did not have the time because of her other interests.

Despite her age, her complexion is still beautiful, and she has very few wrinkles. Her daughter, whose face is quite wrinkled, believes that her moth-er's lifestyle and environment contributed to her lifelong, youthful appearance. Mrs. Whipple grew up on a farm, away from pollutants; she did not drink alcohol for most of her life, and she never drank coffee or used cosmetics.

Mrs. Whipple's creativity exemplifies what is perhaps the archetype of creativity demonstrated by women who were obliged to focus primarily on caring for family and maintaining a home. That creativity is manifested in items made for the home and for family members.

In answering a question about ageism, Mrs. Whipple offered this advice:

> Old people need love and sympathy, and they need company. They need somebody to *talk* to. Of course, so many of them are past the age now when they can take advantage of certain programs, but now, starting with younger people, people in their eighties, need that.

Subject #9: Miss Calder

Miss Calder was eighty-two years old at the time of the interview. The researcher was referred to the subject because of her creative writing and water-color painting, and because of the twenty art courses she created for the local university for whose art department she was the original chairperson.

After retiring, Miss Calder researched a topic for ten years and wrote a book about it which was published when she was seventy-eight years old. Another book of hers concerning Connecticut's cultural legacy was published when the subject was seventy-nine years old. She is currently working on a third book which is being illustrated by the noted naturalist illustrator, Ann Zwinger.

Miss Calder is a recognized water-color painter. Although her painting has been hindered by painful arthritis, she is hopeful that she "will find another way to paint."

Miss Calder worked in home economics and continues to read about the topic. She may publish an article about her experiences sorting and disseminating her possessions and artifacts, because she enjoys these activities a great deal. In fact, she presented the researcher with a leather-trimmed canvas bag in which to store and carry tape-recording equipment.

This subject exemplifies how risk-taking, a characteristic of creative people, was used in a career and in retirement. Miss Calder accepted a position in leadership at a major university at a time when women seldom held such positions. She developed an art department even though her background was in another field. That art department still offers the core courses which she developed. Miss Calder recognizes the risk-taking that was involved in her work at the university. She said, "You see, I was a pioneer," and she requested that the researcher print, in capital letters, her emphatic "AGE DOES NOT COUNT!" She feels that it is not age *per se* which dictates one's drive or limits of accomplishments. She also said, "You still have your mind. You can live as long as you want to, so long as you keep your mind going."

Miss Calder hit upon a point which many who research creativity and giftedness have learned: that one's interests can carry one a long way, perhaps even farther than formal education can. Miss Calder made these comments:

> Some people say that the only way to get along is to have a formal education. And it's certainly true that if you can tack something at the end of your name and have had a variety of experience, it does make a difference if you're going out in the work-a-day world. That's what is recognized. But on the other hand, it is not necessary one little bit if a person is captivated by something that he is going to explore and go farther, many times, than the educated person.

Like many other creative people, Miss Calder had a significant role model and mentor who influenced her life and work. Of the dean who inspired her throughout her career, Miss Calder said, "She was a strength to me all through those years, and she gave me a feeling of promise about anything I was originating or anything I was doing. Whether I was twenty years old or whether I was fifty years old, she was still an inspiration to me."

Miss Calder went out of her way to be helpful to the researcher. Weeks after the interview, Miss Calder alerted the researcher to the fact that a book was recently published which has direct relevance to this study. She had read about the book and its author in her alumni newsletter from The Parsons School of Art and Design.

Miss Calder received news that because of the book she wrote which summarized her research on the life and work of George Freeman, New York State provided $600 for building restoration to the curators of the museum in Plattsburgh, New York, where what is considered to be George Freeman's most important work is displayed. Naturally, Miss Calder was pleased that through her efforts, George Freeman's work will be preserved and housed in a place where more people can enjoy it and learn more about it and his life.

Of creativity, Miss Calder said:

> The creativity comes *after* the creative person finds that he can free himself of outside interferences and then he can become more of himself. People who have retired have an opportunity such as they've never had before to free their minds of all the things that have occupied them before and let them become truly themselves and let them be creative in thought or in ways of working.

Summary and Implications

From 530 pages of data (370 pages of interview protocols and 160 pages of field notes), a great deal of information, rich in detail and broad in scope, was gained. This study examined the subjects' perceptions of their creative development. They tended to downplay the significance of their own creativity, pointing out how their creativity is incomparable to that of famous people, such as Michaelangelo, yet they underscored the importance of creativity in everyday activities and emphasized that that importance should be more generally recognized.

Their creativity was sparked primarily by out-of-school interests, and it was nurtured mostly by their mothers. Teachers in general were helpful to the subjects regarding their creative development, but some teachers were remembered as being especially helpful or especially harmful to that development.

Several subjects want to do writing projects; writing facilitates recollecting and reminiscing about past events, and it incites one to think of new ideas. Writing may be a form of evaluation and planning. All of the subjects described their aspirations; these aspirations build upon their strengths as creative people, and all of them plan to continue doing what they have done and have enjoyed doing. Several of them want to try new activities.

Overall, the subjects' health was seen as both a help and a hindrance to their creative development. In some instances, it was only a help; in others, it was only a hindrance. Neither acute nor chronic illnesses stopped the creative development of these subjects; in fact, acute illnesses often provided subjects with the time and "excuse" to pursue their creative interests.

The subjects do not want their creative abilities or products viewed as being exceptional because of their chronological ages; they want their work to be seen as being exceptional because of its merit and quality. Having an audience for their creative products is of importance to them, and all subjects had at least one aspiration regarding their creativity.

The reasons why people create are varied. One of the reasons relates to the dynamics of dependencies. The research literature concerning dependencies touches upon creativity (Goldfarb, 1969; Kutner et al., 1956). When an individual is able to do something for someone who has helped him/her and is able to give something to that helper, he/she is able to feel as if he/she has reciprocated that help. In turn, such actions help him/her to remain or feel less dependent, if not allowing him/her to be independent. By making cards, baking pies and breads, knitting or sewing clothes, handcrafting jewelry, toys, household gadgets or furniture, people of all ages give of themselves, reciprocate kindnesses and favors and maintain a sense of independence.

Elderly people are at once no different from other people in this respect and they are very different from other people in this respect. They are similar in that they use their time, resources and skills to create and give away or sell their creations to pay for services, repay favors or reciprocate kindnesses. In many cases, their resources are increasingly limited and their health is increasingly frail, unlike the situations most younger people enjoy. On the other hand, younger, working people may have less free time to make handicrafts.

138 KAROL SYLCOX FERGUSON

People at both ends of the age continuum make an effort to create their products. All may benefit intellectually, spiritually and physically from such creative activity.

Conclusion

Thanks to advances in medicine, health care, education and nutrition, one can expect to live longer than his/her ancestors did; hence, there is the possibility of one's being productive for a longer period of time, even if the quantity of ideas/products produced decreases over time (Lehman, 1953). There are documented cases of people who began pursuing their creative interests in old age; people such as Anna Mary Robertson Moses ("Grandma Moses") and Elizabeth Layton ("Grandma") are examples (Jones, 1978; Lengyel, 1971; McLeish, 1976; Skinner & Vaughn, 1983; Torrance, 1977; Torrance & Vesely, 1978; Wilson & Mullally, 1983). Often, one's creative productivity increases with age, and one may produce his/her most important work in old age, as was the case with Sigmund Freud and others (Arlow, 1956; Grams, 1986; Jones, 1957; Munsterberg, 1983). Perhaps those without the advantages of advanced medicine, such as Mozart, felt the pressure of time and/or circumstances and therefore worked hard to be especially productive. Of course, many creative people will be prolific regardless of any real or perceived pressures of time or other factors.

What one contributes, regardless of how long he/she lives, is important, for our society values productivity. The nurturing of creativity among our youth has been considered to be a worthwhile endeavor (Renzulli, 1977; Taylor, 1964). Their ability to generate new ideas, to create new products, and to solve problems is crucial to social progress and world peace. The nurturance of creativity in people of all ages should be the focus, however; the focus should not only be on youth (Andrews, 1968; Butler, 1967; Holahan, 1981; Maslow, 1971; Schaie & Geiwitz, 1982; Torrance, 1981). Older people are faced with new problems and challenges every day as they age. Their ability to generate new ideas, to create new products and to solve problems is important for them and for society-at-large.

References

Andrews, E. M. (1968). *Facing and fulfilling the later years.* Lebanon, PA: Pendle Hill.

Arlow, J. A. (1956). *The legacy of Sigmund Freud.* New York: International Universities Press.

Butler, R. N. (1967). The destiny of creativity in later life. Originally, Studies of creative people and the creative process. In S. Levin & R. H. Kahana (eds.) *Psychodynamic studies on aging: Creativity, reminiscing and dying*. New York: International Universities Press.

Goldfarb, A. I. (1969). The psychodynamics of dependency and the search for aid. In R. A. Kalish (ed.) *The dependencies of old people*. Michigan: Institute of Gerontology, The University of Michigan/Wayne State University.

Grams, A. (1986). Overcoming barriers to creativity. *Perspective on aging*. Washington, DC: The National Council on Aging, Inc., January-February 4-5, 24.

Holahan, C. (1981). Lifetime achievement patterns, retirement, and life satisfaction of gifted aged women. *Journal of Gerontology* 36(6): 741-749.

Jones, E. (1957). The life and work of Sigmund Freud. In *The last phase: 1919-1939, Vol. 3*. New York: Basic Books.

Jones, P. S. (1978). Elizabeth Layton: Alias "Grandma." *Aging* October-November 12-14.

Kutner, B., D. Fanshel, A. M. Togo and T. S. Langner (1956). *500 over 60*. New York: NYC Department of Health, Cornell University, and Russell Sage Foundation.

Lehman, H. C. (1953). *Age and achievement*. Princeton: Princeton University Press.

Lengyel, C. A. (1971). *The creative self: Aspects of man's quest for self-knowledge and the springs of creativity*. The Hague: Mouton.

McLeish, J. A. B. (1976). *The Ulyssean adult: Creativity in the middle and late years*. New York: McGraw-Hill.

Maslow, A. (1971). *The farther reaches of human nature*. New York: Viking Press.

Munsterberg, H. (1983). *The crown of life: Artistic creativity in old age*. New York: Harcourt, Brace, Jovanovich.

Renzulli, J. S. (1977). *The Enrichment triad model: A guide for developing defensible programs for the gifted and talented*. Mansfield Center, CT: Creative Learning Press.

Schaie, K. W. and J. Geiwitz (1982). *Adult development and aging*. Boston: Little, Brown.

Skinner, B. F. and M. E. Vaughn (1983). *Enjoy old age: A program for self-management*. New York: W. W. Norton.

Taylor, C. E. (ed.) (1964). *Creativity: Progress and potential*. New York: McGraw-Hill.

Torrance, E. P. (1977). Creativity and the older adult. In *The Creative Child and Adult Quarterly* Autumn: 136-144.

Torrance, E. P. (1981). Giftedness in solving future problems. In W. B. Barbe & J. S. Renzulli (eds.) *Psychology and education of the gifted*. New York: Irvington Publishers, 294-303.

Torrance, E. P. and A. Vesely (1978). *Art for older Americans: A partial evaluation.* Athens, GA: The University of Georgia and a N. E. Georgia Regional Organization.

Wilson, E. H. and S. Mullally (1983). *Hope and dignity: Older black women of the south.* Philadelphia: Temple University Press.

Chapter 9

Memory, Identity, History and the Understanding of Dementia

KARL E. SCHEIBE

> *We could not understand because we were too far and could*
> *not remember because we were travelling in the night of*
> *first ages, of those ages that are gone, leaving hardly a sign—*
> *and no memories.*

> —Joseph Conrad, *Heart of Darkness*

Living memory enables the binding of time and the realization of human identity. Yet as the experimental or physiological psychologist studies the problem, memory refers to a human capacity that stands outside of time. What are the informational limits of memory capacity? How does information pass form short-term to long-term memory? What are the relationships between sensory modalities and ease of information storage and retrieval?

The importance of these problems, and of the neurophysiology of memory, derives from the pervasive functional role played by memory in all intelligent behavior—speech production and comprehension, decision making, problem solving and the performance of complex motor activities. The term "memory" carries a hint of mentalism, and for this reason it was avoided or used with some embarrassment by strictly mechanistic behaviorists. But now that computer analogies have demonstrated the necessity of employing memory in a functional sense, all of this reserve has evaporated, and memory is here to stay as a central topic in psychology.

While the computer has helped in this way to restore and invigorate research on memory, the computer analogy has at the same time served to obscure the functioning of memory in sustaining human identity, for the memory of a computer does not perform this function. Similarly, the experimental psychology of memory is exclusively concerned with what the person *does* or can *do*. But the psychologist must ask also how memory operates in determining who and what the person *is*. The major purpose of this paper is

to elaborate upon the significance of memory in the development and maintenance of human identity.

In the course of this exposition, it will prove necessary to touch upon the
nature of history and on certain problematic features of historiography. The
significance of history in illuminating the problem of human identity is an
obvious psychological problem, but one that is still a bit strange in contemporary practice. The fundamental premise is that human lives are lived in historical time and in the terms of that time they take their meaning. A particular
person's self-understanding and identity is provided in historically particular
terms—with proper names, specificity of time, an understanding of the particularity of circumstance.

This approach to identity leads inevitably back to the problem of conduct—
of what people do. Actors on an historical stage do not just exist; they act, and
they act out of the conditions of their character and circumstances. Of course,
they must act in accord with the limits and capacities of the nervous and
motoric systems with which they are endowed. In this way, the traditional
experimental study of memory systems complements the study of memory as
a means of developing and sustaining personal identity. Human life is biographical as well as biological, and it is clear that memory has sense from
both of these perspectives.

The following section is an attempt to develop a sense of the role of
memory from the biographical perspective. In order to illustrate this role, it
will be useful to describe some reference cases.

Memories and identities of the aged: Some cases

I choose here to present records of the lives of old people—lives near the
end of their biological course, but possessing a particular biographical richness. In the first two cases, this richness is diminished by impairments of
memory function. These cases will be followed by a composite description of
a set of old people with particularly vivid and active memories.

Marcus L.: Alzheimer's Syndrome and the Fading of Memory and Identity

Alzheimer's syndrome has been identified for a number of years, but only
within the last decade has it received wide recognition as a serious problem
for research. The most typical symptom of Alzheimer's syndrome is progressive memory loss, beginning in late middle age. The syndrome is evidently of
neurophysiological origin, and recent studies have developed promising leads
regarding neural site and possible etiological factors, both environmental
and genetic. The psychological side of the syndrome is of particular interest,

for the memory loss is not typically accompanied by physical or motoric deterioration. At the present time, no therapeutic means exist to halt or reverse the progressive loss of memory.

The case of Marcus L. fits the general profile of Alzheimer patients.[1] A successful lawyer, widely read and well travelled, Marcus L. retired from the bar at age sixty-five. Since he and his wife were divorced, he lived after retirement with one or another of his three children, or with his sister and her family. This arrangement entailed a fair amount of travel, since Marcus would typically stay with one of these relations for less than a year, and in some years would visit all of them.

Memory loss became a serious problem for Marcus L. after retirement, but he often remarked before his retirement that he simply couldn't remember things. As a lawyer, this had bothered him considerably, for memory for case and procedure was vital to his practice. His awareness of memory loss was a factor in his decision to retire before he was required to do so. Memory lapses became most conspicuous in matters of travel and spatial orientation. Marcus would sometimes forget to pick up his suitcase after a flight or bus trip to a relative's city. Or he would forget where the relative lived in that city, and forget their name as well. After several misadventures, it became clear to all the relatives that he could not travel alone without having someone send him off and greet him at the terminal points of his trip, with instructions to attendants to insure his disembarking at the right point. Also, he began to wander off frequently from homes where he was staying, and would be unable to report where he was staying to strangers or to police who picked him up. It became necessary to make for him an identification bracelet, including not only his name, but the name and address and telephone number of the relative engraved upon it. Thereafter, when he became lost, he would show the identification bracelet to someone and thus make contact again with his family. Over the years, these disappearances became increasingly frequent, for while his memory processes were evidently quite impaired, his physical strength and vigor were undiminished, and it was not possible to supervise him constantly or to confine him.

Parallel with spatial disorientation was a loss of memory for names and faces, as well as a loss of memory for matters of personal history. Once at a party, Marcus hastened to introduce one of the guests to "my old friend." The "old friend" was in fact his son, but he could not remember his name. The son's wife and children also lost their names in his memory, though he could still refer to them correctly on occasion as "the wife," "the older child" or "the husband."

In his early seventies Marcus experienced problems of temporal disorientation and confusion about matters of personal apparel. He would sometimes arise in the middle of the night and get fully dressed. Or, he would go through his nightly retirement ritual at four o'clock in the afternoon. He also began to put on shirts over shirts, pants over pants and socks over socks, apparently forgetting that he had already dressed himself with one layer of clothing. Sometimes he would put on as many as six or seven shirts, in summer as well as winter.

At about age seventy-four, Marcus had forgotten everyone's name but his own, which he would invariably pronounce with pride when asked to recite it, often adding a phrase or two about his early boyhood. By this time, he had forgotten that he had ever been a lawyer, and had no idea of where he had lived or what he had done for his entire adult life. He could not remember his age, the city where he was living, the day of the week, month or year. He would also sometimes report as real certain imaginary trips he had made to Russia, to Africa, or to the moon, in company with U.S. astronauts. He still recognized people he lived with, but not by name. At this time, he was admitted to a nursing home. While he was physically quite vigorous and healthy, his memory loss was so complete as to require twenty-four-hour supervision, which could not be provided in his family residences. After admission to the nursing home, which he accepted quite placidly, his mental condition continued to deteriorate. By age seventy-eight he could no longer report his own name and showed no sign of recognition to visiting relatives. The nursing staff would continue to call him by his name, and he did show some signs of recognizing his name. For the last three years of his life, he was almost completely nonverbal, except for frequent bursts of song. During this period he was confined to a bed or to a closed chair, and his physical condition deteriorated markedly. He died at age eighty-two of a pulmonary condition.

Among Alzheimer patients, the emotional concomitants of memory loss are not at all uniform—some remain good-humored and placid, such as Marcus L., while others become violently abusive or severely depressed. But it is remarkable that the emotional consequences for relatives and friends of the suffering person are common in nature and intensity. The failure of personal recognition is highly distressing to a wife or son or daughter. Relatives visiting Alzheimer patients in nursing homes become discouraged after failing repeatedly to obtain a flicker of recognition, and are loath to make further visits because of the emotional burden of such failure. Initially, family members react with anger to memory lapses, mistakes or failed recognition. Later, after struggling with the irreversible problem for years, the family suffers the inevitable guilt accompanying recognition that no amount of love or attention can succeed in restoring the sufferer to his previous condition. Commitment to a nursing home is almost invariably required, and this in turn leads to further feelings of guilt and depression on the part of the family. Their own identities are affected by the gradual disappearance of memory and identity in one who had been of central significance in their lives.

Sudden Stop: Terminal Point Amnesia and Arrest of Identity

The case of Jimmy R. contrasts with that of Marcus L. in many respects.[2] Jimmy, who had been a chronic alcoholic, showed a symptom pattern consistent with Korsakov's syndrome. Jimmy had been in the navy in the Second World War, continuing in that service until 1966, when his chronic alcoholism forced his retirement and his institutionalization. After his institutionalization, Jimmy's memory regressed back to 1945. A bright, energetic and physically able man, Jimmy's life story became permanently arrested at age nineteen. The continued aging of both himself and the world were quite unknowable to him. He had lost the capacity to transfer information from short-term to long-term memory.

As a consequence of this condition, Jimmy's institutional life was in many respects unusual. He could not remember names or faces of doctors, staff or patients in the hospital. On meeting his brother, whom he had known before the border date of 1945, he recognized him, but showed great puzzlement that he looked so very old. After leaving the company of his brother, he entirely forgot their first meeting, and meeting again, Jimmy showed exactly the same confusion.

Jimmy had an identity and a life story, but not one that corresponded with the chronology of his life. He could recall details of his early life in lucid detail, and had an uncanny knowledge of the current events of 1945. But after that, nothing. Were the time of the world to have stopped with Jimmy, there would have been no need to institutionalize him, for his knowledge and behavior were appropriate to that date. But given the arrest of his memory— his inability to provide new material to long-term memory—his identity-narrative was also arrested, with devastating consequences for his ability to get along in the world.

Unlike Marcus L., who showed until his last few years an awareness that his memory was progressively failing, Jimmy's arrest of memory included the limitation of not realizing that he had any memory loss at all. His case is analogous to that of a brain-injured patient, who in addition to the loss of vision, loses as well all visual memory—all recollection of ever having seen and all conception of what the faculty of vision might be. Jimmy was told by his doctor exactly what his problem was, and on the occasion of telling, apparently understood. But a few minutes later, it was as if he had never seen the doctor before, and had no remaining understanding of the limits of his memory, for he had forgotten. Jimmy was stuck in time, and so severely stuck that even the subsequent knowledge that he was stuck could not register.

The Richness of Mature and Intact Memories

Both memory and identity are in a strong sense social. Memory comes alive in the act of narration, and identity is realized when the self is presented to another. Memory is mere latent potential until it is recalled and retold in the form of story, and identity is reduced to the sadness of solitude for those to whom no attention is paid. It is one of the tragedies of our age that those old people who have the most to tell us about our world are left unattended, and their life stories, untold, lie inert and useless even to the beings who possess those lives.

The antithesis of this tragedy is illustrated in a remarkable book by Ecléa Bosi (1979), *Memória e Sociedade,* which recounts the life stories of eight old residents of São Paulo. The stories are composed narratives derived from prolonged series of conversations between Dr. Bosi and each of her informants. Here is represented a series of natural miracles. There sits an old man or woman, waiting in dim solitude to sicken and die. Here comes a researching psychologist, who turns out to be a genuine friend. For this psychologist did not come prearmed with categories and theories into which the stories of lives must be force. Ecléa Bosi presents the rare spectacle of the psychologist simply surrendering to her material, so that the material is in no sense subject to her, but is instead invested with full human dignity.

In these psychological studies, the "subjects" have real names, and the incidents they recount stand on their own terms, without tests of internal consistency, external veracity or interpretive significance. It is useful to think of the contrast of this style of report and the ordinary psychoanalytic case history, where real identities are shielded with an invented name, where nothing the patient says is taken at face value and where the sense or truth of the story is only revealed through the interpretations provided by the doctor. I think it is more than a question of psychological taste to prefer the former sort of story to the latter.

The stories told to Bosi all begin with a recounting of the time and circumstances of birth, proceeding in a roughly chronological way to recount the story of early childhood, the critical transition phase involving the dissolving of the home and family of youth and the formation of the home and family of adulthood. Here are stories of first loves, of disappointments, of successes, of deaths, accidents, marriages, births, travels, adventures, engagement in public life, economic hard times, times of happiness, of sorrow, of folly.

The narrators manifest a joy in the telling, and are often pleased and astonished as memories come into fresh life in the revivifying light of Dr. Bosi's attention. It is as if a sudden egress into consciousness were provided for narrative material that had been mouldering in quiet for years. One consequence of this outpouring is an obvious and developing affection of the old people for their interlocutor. One cannot help but conclude that the narrators also come to feel better about themselves as a consequence of this opportunity to replay their life stories in sympathetic conversation.

There is, finally, an unexpected benefit: Since these eight narrators all lived at roughly the same time in roughly the same place, the reader is provided a rare composite portrait of the ambiance of the city of São Paulo in the early twentieth century. This is history from the inside out, not from the outside in. The ordinary historian is a recorder of events and circumstances, a chronicler of the public and observable. By contrast, we have in these narratives eight separate and distinct views of Paulistana life and culture in the form of personal memories. In some cases entire wars and major crises are passed over, quite unperceived. On the other hand, great importance may be attached to the form and feel of the cobblestones of a particular street. Since all views of history are incomplete and partial, a multiplicity of perspectives provides the best hope of attaining historical truth. These internal stories provide a salutory complement to the formalized external accounts provided by historians. The feel and smell and taste of life are conveyed in these stories with a poignancy that is unattainable for most social histories.

Experienced or psychological time is not at all a constantly flowing stream. Major attention is lavished on the events of a few days; decades are accorded scarcely a word. Commonly, a narrator is able to identify something of an ideal period in the course of the life—the period from which one would select the photograph representing for the narrator a kind of idealized permanent picture of the self. It would be uncharitable to say that the narrators do not think of themselves as they really are, for in this sense we are all guilty of autobiographical distortion. We have, after all, the general custom of giving our ages as our previous birthday, not our next one; except for children, who have an interest in presenting themselves as older than they are. Memory jumps about, is fleeting, ever selective, ever flexible regarding objectivity; now it is blocked, now it flows smoothly, now it cycles and returns to the same point; now it finds a peaceful haven of the harmony of life, now it is drawn irresistibly into dark chambers of horror.

Memory as Active Construction: Implications for Identity

The accepted view within experimental psychology on the basic nature of memory processes has changed considerably in the last fifteen years. In some ways, this change represents a return to the views of earlier writers on the topic, particularly Bartlett (1932), whose studies led him to view memory not as a process of passively storing information, but rather as involving the active organization of mental content around implicit mental structures, or schemata. Before Bartlett, James (1890) had considered the essence of memory to be the active organization of content into semantically ordered structures.

The conception of memory as active construction rather than as passive registration works both for and against the mere efficiency of memory as measured by the ability to recall with accuracy. Memory is partly a matter of recalling that which once was. But in addition, we remember that which never was and forget material which was most concretely and palpably presented to the senses.

In effect, recent studies of memory represent a restoration of meaning to the problem. One hundred years after Ebbinghaus's invention of the non-sense syllable, psychology has finally regained an appreciation of the importance of meaning in memory. As a consequence, there have been many recent studies of memory for prose passages, a tradition that really owes its beginning to Bartlett's work in the 1930s. A general conclusion of this work is that one remembers extended prose in terms of some overall pattern, structure, organization or schema (Thorndyke, 1977). The dramatic studies of Bransford and Frank (1971) showed that subjects reported with high certainty having seen sentences that in fact they had never seen, on condition that those sentences were logically implied by a general story framework provided by other sentences.

That all of this has much to do with the identity problem is shown most clearly in the spate of recent work on "self as narrative" (Mancuso & Ceely, 1980; Mancuso & Sarbin, 1983; Gergen & Gergen, 1983). If memory for external stimuli is selective, constructive and subject to the organizational constraints of predispositions to certain kinds of meaning by observers, then memory for one's own story must *a fortiori* obey the same principles.

Certainly the evidence favors the conclusion that memory for self is selective, constructive and subject to organizational constraints of predispositions to certain kinds of meaning. I do not assert that memory is somehow tailored by individuals to produce for themselves a life story that is singular and integral in its meaning, or polished of flaws, blemishes and contradictions. Rather, I propose the more modest claim that we do not simply register and preserve our life experiences as they are given, but rather take and ignore such experiences selectively, and from them construct narratives of who we are. As we have more than one audience for which such narratives might serve, so we have more than one story. And as we are ourselves a kind of audience-of-one for ourselves, we may be expected to have a special and allowably complex version of our story for internal consumption. The twin questions of *agency* and *interest* must for the present remain open. Even though the self is author and agent of narrative construction, it is clearly not able to construct anything at all by way of a story—but must obey requirements and compulsions seen and unseen. Clearly also one does not always observe some easy henonic calculus of self-interest in constructing or narrating one's story. Oddly enough, one's prewriting of one's story may include one's own suicide, as in the cases of Anne Sexton, Sylvia Plath, Ernest Hemingway and other self-tortured poets. Sometimes the scripts of other lives are taken as models for our own stories, so that the identities taken on are adaptations or versions of stories first lived or invented by others, a phenomenon which Sarbin (1982) has discussed under the heading of the Quixote Principle. these transformations of art to life and back to art provide matter of which psychologists must take account, however complicating they might be to simple theory.

The two cases of memory pathology presented in the previous section are interpretable from this view of memory for self as construction. In the case of Marcus L., the gradual fading of memory over time amounted in functional terms to a gradual fading out or diminution of his identity. It is as if the moment of death were extended for him—played out in slow motion—over a period of fifteen years. As his memory was reduced, his ability to sustain his own story in the company of his family and former associates was likewise diminished. In the end, his own story was obliterated in him, while it continued and doubtless continues to exist in the living memory of these who knew him. Similarly, for Jimmy R. there came to exist a radical disparity between his story as he could retell it and his story as it was understood by the hospital staff and others in his surroundings. For Jimmy was unable to continue to refine and extend his own narrative in tempo with the rest of the human company. And as his identity strayed away from acceptable or tolerable limits of distortions, he was effectively disabled as an actor on the normal human stage.

The cases recounted by Ecléa Bosi serve equally well as illustrations of the connection between reconstructions of memory and the representations of one's own identity by means of narrative. In particular, these stories show the import of what Bartlett referred to in his studies of memory as conventionalization. The story of an old citizen of São Paulo is necessarily told in terms of the conventionalized social institutions, categories and customs particular to time and place. These stories all begin with reference to the birth of the story teller. But these beginnings are never described abstractly, as "I was born." But rather, "I was born on August 15, 1902, on Rua _____, in the city of São Paulo." Then begins an account of who the father and mother were, again not abstractly, but in terms of particular historical facts and circumstances. These narratives are intelligible only in contextual terms. Someone knowing nothing of the religious, political, cultural and familial traditions of Brazil in the early twentieth century would find these stories quite unintelligible, and were they to be retold by such a person, they would of necessity be conventionalized in other and alien terms. Thus one might consider rendering a version of the life of St. Augustine in Marxist or Freudian terms, but in so doing, one must recognize that such an exercise is an enormous biographical crime, for it implies a magisterial negation of the conventions of Augustine's own time and context, however remote these might be to us. One of Bosi's informants asserts, near the end of her story, that she has always been a rebel, has always "... rowed against the current." But even though she defined herself in contradiction to the dominant conventions of her time, still her identity takes its true meaning only by relation to those conventions.

Bartlett was hardly thinking of the problem of identity when he wrote of the operation of memory. And yet we can make a ready application of his characterization:

> It looks as if what is said to be reproduced is, far more generally that is commonly admitted, really a construction, serving to justify whatever impression may have been left by the original. It is this 'impression', rarely defined with much exactitude, which most readily persists. So long as the details which can be built up around us are such that they would give it a 'reasonable' setting, most of us are fairly content, and are apt to think that what we build we have literally retained (Bartlett, 1932, p. 176).

Similarly, Tversky and Kahnemann (1973) have demonstrated the enormous significance of vividness of imagery in facilitating and also in distorting memory. One's memory is selectively retentive for particularly vivid or meaningful material, or for material that "fits in." The act of recalling is not a matter of simply reproducing that which was presented, but of reconstructing what must have been presented, in order that some meaningful or vivid image of a story might be supported. Studies of factors influencing the accuracy of eyewitness testimony likewise have demonstrated convincingly the importance of the observer's particular patterns of meaningful construction in determining what is observed, or what is remembered as having been observed.

The most general point I wish to make is given clear illustration by Bartlett's series of original studies on remembering. Using the method of "serial reproductions," Bartlett demonstrated that visual and prose materials tended in their successive reproductions by memory toward simplification, conventionalization and sharpening of detail, in accord with the selective principles of the observer. Thus, a very irregular face mask is sifted through memory and emerges as an ordinary and highly simplified sketch of a human face. Odd and incongruous elements are dropped out of stories; in successive repetitions, stories are told in such a way as to make sense from the framework of beliefs of the retelling subject, not the framework of the culture from which the original story was taken. Bartlett commonly observed in these successive retellings of stories a complete reversal in the main point or moral sense of a tale. For example, a folktale emphasizing the deep respect the young have for the wisdom of the old is transformed in its retelling into a story describing the relief of a youth in escaping the punishment and domination of his father.

The sort of life story told by an old person is a construction, a fabrication that reveals certain truths both about the agent of construction and about the world from which the materials of construction are borrowed. In the case of a failing or arrested memory, the power to construct and maintain a narrative is diminished or destroyed. In the case of intact and functioning memories, we observe arrangements of details of life lived around some central self-impression, which, as Bartlett observes is ". . . rarely defined with much exactitude." But the details and their arrangement reveal two sorts of reality—one inner and one outer. The inner reality, itself without articulate voice, is revealed by the conformation of arranged detail—a kind of visible shell constructed over an invisible and impalpable core. The external reality, of course, is revealed by the very substance of the details appropriated by the story teller from that person's providential location in time and circumstance. The "I" is unintelligible out of its circumstances. And circumstances can only be understood from the tacit position of "that which they are about." This is, I believe, what is meant by Ortega y Gassett's enigmatic expression, "I am I and my circumstances."

Another of the conceptions of contemporary cognitive psychology is of great use in illuminating the relationship between identity and memory. Tulving (1972) first coined the distinction between episodic and semantic memory. Episodic memory is located in time, is tokened by the recall of specific events in specific historical context, as in "Last February, just at the end of a bitterly cold and snowy month in Connecticut, I embarked for a week's vacation in the Caribbean." Semantic memory is of a different sort, and has to do with the recognition of conventionalized patterns of meaning, quite apart from historical or temporal context. Thus, Jimmy R., no longer able to register episodes into a continuing story of his life, could nevertheless remember quite well that the food on his plate is for eating, the bed for sleeping and language is for talking. He used language with great precision of meaning, and could solve difficult puzzles if they did not require memory for events as opposed to memory for meaningful relationships. While recent interpretations suggest connections and certain grey areas in these two types of memory, it is generally accepted that the functional distinction is useful. In describing cases of damaged or disordered identities, the distinction has obvious applicability. For a semantic sense of identity may remain after one literally has become disconnected from time through destruction or atrophy of episodic memory.

Even though one's chronological story might effectively cease to be known or controlled from the inside, it is not proper to conclude thereby that an inner sense of identity does not exist. In this condition, "I am I and my circumstances" would mean that I am able to understand and be related to the palpable and immediate reality of the present—that episodes of the past and possible episodes of the future do not form part of these circumstances. Even though identity is thus reduced in the dimension of time to an apparently motionless present, it cannot be said to disappear, for it can retain its own existential semantics. "A man does not consist of memory alone. He has feeling, will, sensibilities, moral being, matters of which neurophysiology cannot speak" (Luria, in Sachs, 1984, p. 12). In this statement, Luria is referring directly to loss of memory of the episodic kind, suggesting that a continuous sense of existence remains in someone like Jimmy R., even though that continuity has nothing to do with what is ordinarily thought of as an historical line.

Bosi employs a distinction between 'information' and 'narration' in a way that parallels the distinction between episodic and semantic memory. Semantic memory allows for the processing of information and its effective and correct interpretation. Computers process information—they register it, store it, manipulate it, transform it, retrieve it and reproduce it. Human beings are simulated by computers in these functions, but only insofar as their semantic memories are concerned. When it comes to episodic memory, the computer analogy becomes strained and awkward. For human beings are not mere processors of information, they are inventors and makers of narratives, including narratives about themselves. Human episodic memory is a means by which selves are related to history and to the particularity of circumstance. This process is creative, original, constructive and not always subject to the constraints of realism.

Human episodic memory makes it possible for a person to continue the development and refinement of their self-narratives. This in turn makes it possible to retain a knowable social identity and thus to enter into normal social interactions, conversations and relationships that are conceived as transcending the limits of the present (see Scheibe, 1979). The truncation of episodic memory entails a corresponding truncation in social identity, or the development of what sociologists refer to as socially atomized persons. The socially atomized person retains semantic memory, and thus is able to function meaningfully in the present. But relationships—such as marriage, filial identity, brotherhood, loyalty to clan, religion, race, or nation, or to employer, or to any social entity remote in time or place—all of these are impossible to the socially atomized person. The social atomized person is unloosed from all historical connections through the disappearance of episodic memory.

Memory, History and the Question of control

Who controls the present controls the future, and who controls the past controls the present.
                                            —George Orwell, *1984*

The previous section suggests some of the ways in which an individual's capacity to remember is related to that individual's ability to construct and maintain an identity. In this section, I propose to examine the extension of this argument to the memory or collectivities of individuals—that supra-individual memory known as history.

It is, of course, outrageous to regard history merely as that which happens to be remembered. But a psychological perspective on the meaning of history enables us to set aside for a time all the vexed questions of what history might be, in favor of a straightforward functionalist view of the matter. What matters as providing an outside frame and context for the meaning of the story of the individual is not history as it may have really happened, or history as it is recorded in the most authoritative books, or history as it is revealed in the interpretative modes most in current vogue, but rather history as it happens to be transmitted to and understood by the individual. We can see from this perspective another outrageous fact: As the narrative form and content of history can be revised or renegotiated by those in a position to control the telling of history, so can the meaning and content of an individual's life be radically reconstrued by such changes. The life of Napoleon was whatever it was. But the way we regard the life of Napoleon—who we think him to be, and of what quality—is very much a function of the historical frame in which his life story is placed. This is no fixed matter, but a matter of continual negotiation and interested change.

The pigs in *Animal Farm* crawled up on the side of the barn at night and revised the principle of universal equality by introducing the qualifier, "... but some animals are more equal than others." Similarly, in *1984*, the work of the Ministry of Truth was to comb published historical records and to delete inconvenient passages, making revisions according to the needs of the moment. These caricatures were meant by Orwell to represent a real danger—that of allowing historical memory to be controlled by a single interested group. Indeed, the controllers of history can turn the truth inside out, upside down or simply obliterate it. Just as Bartlett demonstrated the strong effect of social conventionalizations in the operation of individual memory, so is collective memory—history—conventionalized by the currents of present interests. Totalitarianism, in this interpretation, is simply the centralization of the control of transmitted history. Thus is controlled the sense of the meaning of the present. In turn, the options for future courses of action are limited and defined. If this control is centralized and complete, then War can become Peace, Freedom can become Slavery and Love can become Hate. Examples of these perverse transformations are all about us, as when armies are called, "Peace-keeping-forces," when harbors are mined by the U.S. in Central America in order to preserve "democratic choice," when concentration camps are referred to as "reeducation centers" etc. Somehow Christianity, a religion based

on brotherly love, love of one's enemy and turning the other cheek, is used as
a basis for justifying genocidal campaigns; and Marxism, a doctrine committed to the elimination of all forms of human oppression, becomes in interested hands, a doctrine most flexibly applicable to the justification of mighty
and generalized oppressions.

Our present view of history, while it does contain vast margins of doubt
and ignorance, is nevertheless quite fixed in many of its central features. Yet
what is now taken as given—the sanctity of the U.S. Constitution for instance—
was once a matter of urgent debate and honest doubt. The genius of Gabriel
Garcia Marquez's *One Hundred Years of Solitude* is that he manages to demonstrate through a work of fiction the way in which history has been made
and remade and remade again in Latin America. Somehow, in Macondo, the
mythic bedrock of history has not yet been touched.

It is worth contemplating how historical bedrock sometimes turns to sand.
Why should King Henry VIII have cared greatly whether or not he was to be
excommunicated on account of his desire for divorce? What is status in the
Roman Church but a matter of established and mutable convention? And
what is marriage, after all, but a fictive arrangement of convenience that may
be nullified at any time? To ask such questions seriously, of course, is to
betray an enfeebled sense of the enveloping power of historically carried beliefs
and conventions. "What the whole community believes in and conceives to be
true grasps the individual as in a vice," said William James. The most powerful controllers of our lives are such deeply engrained conventions that they
seem not to be conventions at all, but immutable truths. Money, for example,
is nothing at all unless it is conventionally agreed to be a legal medium of
exchange. And neither has gold any intrinsic value, apart from common assent.
The Indian has a full right to his belief that land is not ownable by mere men,
but belongs eternally to the Great Spirit, but this view is laughable in our
courts. Slavery, where it exists, is justified by a congenial history. Hitler, in
mounting with insane racist ambition the program of a thousand-year Reich,
tried to command into existence a history and a prehistory, supported by
scholarly and anthropological authority, to make fully reasonable and legitimate his program. Now in the United States, historians have discovered to
their chagrin that the country's story has been transmitted with overwhelmingly
powerful biases against women, blacks and other minorities, so as to provide
a tacit justification for the continued social deprivation of such groups. Now
that social historians are trying to provide a corrective to the errors of the
past, they are themselves charged with using history as polemic or apologia
for some desired social change. Meanwhile, prominent figures of the past are
not even free in death from changes in the historical frame. Corpses in Moscow
are hefted about to and from less and more honored sites. Mao Tse Tung is
now built up as a saint, now derided as an evil menace, now redeemed again.

Thomas Jefferson is drawn as a slave-owning philanderer, and not even Abraham Lincoln is free from the reconstructors of his story.

In Brazil currently, the government would like to have people beleive that the past twenty years have seen an enormous surge of prosperity and development because of the sure and firm hand of the benevolent and far-seeing military leaders. But as soon as this government allowed an "abertura," it became possible to counteract this official story with other and less flattering versions of the historical forces that have been flowing and acting for the past twenty years. The film *Jango* is an attempt to provide a rereading, not only of the character and quality of the last elected president of Brazil, but also of the entire flux of the historical currents that led to his downfall and to the establishment of the military government.

Such examples can be multiplied at will. Indeed, it is the daily work of newspapers, journals, scholarly reviews and political and historical writings to remake and reread the past. From whatever systematic or haphazard contact the developing person has with all of this historical working and reworking, the terms of one's own story are defined and provided. The story of a particular person's identity must be worked out with the materials that are given to it on a particular stage of history.

Given the conditions of a particular stage of history, individuals come to enact a particular form of story, or become a particular kind of person. Sometimes this is described as learning of one's vocation or calling, as if there were some voice out there making heard its claim for a particular form of service. Indeed, there are many such voices. The developing young person is not allowed to drift passively into the future, but must perforce have a plan, a program, a profession, a career or plans for an adventure or for a family, or even for a life of reflection and meditation. The social nexus will not rest until the developing young person has covered the nakedness of a vacant life with some serviceable story, entailing some sort of progression or dramatic development.

Russell Baker's biography, *Growing Up*, contains a description of how Baker acquired a legitimate career story for himself:

> The only thing that truly interested me was writing, and I knew that sixteen-year-olds did not come out of high school and become writers. I thought of writing as something to be done only by the rich. It was so obviously not real work, not a job at which you could earn a living. Still I had begun to think of myself as a writer. It was the only thing for which I seemed to have the smallest talent, and silly though it sounded when I told people I'd like to be a writer, it was one way of thinking about myself which satisfied my need to have an identity (Baker, 1983, p. 121).

Fortunately, the world was sufficiently cooperative with this protean self-definition to allow its full realization. The consolidation of a presentable life-story is always a joint product of internal interests and external forces. In the best of cases, these pressures converge to produce roughly the same story.

Life is begun without a story. Even so, the fundaments of the developing person's story are laid down before that person knows of them. These fundaments are matters of sex, social class, kinship, national, religious and racial heritage. These form the conditions of the birthright grant, upon which a large but limited number of life stories can be erected (see Sarbin & Scheibe, 1983). Normally, individuals integrate these historically-given conditions into their life stories effortlessly, and memory has no trouble in preserving them. As the story of one's life develops, the historical ambience plays an equally important role, but now it is the provision of opportunities or possibilities for movement into the future.

Neither the conditions or birthright grants nor the opportunities provided by the current historical ambience are constant, though like the clouds on a still summer day, they may seem to be so. By appropriate revisions of the dominating views of the past, a present institution such as slavery can be undermined. Once destroyed, a new birthright is conferred upon individuals who were once condemned by the vagaries of history. And once liberated, these individuals have a new range of choices for the development of life presented to them. Sadly, the movement that abolished slavery did not at the same time accomplish the sort of historical transformations that would result in the provision of opportunities for life development commensurate with opportunities offered to others. A lived life is a story traced within the confines of historically-given circumstances. Both the continuity of the tracing and the giving of historical circumstances are ultimately dependent upon fallible human memory.

Concluding Considerations

People awaken to consciousness in a society, with the inner story of experience and its enveloping musicality already infused with cultural forms.

—Stephen Crites, 1971
The narrative quality of experience

If the facts of collective history and individual memory are secular matters, the facts of *having* a collective history or of *having* an individual memory most assuredly are not secular, but universal. The particular dramas we enact, the dances we dance, the music we know, the language we speak—all of these derive from particular historical episodes of invention, transformation and propagation. But *that* we enact dramas, have dances, know music and speak in languages—these are universally given as part of the human condition. Moreover, the basic forms of language, and of drama, art and music are timeless—given to us as universal (see Crites, 1971).

This point allows us to see the profoundly social bias of all the preceding discussion of the relation between identity and memory. Memory of the nonepisodic sort might not even be socially acquired, but might simply be given as a natural endowment. To be sure, the nurturance of the socius is required in order for this protean or inchoate endowment to be realized in any particular way. Carl Jung, in his *Memories, Dreams and Reflections,* describes his main reality as inner and timeless. For Jung, commerce with the socius was always regarded as a kind of concession to necessity.

Jung developed and used a striking metaphor to describe this relation of the temporal and the timeless. The collective human nature, product of millenia and without consciousness or voice, is like a vast perennial rhizome (root mass), lying beneath the surface, invisible. An individual human life is like a single green shoot growing upwards into light and air from this vast subterranian rhizome. For its brief period of life, these historically particular growths are able to see and have commerce with their contemporary neighbors. But the possibility of this social commerce is dependent upon the common but invisible nature shared by individual forms. Much of Jung's interest was in plumbing the depths—in vertical exploration. Commerce with his fellows was mainly an auxiliary to this major interest.

Jungs's memories, then, are of two kinds. Conventional memories are of going to school, of parents, of medical school, of his relations with Freud, of his patients, of his writings, of his wife and family and so on. These memories comprise his conventional social identity. But Jung gives great importance to less time-bound memories—memories of particular dreams, particular obsessions, achievements of insightful and arresting interpretations, fruits of solitary meditations. These are Jung's attempts to gain an understanding of universals, or in different terms, the sacred or the primordial. Without question, the category of "vertical" or timeless memories have priority for Jung, while he realizes full well the utter necessity of an ordinary secular existence and memory to enable his exploration of the timeless and the sublime (see Juhasz, 1983, for an exposition on timeless polarities of human nature).

What sort of evidence is there that we should take seriously these half-mystic ruminations of Jung? To the already convinced, no evidence is needed, and to the skeptic, no amount of evidence will suffice. But I offer at least a shred of an observation which seems consistent with Jung's conception of a non-social but human identity.

Jimmy R., whose temporal memory was permanently arrested at age nineteen could still participate meaningfully in Catholic Mass.

> ... If he were held in emotional and spiritual attention—in the contempla-
> tion of nature or art, in listening to music, in taking part in Mass in chapel—
> the attention, its 'mood', its quietude, would persist for a while, and there
> would be in him a pensiveness and peace we rarely, if ever, saw during the
> rest of his life at the Home (Sachs, 1984, p. 19).

The coherence of this sort of experience for Jimmy could not depend upon memory of a secular kind, but rather upon memory derived from some universal sense of semantics, of significance. Music, the Mass and art can be seen as particular secular expressions of universal forms, and the apprecia-tion of these forms could just be given in the nature of things, and not be a matter that is dependent on secular memory. Both Jimmy R. and Marcus L. seemed to have lost their sense of temporality. But is is by no means certain that this rupture of the temporal also entailed for them a loss of their "verti-cal" consciousness, their inner sense of timeless identity. We can say of the aged and the senile that their temporal stories are finished—that nothing more of consequence will happen to them, save their death. But while life remains, it is presumptuous and inhumane to affirm that, with the disappear-ance of chronology, their identities in the inner and vertical sense are also thus dissolved. Something there is of the sacred in human life. Of course, in temporal and historical terms, I am now talking nonsense.

The thinker is the thought, said James. And the thought, in turn, is not some fixed and formed entity, but a process—and on-going, ever-shifting and contin-ual reforming of content. Thus, thought is like a stream, and memory allows one to have a sense of the stream of time and a sense of continuous identity in that time. But the streams are surrounded by oceans, and these are timeless, eter-nal. Our identities are stories told in the terms of the streams of our thought, as these streams are conducted through the courses of grounded circumstance. But the streams presuppose both an origin and destiny in their endless cycles, and these are not matters of story, but of voiceless and universal verity.

> *This is the use of memory: For liberation—not loss of love*
> *but expanding Of love beyond desire, and so liberation From*
> *the future as well as the past.*
>
> T. S. Eliot, *Four Quartets*

Notes

1. I maintained personal contact with Marcus L. and his family over a number of years. I have modified certain identifying details in this description. The description is based on my own observations.

2. This summary report is based upon a fuller presentation of the case of Jimmy R. in Sachs (1984).

References

Baker, R. (1983) *Growing up.* New York: Norton.

Bartlett, F. (1932) *Remembering.* Cambridge: Cambridge University Press.

Bosi, Ecléa, (1979) *Memória e sociedade.* São Paulo: T.A. Queiroz.

Bransford, J.D. and J.J. Frank (1971), The abstraction of linguistic ideas. *Cognitive Psychology.* 2:331-350.

Crites, S. (1971), The narrative quality of experience. *The Journal of the American Academy of Religion* 39: 291-311.

Gergen, K. and M. Gergen (1983), Narratives of the self. In T.R. Sarbin and K.E. Scheibe (eds.), *Studies in social identity. New York: Praeger.*

James, W. *(1890), Principles of psychology.* 2 vols. New York: Holt.

Juhasz, J. (1983), Social identity in the context of human and personal identity. In T.R. Sarbin and K.E. Scheibe (eds.) *Studies in social identity.* New York: Praeger.

Mancuso, J.C. and S.G. Ceely (1980), The self as memory processing. *Cognitive Theory and Research,* 4: 1-25.

Mancuso, J.C. and T.R. Sarbin (1983), The self-narrative in the enactment of roles. In T.R. Sarbin and K.E. Scheibe (eds.) *Studies in social identity.* New York: Praeger.

Sachs, O. The lost mariner. *New York Review of Books,* February 16, 1984, 14-20.

Sarbin, T.R. (1982), The Quixotic Principle. In V. Allen and K.E. Scheibe (eds.) *The social context of conduct.* New York: Praeger.

Scheibe, K.E. (1979), *Mirrors, masks, lies, and secrets.* New York: Praeger.

Thorndyke, P.W. (1977), Cognitive structures in comprehension and memory of narrative discourse. *Cognitive Psychology,* 9: 97-110.

Tulving, E. (1972), Episodic and semantic memory. In E. Tulving and W. Donaldson (eds.) *Organization of memory.* NY: Academic.

The In-Depth Interview

Chapter 10

More Than Counting Years: Social Aspects of Time and the Identity of Elders

SUSAN A. EISENHANDLER

Introduction

For the individual social actor looking out at a graying social world, a major component of successful aging involves coming to terms with becoming older—understanding what old age means to her and to those around her and what it may come to mean in the future. Another element of successful aging is facing and responding to the sometimes foreseeable, yet just as often unforeseeable, changes in health. Changes in health are often powerful enough to thrust elders into the kinds of roles and social contexts that are largely unfamiliar to them at the same time that they relegate familiar roles and contexts to the attic of social relations, bygone aspects of self. These same changes in health impinge upon what phenomenologists have called the "life world," and somewhat paradoxically they offer elders the chance to enlarge, redefine and reintegrate aspects of self and identity.

The idea of the future, a projection of the continuous and customary patterns of one's existence, is not generally shaken by a touch of the flu, some broken bones or a scalpel's stroke. However, these difficulties may challenge an elder's presumption that the future and the self will emerge undisturbed from what had previously been construed as temporary bouts of ill health. Through difficulties with physical well-being in late life, elders are introduced to novel ways of looking at the future and simultaneously the present and the past. What was once the taken-for-granted social landscape of late adulthood, including the perception of time and the perception of self, may be dramatically altered. Indeed, a definition of the self as old, may be more readily admitted as part of one's identity once health becomes problematic.

This chapter discusses the social aspects of time and the process of growing old by considering the relationship between health and the meaning of old age as evidenced in the lives of a sample of community elders. A central thesis is that events that block usual patterns of interaction create a disjuncture in social time and hence in identity. A change in health is often the precipitating factor in the shift of identity and social time because it emphatically transforms the individual's relations and ties with the social world as well as with the life she has lived and the life she expects to live by blocking typical conduct. Although such disruptions are not exclusively restricted to the lives of the old, they are more frequently encountered at this stage of life in post-industrial societies where the general increase in life expectancy has reserved a multitude of health problems for late adulthood.

Theoretical Perspectives on Time and Old Age

Social gerontologists have been sensitive to the nuances of time and the process of human aging. Yet this sensitivity to social aspects of time has been a relatively minor theme in the burgeoning scholarly literature of the field. When scholars have pursued the idea of time and human aging, this work has typically been represented by concepts like the distance from death (Lowenthal and Haven, 1968), finitude (Marshall, 1985) and the more general theoretical concern for ideas about the future. Although discussions about the meaning and measure of time do appear in a fragmentary form in many significant studies, it is not often a recurring theme nor is it treated as a major theoretical or substantive theme in most sociological studies of aging. Nevertheless, several scholars (Clark and Anderson, 1967; Quinn and Reznikoff, 1985; Epinay, 1986; Rakowski, 1986) have addressed pieces of the puzzle of social time. Acknowledging the risk of oversimplification, one may discern two general perspectives on time that are relevant to the analysis of health and identity among elders. The first theoretical perspective (Simmel, 1964, 1971; Mead, 1959, 1962, 1964; Schutz, 1967, 1970) is one that treats time as an emergent process—a phenomenon that is to be understood by understanding the various definitions people attach to its passing. The second perspective is represented by an amalgamation of works (Clark and Anderson, 1967; Quinn and Reznikoff, 1985; Rakowski, 1986; Reker et al., 1987) that discuss the orientation to time (how individuals and groups place themselves in the stream of time) and the consequences such orientations have in the lives of elders. Both perspectives place a special emphasis on the social definition of time as an important analytical element in the study of aging.

Time as an Emergent Process

A number of sociological theorists have considered the relationship between time, meaning and identity. Featured prominently in this group are

Georg Simmel, George Herbert Mead and Alfred Schutz. In an essay on home-coming and the experience of the familiar becoming unfamiliar, Schutz (1970, p.304) remarked that inner time was irreversible and argued that "the mere fact that we grow older, that novel experiences emerge continuously within our stream of thought . . . bar a recurrence of the same. Being recurrent, the recurrent is not the same any more." Seen in this way, old age is not an end-point. Even for the oldest of the old, events continue to unfold and to change the individual in a variety of ways. In a real sense, one never is the same so long as one lives and simultaneously ages. Aging is itself a push against social inertia. Elders, like younger adults, keep pace with the "wider community of time." Falling out of step with the flux of time, entraps and enfeebles the individual. The image of Dickens's Miss Havisham comes to mind as an exam-ple of an individual who has resisted and retreated from the unfolding of the time that surrounds her. In addition, Mead's (1962) writings on adaptation and creativity in the continuous mutual adjustments self and society make toward one another presents an analogous point.

Simmel's commentary on the "profound inner configuration" of adven-ture is also instructive with regard to time as process. A certain timelessness is, according to Simmel, associated with understanding life as an adventure.

> No matter how much the adventure seems to rest on a differentiation within life, life as a whole may be perceived as an adventure. For this, one need neither be an adventurer nor undergo many adventures. To have such a remarkable attitude toward life, one must sense above its totality a higher unity, a super-life, as it were, whose relation to life parallels the relation of the immediate life totality itself to those particular experiences which we call adventures. (1971, p.192)

However, Simmel did not believe that this form of experiencing life fell within the purview of the old. He suggested that the experiential tension necessary to produce the spirit of adventure was lacking among the old.

> The old person usually lives either in a wholly centralized fashion, peripheral interests having fallen off and being unconnected with his essential life and its inner necessity; or his center atrophies, and existence runs its course only in isolated petty details, accenting mere externals and accidentals. (1971, p.198)

Despite Simmel's stereotypical contention that it is not possible for the old to see life and self afresh, adventurously, he recognized the adventurer as the "man who lives in the present." Therefore, to the extent that the old live in the present, perhaps more than any other age group, it may indeed be possi-ble for the old to experience life as an on-going process. In the words of phenomenology, the immediacy of life events mutes the fact of only being old.

Contemporary social gerontologists (Hendricks and Hendricks, 1976; Hendricks and Peters, 1986) have been encouraged to pay more attention to the temporal dimensions of aging and to the emergent qualities that drive the process of growing old. For example, Hendricks and Hendricks caution against using the static experiential attributes Simmel imputed to the old as a basis for understanding old age.

> When time is seen as a process, continually becoming, man is free to attribute a variety of meanings to his temporal experience. The imposition of quantitative measures on temporal flow exerts a restrictive force on man's experience. Unfortunately the latter approach does not take account of man's active participation in the construction of his temporal world. Students of aging, whatever discipline they represent, would increase the scope of their understanding if they adopted a more flexible conception of the part played by time in aging processes. (1976, p.49)

Put simply, it is not useful or accurate to view old age as a developmental stage that signals the end of the creation of meaning and identity, the end of adventure, the end of a process. Consistent with this view of time as process, is the idea that the developmental resolution of integrity versus despair (Erikson, 1963, p.168) involves "a comradeship" with lived time. For Erikson, this resolution is the principal developmental work of old age.

> It is the acceptance of one's one and only life cycle as something that had to be and that, by necessity, permitted of not substitutions . . . it is a comradeship with the ordering ways of distant times and different pursuits, as expressed in the simple products and sayings of such times and pursuits.

Orientation to Time

Another perspective that treats time as a significant dimension in the study of aging, but is not necessarily wedded to the theoretical construct of process, considers the orientation to time and its impact on elders. This perspective is highlighted in one study (Clark and Anderson, 1967) that includes a brief discussion about the relationship between time orientation, self and mental health. The authors (1967, p.191) suggest that "an image of the self as continuous or evolving is related to mental health, whereas a deteriorative or retrospective self-view is more likely to accompany mental illness." In a similar vein, Lieberman and Tobin (1983, p.313) have recently written that, "Most elderly people who have suffered through painful life circumstances do not exhibit hopelessness. Indeed, many whose bodies have withered and who have lost numerous significant others through death are able to cope with their present reality and simultaneously relate to their personal past." This ability to come to terms with the passage of time and one's own aging even in the face of social deprivation and the death of loved ones is interpreted as a hallmark of cohesive identity.

Moreover, Clark and Anderson (1967, p.194) delineated factors that contributed to the social-psychological integrity of identity. Healthy elders hold an orientation to the present that allows them to focus on "what they still have, rather than what they have lost." Consequently, there is a substitution of new behaviors and values for ones that can no longer be enacted. This adaptive orientation to time involves a readjustment in the optimal level of aspiration. Elders who do not calibrate their aspirations to real changes in their circumstances are not as connected to the present as they are to the past. The lack of recalibration makes day-to-day living unpleasant because one can hardly be a part of a continuous unfolding of time if self and identity are associated with aspirations better suited to a past that can only be reconstituted imaginatively than to an imperfect but real present.

Other studies in the perception of time (Joubert, 1984, p.335) suggest that long periods of time are perceived as passing quickly when social roles and their attendant obligations are numerous. Thus the experience of time acceleration is a function of "the proportion of structured time that is demanded of the individual at different ages." Recent analyses (Quinn and Reznikoff, 1985) of time orientation among physically healthy elders sustain Clark and Anderson's original idea that a concentration on the here and now is positive adaptation to aging. It may also account for continuing evidence (Levkoff et al., 1987) that the old, despite their greater experience with ill health and disability, are less likely to report disease. The noninstitutionalized old may not be health optimists so much as they may be those who do not have the time (due to increasing time acceleration and truncated futurity) to dwell upon the vicissitudes of health as an important part of daily life. It is perhaps a testament to the pervasiveness of ageism and stereotypes of the old that many commentators find this to be an alarming circumstance rather than a reassuring one.

Qualitative research by Myerhoff (1978, p.196) provides a glimpse of the relationship between the social meaning of time and the awareness of being old. One woman's words, taken from a group discussion about changes in the behavior (religious and familial) of adult children, illustrate the point that time and the meaning of life are socially constructed daily and are directly related to engagement in interaction.

> For some people old age is a terrible ordeal because of the loneliness. But if you manage to find yourself you take a big step. You stop thinking about death. *When you have every day something to do, you begin to live all over again.* [emphasis mine]

The ideas of time and chronology give a structural order to lives and facilitate discourse about social behavior. The study of gerontology as it relies principally upon the idea of time and the changes that occur with the passing of time (e.g., shifts in health status), gauged cumulatively in what is recognized socially as aging, implicitly understands time as flux or process. Indeed, as elders tell it, aging and living are much more than the counting of years as a way to mark time.

What Community Elders Revealed About Time, Health and the Perception of Being Old

A Brief Word about the Community Sample of Elders

The empirical core of this chapter is based upon a study of old age and identity among community elders. These fifty elders represent a three percent sample of the population aged sixty and older in one western Massachusetts town. Interviews were obtained from the sample during the early months of 1982. The interview schedule followed a semi-structured format which was organized to elicit biographical or retrospective material as well as detailed commentary about the present and the future. The questions were primarily open-ended. This allowed respondents to answer in their own words, to adjust their responses in any number of ways, and in so doing, to shape part of the inquiry itself. Selected descriptive statistics of the sample are included in a short appendix at the end of this chapter.

Typical Perceptions of Being Old

One eighty-three-year-old woman conveyed a realistic appraisal of coming to terms with being old by noting a positive feature. This sentiment was expressed with slight variations by many other elders.

> Well I would say I wouldn't mind being sixty-three or seventy-three even. But I tell you, one thing about older people, not necessarily in their eighties, but in the seventies, I think we are more carefree in a lot of ways. We don't have the problems that the young people have like dating and finding the right one to marry and . . . financial worries as a rule. That's all past us.

These remarks are all the more indicative of both living in the present and acting on an optimal set of aspirations when one considers that this woman has been widowed twice. The most recent time was three years before this interview when her second husband died of a heart attack at the breakfast table.

A younger full-time worker, a sixty-two-year-old man, offered this general assessment about his present age in comparison to previous ages.

> It isn't that much different, but I noticed something, I'm not as quick as I was ten years ago, . . . it sneaks up on you so gradually you really don't notice it there. But I've been cutting down. My garden was the full width of the lot, now it's only half. And I find it a lot easier to put things off too. Oh, I'm not kidding myself; I'm sixty-two and I know it. I do what I'm able to and fortunately the job I have doesn't involve heavy work. I'm glad it doesn't, for there was a time when it didn't bother me any.

The recognition and acceptance of the changes that aging has brought is evident. The adjustment to change has thus far occurred so quietly that the respondent talks about age sneaking up. Twenty-one elders were absorbed in on-going activities, such that the process of aging and the adjustments to the individual's experience of aging had already been incorporated into a definition of self that had little correspondence with stereotypes of what old age ought to be like.

Eighteen elders concede, however, that chronological age has substantive meaning th. ough the mediating factor of health problems. Old age played a significant role in identity when it was linked to troubles with health, memory and changes in the perception of time. References to health problems run the gamut from minor to severely debilitating diseases, and have a focus that is not entirely centered on the individual interviewed.

Links between Health, Old Age, Time and Identity

A useful definition of good health has been presented by Maddox and Douglass (1973, p.87). They stipulate that good health "generally implies the absence of debilitating illness that significantly interferes with personal and social functioning, not necessarily the absence of morbid conditions." Another factor treated by Maddox and Douglass (1973, p.92), and one of long-lived interest to Maddox (1962), is the reliability of subjective reports about health. It is their view that the "self-assessment of health is not random but is persistently and positively related to objective evaluations of health status." Accordingly, such questions were used to assess health status in this study.

In terms of health, the elders correspond to patterns that are found in the larger population of the old. Sixty-eight percent of the young-old (those under seventy-five) describe their health as excellent or good. This is not characteristic of the old-old of whom only thirty-one percent use the same terms. Overall, the sample is almost equally divided between elders with excellent health and elders with fair to average health, twenty-seven in the former, twenty-three in the latter category. Only one person reported poor health and five called their health excellent. Men were slightly more likely to describe their health as good, twelve to eight, but women split equally between good, fifteen, and fair, fifteen. This should not be construed to mean that elders had no serious chronic conditions. Many were being treated for grave medical problems (heart, respiratory, cancer, arthritis) yet even with daily regimens of prescription and exercise/dietary treatments as well as periodic medical intervention, elders appeared to draw careful distinctions about how their health was on the whole and how a specific health problem was affecting them.

An examination of responses to questions about health and identity discloses that elders who rated their health as good to excellent were less likely to impart meaning to being an age. When asked the question, "What's it like to be (the person's chronological age)?", they did not provide clear or sharp images or statements. This remained the case, even after extensive probes. In addition, healthy elders were less likely to feel their age and to think of themselves as old.

Elders who termed their health fair to poor were more likely to describe being an age with references to physical health and fitness. They gave qualified responses about feeling their age and many said, yes, and expanded on their responses when asked if they thought themselves old. The oldest elders were also more likely to term their health fair or poor. This departs from findings reported by Ferraro (1980) and Cockerham et al., (1983) to the effect that the old-old may be more "health-optimistic" than the young-old.

There was some variation in the health status reported by men and women in this sample Men were more likely than women to assess their health as good. An analysis of a much larger data set (Payne and Whittington, 1976) concluded that there was no significant difference between the objective or subjective ratings of health given by men and women. Men in the community sample, however, did assess their health in more positive terms than the women. This may be a reflection of greater sensitivity to topics of health and disability.

Elders had difficulties with a wide array of illness and disability. Arthritis, cancer, emphysema, heart disease, stroke (nearly always described colloquially as a 'shock') and diabetes were some of the problems mentioned. Morbid conditions did abound, but all elders were functioning sufficiently well to participate in a variety of daily activities. Most believed themselves to be doing considerably better than that. Yet it is true that health problems, ones that disrupted the usual and enjoyable round of daily activities, and ones that caused others to tell elders that they had to go easy on daily activities, subtly pushed respondents into re-thinking their sense of identity. One respondent indicated his awareness of the relationship between health and a changed identity when he remarked on his own situation.

> Well, back this fall, I developed a rupture somehow. I threw my back out, so I had a slipped disc. Well, there was probably three, four, five weeks I felt my age. But I'm perfectly all right now . . . but I know I can't do all the things I used to do . . . I told the doctor after I had that slipped disc, 'Doctor, you made an old man out of me overnight. You told me I can't do things I've always done.'

This elder continued to work part-time in a family-owned small business even though his back problems did not go away. Now, however, he was very much aware and sensitive to the influence old age had on the way others treated him. "I know when people come in, if I start to pick up something and they want to pick it up for me and do it, that's a sign. They must think I'm an old man."

Rarely did elders link old age to a specific condition. The tenor of their remarks suggests that actual limitations and adjustments imposed by uncertain health rather than an illness precipitates an identification with old age, and foreshadows a change in identity. The significance of limitations in the life world is that time acceleration slows, the orientation to time is changed. In other words, problems in health constrict time and elders become aware, in elegant colloquial terms, that time catches up with them. Hence the relatively new sense of being old permeates identity.

The caveat is that many health problems can be managed. As one woman noted, the sense of being old can be short-lived.

> The only thing is, that I noticed the years kind of coming on is when I started to develop cataracts. And I had both eyes operated on. So this is the only thing. I can see and everything, good, but of course it's not like your own eyes. At that time, you feel like you're really getting along in years.

Contained within the core of this response as well as most others is the clear reference to the situational dimension or health-dependent aspect of old age. When the disease or disability is controlled, the once-strong, perhaps overdetermined, identification with old age is attenuated and ceases to be as forceful in the elder's identity. Of course, renewed episodes of ill health or the appearance of new health problems create the kind of uncertainty and disruption of life worlds that may bring old age to the fore again. The particular direction and form this identity as old takes is closely connected to the perception the elder forms of the responses that significant others, and others in general, make when confronted with this changed health status.

Pain

Despite the fact that only two elders in a sample of fifty equated being old and feeling old with the pain of cancer and the discomfort brought by treatment for the disease, their comments about pain graphically illustrate how time is halted and how old age comes to dominate identity. One woman who had become housebound by cancer and therapy stated her views forthrightly.

> I have no desire to live on endlessly. The going is getting rough when you can't get away from the pain for twenty-four hours a day. Then it [old age] begins. Like I say, it's like I'm backed into a corner with a tiger attacking me all the time. If you can't sit, you can't walk, you can't lie down without discomfort, what is there?

The intensity of this disease does not permit the elder much latitude in staking out or participating in different (non-age-related) aspects of identity. There is only old age and death. They come to dominate most aspects of identity because there is little chance to participate in social relationships without the constant companion of pain. Pain associated with disease or with treatment has the main effect of producing social isolation. The social isolation then reinforces the individual's orientation to time as winding down and her sense of self as old.

Others and Health

Eighteen elders spoke about their experience of old age as bound up with health. However, most of the elders in this sample were aware of old age and the passing of time through the ill health of other elders. Quite often changes and continuity of self can only be perceived when juxtaposed with the experiences of others. Some elders could not accommodate the transformation. For example, one sixty-seven-year-old married woman described the case of a widowed friend (sixty-one) whose experiences in young-old age shifted the basis of her identity and isolated her from elderly friends who now defined her as someone old and different from them. Despite this couple's attempts to include the widow in activities, there was a gulf between them. The gulf was created by old age and the complex shift in the friend's identity and the respondent's shift in the perceptions of her friend.

> . . . she depended on him a lot and it's been very difficult for her . . . she hasn't been well either [a number of her immediate family have died and her elderly father is senile] . . . she gets so very depressed . . .. Well, that isn't all health, it's partly health, but it also is situations . . . that you get tied up. It just seemed like she'd been whacked down, she gets up a little bit and then gets whacked down again . . . that can do something to you. That can make you old, I'm sure.

In this instance, the presence of old age is diluted because it is not the direct experience of the individual. When ill health comes indirectly to the individual through the experience of significant others it figures in an elder's identity, but it does not have the strength and intensity that an immediate encounter has for the individual. The actual experience of another's pain or ill health is only accessible symbolically. Even previous experience with a disease cannot mediate an experience that someone else has now. At best the previously affected individual may be able to respond in an empathetic way; however, empathy is only one possible outcome. Disdain, contempt, indifference and discounting the experience of illness are other possible responses to learning that someone your age is ill or has health problems. No matter how close one is to another person, one's life world is indirectly disrupted by the difficulties others face in growing old.

Yet it is also true that elders often noted how changes in the health of friends interjected old age into aspects of their own identities. One woman made the following observation.

> Well, I find that I'm slowing up for them lots of times. I mean I have a friend [two years younger, seventy-one, with asthma] that finds it very hard to walk... so it's more as if I'm slowing up for their pace the way I probably did for my mother, as she was getting older than I—although she was very active for a person eighty-four, but still there were things you would do for her because she was eighty-four.

Sometimes the aging and poor health of an adult child was both a cause for concern and a firm nudge about one's own old age. As one eighty-two year old stated, "Why even my oldest son is getting to be a senior citizen, he's sixty. That bothers me more to have them get older than for me to get older. He has angina."

Although the most dramatic reminder of old age and the precipitating factor in seeing oneself as old was the presence of uncertain health in self, the ill health of a spouse could thrust old age into identity. One very ill woman (cancer) worried about surviving her presently healthy spouse, '... if I should survive my husband, what will I do? And, I don't want to be an anchor around my daughter's neck either." Surprisingly, such comments were not often made by the twenty-eight married elders. Spouses were not typically mentioned as constant or important reminders of being old. This is rather perplexing because despite some discrepancy between the chronological age of self and spouse, most couples were separated by only a few years. One might expect that the experience of growing old together would heighten the awareness of old age and identity. However, that was not the case among these elders.

Many respondents initially answered by speaking of being sixty-five and having arthritis, yet their replies often departed from their experience and drifted to the health problems of close family members about the same age or

non-family age peers. The genesis of this shift may be a matter for speculation, but the function of this shift is to set the individual's reply aside and to
extend the remarks to the respondent's perception of the situation for others.
For instance, one seventy-three-year-old widow answered in the following way:

> To me, it's not that bad. But I can see that for people who don't have their
> health it could be bad. Nobody wants to, we're all getting older, nobody's
> getting younger. It's just something we can't do anything about. I don't think
> anyone likes to get old, but we all have to.

The respondent notes that aging and old age are not volitional. one can,
of course, attempt to forestall the organic process, particularly through
adjustive and adaptive measures. Yet in the main, aging as it is manifested in
the uncertainties surrounding poor health and disability, is not a process
amenable to direct control of the individual. Hence even when the meaning
of chronological old age is synonymous with health, it is understood to be a
facet of the evolutionary process of identity. Because the process is, on balance, beyond the direct control of the individual, ill health may define identity
for some elders, but it does not carry the attribution of personal accountabil-
ity with it. Elders are not stigmatized in their own eyes even though they
associate ill health with being old and emphasize that some situations foster
health problems. Still they do not often characterize themselves or their peers
as being old.

The largest number of elders, twenty-seven, recounted wide-ranging concrete and general instances or occasions that had the effect of making them
"feel their age." Again, many of these reminders of old age were closely connected to health. For instance, a seventy-six-year-old widow replied, "no, only
when I'm in pain, that's the only time. I want to work to get at it (the pain). I'm
not going to lay down and let it get the best of me, not me (R laughs). I'm a
fighter in other words." Or, as another woman (eighty-six and married) stated,
"How can I explain it? I boast, I can tell you frankly, every time that I make a
mistake which happens terribly often now—that I forget anything, or that I
stumble which I often do when I walk, I say okay, what can you expect when
you are eighty-six?" This respondent also added that her failing eyesight makes
her feel her age, but she closed by asking, "So how can you complain about
that when you are that age?"

Conclusion

A principal component of identity in old age and the social construction
of the aging experience is the perception of one's health. In this study there is

an additional caveat: the elder's perception of the health of significant others influences identity, especially the awareness and understanding of old age, insofar as the significant other's uncertain health status penetrates the life world of the person. Moreover, health problems influence the elder's orientation to time and with that the continuity or constriction of his or her identity.

To the extent that the "wide awakeness" (Schutz, 1970, p.68-69) of the self is tied to acting in the present, elders who remain engaged with life are more likely to see their own old age as unproblematic. Old age does quite literally sneak up and into a coherent identity. The comments of a seventy-six-year-old married woman buttress this point.

> Of course. The funny thing, part of it is, I don't consider myself old and when you called and said you wanted to talk to an older person, I thought, 'Oh gee. Am I getting to that stage?' Because when you have good health and you continue in your activities that you don't think about growing older. But my attitude has changed because I had a heart attack. I was in the hospital for seventeen days and I'm just getting over it. So now I'm beginning to feel, well, old age has finally crept up with me and I have to consider myself, old, I guess now, although I hadn't before.

There is scant indication of age making inroads into the personal identity of elders. The biographic and cumulative material, personal identity, elders bring into old age is the stuff that provides them with a sense of direction and continuity in struggles against the declines in health they and significant others experience. Even Simone de Beauvoir's (1973, p.769) dour perspective on aging admits this possibility.

> It may happen that old age, carrying on the life of the middle years without a break, may as it were pass unnoticed. For this to happen, it must develop in favorable circumstances. And the old person's earlier life must have provided him with a constellation of intellectual and emotional interests that will stand up to the weight of the years.

This begins to explain how health becomes such a powerful proxy for old age in situated identity, and how it is the sole factor that does eventually work its way into personal identity. Ill health disrupts patterns of interaction with the life world and creates uncertainty in social relations as well as it brakes the acceleration of time. Even with successful adjustment to health problems it becomes difficult for elders and others to put old age aside; it is now some part of situated identity, and less often part of a personal identity.

Most elders were caught up in attempts, not so much to acquire, as to hold onto a modicum of good health because without the certitude that health gives to the unfolding of time and self, an identity unrelated to age becomes almost impossible to sustain. It is no wonder that poor health status is synon-ymous with the perception of being old, at any chronological age along the life course.

Elders do not want to be any younger. They merely want to grow older without surrendering aspects of identity crafted and reworked over a lifetime to the misidentifications others have regarding old age. What they cannot accede to, as long as they are still engaged in social relations within a life world made possible by adequate health, is the idea that they are old and that they should see themselves as old. Growing old is not so much a function of counting up years and running out of time. It is a function of adapting to the reality of eroding health, and in the words of a seventy-six-year-old widow it means accepting the idea that you can't "ever make other people's time right or good . . . you have to live your own life."

Appendix
Percentages of Selected Variables

Table 1
Marital Status, Health, and Memory by Sex and Age

		SEX		AGE	
		Male (N 20)	Female (N 30)	60-74 (N 31)	75-92 (N 19)
MARITAL STATUS					
	Married	32	24	42	14
	Other	8	36	20	24
HEALTH					
	Excellent/Good	24	30	42	12
	Average/Poor	16	30	20	26
MEMORY					
	No Problems	30	36	50	16
	Some Problems	10	24	12	22

Table 2
Age Identification Questions by Sex and Age

	SEX		AGE	
	Male *(N 20)*	*Female* *(N 30)*	*60-74* *(N 31)*	*75-92* *(N 19)*
AGE QUESTIONS				
What is it like to be (an age)?				
Like any other age	14	28	26	16
Health predominates	20	16	20	16
Ambiguous	6	16	16	6
Do you feel your age?				
Yes	10	8	10	8
No	8	24	26	6
Ambivalent	18	18	18	18
Cannot say	4	10	8	6
Do you think of yourself as old?				
Yes	2	8	4	6
No	32	46	52	26
Ambivalent	6	6	6	6

Table 3
Primary Concern, Outlook on Future by Sex and Age

			AGE	
	Male *(N 20)*	*Female* *(N 30)*	*60-74* *(N 31)*	*75-92* *(N 19)*
PRIMARY CONCERN				
Staying Healthy	16	22	22	16
Staying Active	8	14	16	6

Table 3—Concluded
Primary Concern, Outlook on Future by Sex and Age

	Male (N 20)	Female (N 30)	AGE 60-74 (N 31)	75-92 (N 19)
Becoming a Burden	6	4	6	4
Memories of the Past	4	4	0	8
Societal Image of Age	2	4	6	0
Forced to Feel Useless	0	6	4	2
Living with Other Old People	2	2	2	2
Finances	0	4	4	0
Safety	2	0	2	0
OUTLOOK FOR THE NEXT TEN YEARS				
Optimistic—Global	18	12	24	6
Expects Positive and Negative Changes	6	14	16	4
Only Reflects on Life Day by Day	8	10	8	10
Apprehensive/Anxious	4	14	10	8
Won't Be Around Then	4	10	4	10

References

Beauvoir, Simone de. (1973). *The coming of age.* New York: Warner.

Blumer, Herbert J. (1969). *Symbolic interactionism: Perspective and method.* Englewood Cliffs, NJ: Prentice-Hall.

Brittan, Arthur. (1973). *Meanings and situations.* Boston: Routledge and Kegan Paul.

Clark, Margaret and Barbara G. Anderson. (1967). *Culture and aging: An anthropological study of older Americans.* Springfield, IL: Charles C. Thomas.

Cockerham, William C., Kimberly Sharp and Julie A. Wilcox. (1983). Aging and perceived health status. *Journal of Gerontology* 38:349-355.

Cole, Thomas R. (1984). Aging, meaning, and well-being: Musings of a cultural historian. *International Journal of Aging and Human Development* 19:329-336.

Cowley, Malcolm. (1982). *The view from eighty.* New York: Penguin.

Cowley, Malcolm. (1985). Being old old. *New York Times Magazine* May 26:58.

Dewey, John. (1910). *How we think.* Boston: D. C. Heath.

Epinay, Christian Lalive D'. (1986). Time, space and socio-cultural identity: The ethos of the proletariat, small owners and peasantry in an aged population. *International Social Science Journal* 38:89-104.

Ferraro, Kenneth F. (1980). Self-ratings of health among the old and old-old. *Journal of Health and Social Behavior* 23:377-383.

Halpert, Burton P. and Mary K. Zimmerman. (1986). The health status of the 'old-old': A reconsideration. *Social Science and Medicine* 22:9:893-899.

Haug, Marie, Linda L. Belgrave and Brian Gratton. (1984). Mental health and the elderly: Factors in stability and change over time. *Journal of Health and Social Behavior* 25:100-115.

Heidegger, Martin. (1962). *Being and time.* tr. J. Macquarrie and E. Robinson. New York: Harper and Row.

Heidegger, Martin. (1969). *Identity and difference.* tr. J. Stambaugh. New York: Harper and Row.

Hendricks, C. Davis and Jon Hendricks. (1969). Concepts of time and temporal construction among the aged, with implications for research. In J. F. Gubrium (ed.) *Time, roles and self in old age.* New York: Human Sciences Press, 13-49.

Hendricks, Jon and Calvin B. Peters. (1986). The times of our lives. *American Behavioral Scientist* 29:662-678.

Hyman, Herbert H. (1983). *Of time and widowhood: Nationwide studies of enduring effects.* Durham, NC: Duke Press Policy Studies.

Joubert, Charles E. (1984). Structured time and subjective acceleration of time. *Perceptual and Motor Skills* 59:335-336.

Levkoff, Sue E., Paul D. Cleary and Terrie Wetle. (1987). Differences in the appraisal of health between aged and middle-aged adults. *Journal of Gerontology* 42:114-120.

Lieberman, Morton A. and Sheldon S. Tobin. (1983). *The experience of old age: Stress, coping and survival.* New York: Basic.

Lowenthal, Marjorie F. and Clayton Haven. (1968). Interaction and adaptation: Intimacy as a critical variable. *American Sociological Review* 33:20-30.

Maddox, George L. (1962). Some correlates of differences in self-assessment of health status among the elderly. *Journal of Gerontology* 17:180-185.

Maddox, George L. and Elizabeth B. Douglass. (1973). Self-assessment of health: A longitudinal study of elderly subjects. *Journal of Health and Social Behavior* 14:87-93.

Maddox, George L. and Elizabeth B. Douglass. (1974). Aging and individual differences: A longitudinal analysis of social, psychological, and physiological indicators. *Journal of Gerontology* 29:555-563.

Marshall, Victor W. (1985). Age and awareness of finitude in developmental gerontology. In S. Wilcox and M. Sutton (eds.) *Understanding death and dying.* Palo Alto: Mayfield, 150-161.

Mead, George Herbert. (1938). *The philosophy of the act.* (ed.) C. W. Morris. Chicago: University of Chicago Press.

Mead, George Herbert. (1959). *The philosophy of the present.* (ed.) A. E. Murphy. Lasalle, IL: Open Court.

Mead, George Herbert. (1962) *Mind, self, and society.* (ed.) C. W. Morris. Chicago: University of Chicago Press.

Mead, George Herbert. (1964). *George Herbert Mead: On social psychology.* (ed.) A. Strauss. Chicago: University of Chicago Press.

Merleau-Ponty, Maurice. (1962). *Phenomenology of perception.* (tr.) C. Smith. London: Routledge and Kegan Paul.

Merleau-Ponty, Maurice. (1964). *Signs.* (tr.) R. C. McCleary. Evanston, IL: Northwestern University Press.

Myerhoff, Barbara. (1978). *Number our days.* New York: Touchstone.

Payne, Barbara and Frank Whittington. (1976). Older women: An examination of popular stereotypes and research evidence. *Social Problems* 23:489-504.

Quinn, Patrick K. and Marvin Reznikoff. (1985). The relationship between death anxiety and the subjective experience of time in the elderly. *International Journal of Aging and Human Development* 21:197-210.

Rakowski, William. (1986). Future time perspective: Applications to the health context of later adulthood. *American Behavioral Scientist* 29:730-745.

Reker, Gary T., Edward J. Peacock and Paul T. Wong. (1987). Meaning and purpose in life and well-being: A life-span perspective. *Journal of Gerontology* 42:44-49.

Schutz, Alfred. (1967). *The phenomenology of the social world.* (tr.) G. Walsh and F. Lehnert. Evanston, IL: Northwestern University Press.

Schutz, Alfred. (1970). *On phenomenology and social relations.* (ed.) H. R. Wagner. Chicago: University of Chicago Press.

Simmel, Georg. (1964). *The sociology of Georg Simmel.* (tr.) and (ed.) Kurt H. Wolff. Glencoe, IL: The Free Press.

Simmel, Georg. (1971). *On individuality and social forms.* (ed.) D. N. Levine. Chicago: University of Chicago Press.

Stoller, Eleanor P. (1984). Self-assessments of health by the elderly: The impact of informal assistance. *Journal of Health and Social Behavior* 25:260-270.

Chapter 11

'Successful Aging' Among Elderly Men in England and India: A Phenomenological Comparison

L. EUGENE THOMAS
KIM O. CHAMBERS

We have long been interested in the fact that some people, as they grow older, become more thoughtful, exhibit more wisdom, and become more "gracious." Others, however, become more petty and petulant, and are anything but gracious in their old age. Like others, we have wondered what makes the difference. Is it native disposition? Is it early conditioning? Is it the result of their current environmental situation? Is it a function of the beliefs that the person holds? Or what?

As persons facing aging ourselves we find these questions fascinating. We wonder how we will age, how our families and colleagues will react to the aging process. Are there secrets or strategies that can be learned from those who have successfully navigated the shoals of aging? Indeed, can they help us understand what it is to age well?

We shared some of these thoughts with a well-known gerontologist several years ago, and were somewhat shocked when he questioned the whole concept of "gracious" aging. He suggested that the concept is only a term applied to elderly who are docile and meet society's preconceptions of what the elderly should be. On the contrary, he argued, those who are most successful in their later years are aggressive, self-centered scrappers who are anything but pleasant to be around.

Despite his discouragement, we have continued to follow our interest in trying to understand those qualities of aging which we had termed "gracious." But his warning alerted us to the necessity of being careful in defining what we mean by the term. Indeed, much of our work since then has been seeking to define more precisely those qualities which constitute "successful" aging.

In this chapter we would like to try to indicate how one might go about studying a topic that presents conceptual and methodological problems, but which is of considerable substantive interest. First, care must be taken in phrasing the question. As will be indicated below, the notion of "gracious aging" raises all manner of theoretical questions that must be faced before any meaningful research can be undertaken. Then one must choose a sample that will help illuminate the issue, and develop a method for analyzing the data. Whether following a quantitative or a qualitative approach, this must entail data reduction, or the researcher will drown in a sea of details. In going from the details to the larger picture, and back again, the hermeneutic circle must be traversed several times in order to make sense out of the data. And finally one must relate the findings to the larger issues under consideration in such a fashion that colleagues can evaluate the validity of the claims made.

Phrasing the Question

White (1966) has noted that our definitions of emotional health tend to be derived by cataloguing the traits characteristic of mental illness, and designating their opposite as constituting mental health. The fact that depression is seen (at least by middle-aged researchers) as the most problematic psychological aspect of aging probably accounts for the widespread use of measures of morale in investigations of "successful aging."[1]

In a cautionary note concerning cross-cultural gerontological research, Nydegger (1980) warns that happiness might not be a universal concern of the elderly. Indeed, one of our early interviews brought this forcefully to our attention. Mr. Oakley, a ninety-two-year-old emigré from Russia, now living in London, responded to a typical morale question in the following way:

> (On the whole would you say your life today is: very happy, somewhat happy, not too happy or very unhappy?) Happiness wouldn't enter into it at all. I would say I was satisfied with my life. I'm trying to get a right, good, a real light. Yes, light would be the word. If I could do that I would be happy. But I won't get it. I haven't got the strength, the knowledge, the heart to get it. That's what I'm longing for. To be quite clear in my life. (You don't feel like you have it yet?) I haven't got it yet. But I hope I will get it. (Would you say you're a very unhappy man?) No, I . . . (Somewhat happy?) I have been happy in my life, yes. Not in the proper sense of happiness. I would say I was satisfied with my life. (Satisfied?) Yes.

The term that he uses, "satisfied," was echoed again by an elderly therapst who came up after a presentation of our research and suggested that in future interviews we might want to ask the question, "Are you satisfied with your life?" She said that she found that with patients, and in informal conversations, people respond to that question readily. Almost invariably they have given it thought, and appreciate having a chance to share their thoughts with others.

The advantage of the concept of "life satisfaction" (in addition to the fact that the Neugarten-Havighurst Life Satisfaction Index has given wide exposure to the concept) is that it is something which a respondent can answer for him/herself. Unlike more normative concepts, such as "maturity," which respondents can't answer directly for themselves, and which have to be inferred by the investigator, individuals are able to say whether they feel satisfied with their life.

But the term "aging gracefully" implies more than the individual's sense of subjective well-being. There is implied in the concept an evaluation by others of the degree to which the individual has been successful in aging—indeed, to what extent they might serve as a role model for younger persons. The schizophrenic on the back ward may express gleeful morale (if he is of the hebephrenic variety), but this is hardly what most people would think of as successful aging.

Clark and Anderson (1967) make a distinction between tasks of aging that are "adaptational" and those that are "developmental." The former are related to the cultural value system in which the individual lives, and can be expected to vary from one culture to another. Developmental tasks, they suggest, are more universal, or "pan-cultural," since they are tasks that are faced by every individual. "Life satisfaction" is more related to the task of "adaptation"—it would represent the evaluation the individual makes of his or her life in light of cultural expectations and values.[2] The success with which an individual has maneuvered the relevant development tasks, on the other hand, would be more apparent to an outside observer than to the individual.

Peck (1968) provides one of the most complete formulations of the developmental tasks of the latter third of the life cycle. Taking Erikson's life-span formulation, he has expanded the tasks confronting the individual in the final years of life. First, individuals must come to terms with inevitable bodily decline and illness as they age, presenting the task that Peck terms "body transcendence vs. body preoccupation." Finally, everyone must face the inevitability of death, and the task of "ego transcendence vs. ego preoccupation."

For present purposes, then, the provocative but vague term "aging gracefully" will be defined in this dual manner: first, self-evaluated "life satisfaction," relating to the adaptive tasks of aging, and, second, an external evaluation of the success with which the individual has handled the developmental tasks of coming to terms with the problems of bodily decline and eventual death. And to keep terminology more in line with present gerontological usage, the combined concept will be labelled "successful aging" (placed in quotation marks to indicate the special meaning attached to the term), rather than "aging graciously."

Given this redefinition of "gracious aging," the question arises as to how it can be researched. Even if the term can be operationalized (to use a positivist term), it is clear that an experimental design can not be utilized in examining antecedents of such behavior. At best we can hope to find "natural experiments" in which there are significant variations in cultural beliefs and experiences and then examine the outcomes. For this purpose, the most promising approach is to examine cultures which provide widely differing environments and values relevant to the handling of old age. Let us turn now to a discussion of the choice of a sample which maximizes cultural variation in relevant value-orientations.

Choosing a Sample

In their study of elderly men and women in San Francisco, Clark and Anderson (1967) found that those who were maladjusted continued to subscribe to the dominant cultural value-orientations (individualism, ambition, competitiveness, etc.). The sample of adjusted eldery, on the other hand, tended to subscribe to secondary value-orientations (congeniality, cooperation, relaxation, etc.). The authors suggest that aging is made difficult in Western society because the individual has to make a shift in value-orientations, without guidance of institutionalized alternatives. Cultures in which dominant value-orientations are more consonant with the realities of the latter part of the life cycle (physical decline and eventual death), they suggest, produce less stress for the aging person.

If this analysis is valid, one would expect to find elderly persons in societies with more congenial dominant value-orientations better adapted than those in Western countries. The "natural experiment" we were seeking, then, would appear to be provided by examining the elderly in such a culture, and comparing them with elderly in Western society.

Indian society, with its strong identification with cultural Hinduism, would appear to provide an ideal setting for such a study. Although influenced by Western culture over the past several hundred years, there is reason to believe that it still retains distinct value-orientations. Western observers (Dumont, 1977; Minturn & Hancock, 1963; Vatuk, 1980), as well as Indian scholars (Das, 1979; Kakar, 1982; Madan, 1982) have noted differences in beliefs about individualism between Indian and Western societies, as well as differences in other core values. Further, the Indian cultural ideal, still influenced by Hindu scriptures, prescribes withdrawal in the last two periods or "asrama" of life (Tambiah, 1982; Vatuk, 1980). Finally, in India there are institutionalized alternatives to provide guidance in seeking "Purusartha" or "the good life" (Malamoud, 1982).

The present study is based on interviews with a sample of elderly Indian men residing in New Delhi, India, along with a sample of English elderly residing in London, England. Interviews were conducted with fifty English-speaking Indian men seventy years of age or older, living in the community and in relatively good health. Since fluency in English was a criteria for selection, the group tended to have a high educational level and to have been employed in technical or professional occupations. Respondents were selected by means of multiple-entry chain sampling, with an attempt to locate respondents in various sections of New Delhi known to have relatively high concentrations of elderly persons. Ninety-five percent of the men approached agreed to be interviewed.

The English sample, which was located after the Indian interviews were completed, was matched as closely as possible with the Indian sample. Interviews were conducted in London which, like New Delhi, is the national capital and a large cosmopolitan city. Multiple-entry chain sampling was utilized, beginning with enrollees in a continuing education program, members of senior hobby groups, church and synagogue groups and social service programs. Most of the respondents had held technical or professional occupations, but their educational level was somewhat lower than their Indian counterparts. The refusal rate for the English sample was higher (24%) than for the Indian sample.

One other significant difference between the groups was the greater tendency of Indian respondents to live with extended family. Otherwise the two groups are quite similar demographically, with the obvious exception of religious affiliation. Table 1 summarizes the demographic chacteristics of the samples.

Table 1
Demographic Characteristics of Samples

Indian (N 20)		English (N 20)
	Age	
78.0	Mean	77.1
	Education	
3	To Age 16	9
0	Vocational	1
1	Some College	1
8	College Grad	4
5	Advanced Degree	3
3	Not ascertained	2

Table 1—Concluded
Demographic Characteristics of Samples

Indian (N 20)   *English (N 20)*

Marital Status

Indian		English
1	Never Married	3
5	Widowed	2
1	Divorced	1
13	Married	14

Living Arrangement

Indian		English
3	Alone	6
7	Wife with Relatives	0
4	Alone with Relatives	0
6	Wife Alone	14

Religion

Indian			English	
17	Hindu		Ch. England	6
2	Sikh		Protestant	2
1	Moslem		Catholic	3
0	Other		Jewish	3
0	None		Other	2
			None	4

Devising a Method

Having defined "successful aging," and devised a strategy for comparing elderly in cultures believed to provide different levels of psychological stress for their aged members, the question remains as to how to measure the concept. The temptation is to utilize standardized measures of subjective well-being which have been developed and are widely used. There are two problems connected with this solution, however. In the first place, to do so would impose Western categories on members of a culture known to differ in core values. We can't be sure that the components of the Life Satisfaction Index (Neugarten, Havighurst & Tobin, 1961), for instance, are salient for non-Western elderly. Indeed, as Nydegger (1980) has speculated, and Mr. Oakley articulated in his interview, the issue of morale may be far less salient to some elderly than our theories and standardized instruments assume.

Further, standardized instruments of subjective well-being fail to provide insight into the way respondents have negotiated the relevant developmental tasks of the latter part of the life cycle. To be sure, one would assume failure to deal with these developmental tasks would lead to lower levels of life satisfaction, but there is no assurance of a perfect correlation. And, if such instruments are inadequate for non-Western elderly, the problem is even more complicated.

For these reasons it was felt that the study should allow informants to describe their experience and perception of the world in their own terms. Open-ended interviews were conducted, in which respondents were encouraged to talk about themselves and their past experience (their youth, past successes and failures, persons who had influenced them, etc.), as well as their present situation. Two interviews were conducted with each informant, spaced four to six weeks apart. The Indian interviews were conducted by a professional Indian male interviewer (with the first author present); the London interviews were conducted by the first author. Responses were tape recorded and subsequently transcribed for analysis.

It is easy enough to enter into dialogue with respondents on topics of personal interest to them, and most informants enjoyed the interaction very much. The researcher ends up with many impressions, and several hundred pages of typed protocols. Having foregone the security of quantifiable data, there is the threat of drowning in the data, however. What is clearly needed is some form of data reduction in order to gain perspective on the information and arrive at overall conclusions.

One solution is to develop categories (e.g., zest for life, mood tone, etc.), and score the protocols for each dimension. Such an approach has several advantages. It is possible to obtain reliability ratings by having a second or third researcher rate the protocols. More importantly, one has reduced the mountain of data to a manageable set of numbers, which can then be manipulated statistically in order to reach conclusions about levels of life satisfaction.

The problem with this approach is precisely the same as the problem with standardized instruments: it imposes the researchers' categories on respondents. When a Western researcher does this with a Western sample, the problem is not so apparent (though perhaps equally real). But when one does this with a non-Western sample, especially one which is known to hold different value-orientations, it defeats the very purpose of conducting cross-cultural research. The very differences that one is looking for may well be masked. As someone has remarked, it is like a biologist announcing that the sea contains no fish smaller than two inches, after having seined the ocean bed with a two-inch gauge net.

What is needed, then, is a more phenomenological approach, whereby the researcher is enabled to see the world through the eyes of his or her informants. To do this it is necessary to bracket, or hold in abeyance, one's assumptions and expectations.[3] At the same time, the data must be reduced to a manageable size in order to gain any perspective on the issues under investigation.

The method adopted was a modification of the phenomenological procedure developed by Colaizzi (1978). As a first step each protocol was read for an understanding of its content. Then each meaning unit (a phrase or sentence containing a complete idea or thought) was extracted from each protocol. At this point the researcher seeks to avoid imposing categories or ideas on the protocol. A second coder would be expected to identify roughly the same meanings units, working independently.

Once the meaning units have been identified, the researcher conducts a kind of verbal factor analysis to seek to identify the salient themes that emerge. A theme consists of several meaning units that can be identified as related to a common topic: major themes are those for which there are the greatest number of related meaning units; minor themes are supported by fewer meaning units in the protocol. At this stage of the analysis the researcher will, to an extent, impose order on the material, though the attempt is made to remain as close to the lived world of the respondent as possible. That is, the major and minor themes that are identified must arise out of the interview protocol, although the exact wording of the theme may not be stated specifically by the respondent. A second investigator may or may not agree with the particular themes which are identified, but he or she should be able to recognize what the first researcher saw that led to identifying the theme.

At this point in the analysis a modification of Glaser and Strauss's (1967) "constant comparative method" was utilized. As each protocol was analyzed, the coders determined if significant new themes were emerging. When "saturation" was reached, that is, when it became clear that analysis of additional interviews was not materially adding significant new data, this phase of the research process was terminated. After ten protocols had been examined for each group it was clear that saturation had been reached. In order to be conservative, an additional ten protocols for each group were analyzed, and the remaining interviews were not utilized for this piece of research (in Glaser & Strauss's model, interviewing itself would have ceased at this point).

The reader should be reminded that this procedure, which in traditional quantitative data analysis would be seen as "throwing away data," and highly suspect, does not violate the human science paradigm. In this paradigm numbers are not themselves any guarantee of truth claims that are made. Rather, the criteria is gaining understanding of the phenomenon under investigation. In fact, overwhelming numbers can stand in the way of understanding if it prevents the type of analysis appropriate to the topic under investigation (Kvale, 1987).

Analyzing the Data

Two coders rated the protocols independently, achieving near perfect agreement in identifying the meaning units. Though not in exact agreement, the thematic analysis of the two coders produced comparable results.[4] Table 2 gives the resulting thematic analysis for one of the Indian respondents. The number by each theme indicates the number of meaning units which related to this theme in the protocol.

Table 2
Indian Subject #17

MAJOR THEMES	Meaning Units
Importance of Children	11
wishes they be content	
like to give them financial provision	
they respect him	
Belief in religion, God	6
accept God's plan	
death beginning another chapter	
Does not want to live much longer	5
ready to die	
not afraid of death	
Importance of his holy man (guru)	4
MINOR THEMES	
Does not want to become dependent	2
Misses friends who are deceased	2
all friends have died	
Does not want to be a liability to anybody	2
Had a good life, happy marriage	2
SUB-THEMES	

Thinks of death often
  death inevitable, not bother

Neighbors treat him well

Table 2—Concluded
Indian Subject #17

SUB-THEMES, cont'd.	Meaning Units

Never feels bored
  reads books in spare time

Poverty moves to tears

Tears at surprise 60th wedding anniversary

Feels like he is 50

Is not good looking

Sex has no meaning to him

The first data reduction, then, consisted of identifying the major and minor themes for each of the interview protocols. A second data reduction was necessary to identify common themes for each sub-sample as a group. The themes were combined for the English and for the Indian samples. A procedure similar to that used for individuals was utilized, with raters taking the list of major and minor themes for the two groups and submitting them to a further "verbal factor analysis." Table 3 gives the "Overarching Themes" which emerged for the Indian sample, and Table 4 gives those for the English sample.

Table 3
Indian Overarching Themes

Theme	Frequency of Occurrence
Importance of family (extended)	17
Religious beliefs and practices	16
Satisfied with life, past	15
Pleased with self, appearance	15
Improve society, help others	11
Critical of Indian society	8
Dissatisfied with life, past	8
Not afraid of death	5
Concern for health	5
Importance of career and work	5

Table 4
English Overarching Themes

Theme	Frequency of Occurrence
Dissatisfied with life, past	16
Satisfied with self, appearance	15
Importance of Family (esp. wife)	12
Concern for health	9
Dread of Being dependent	7
Desire to be active	7
Religious & philosophical beliefs	6
Thoughts about death	5
Satisfied with life	5
Religious experience, practices	4
Dissatisfaction with self	3

Before writing the overall summary, which attempts to state the common salient features for the particular sample, the researchers returned to the original interview protocols to determine if there were any important elements there that did not appear in the data reduction. Conversely, they sought to make sure that all of the identified themes were clearly present in the original protocols, before writing the overall summary. This completion of the hermeneutical circle helps insure both the reliability and validity of the conclusions which are drawn from the mass of verbatim interview data. Tables 5 and 6 give the overall summaries for the Indian and English samples.

Table 5
Overall India Summary

Directly and indirectly religion and life satisfaction are the dominant issues that emerge from these interviews. Importance of family, particularly the success of children, and interest in "social work" (being of service to others), reflect concern with fulfilling one's religious "dharma" in the Hindu tradition. Level of life satisfaction, both past and present, attests to the fact that these men see themselves as having accomplished much of what is expected of them. And their religious beliefs and practices, in turn, enhance present life satisfaction.

In viewing their lives in light of these ideals there are notes of dissatisfaction and regret. There is a fairly strong note of criticism of present-day Indian society in some of the interviews. Some of the men regret past failures or mistakes, and to a lesser extent, blame others for their situation. But these are secondary to the overall note of satisfaction and contentment expressed by the majority of respondents.

There is also an acknowledgement of declining health and physical strength in many of the interviews. Often the greatest concern is expressed for their decreasing ability to be of use to their families and to engage in "social work." The prospect of increasing frailty is generally accepted as an inevitable part of growing old, and to be expected, along with the acceptance of the inevitability of death.

These men feel by and large that they have performed their expected duties and obligations. Embedded within their family and the larger religious tradition with which they identify, they can look back on their lives with a sense a completion and satisfaction. For the present they express contentment with life, even as they continue to be engaged in religious practices and concern themselves with the welfare of family and doing "social work."

Table 6
Overall English Summary

On the surface the two dominant major themes in these interviews appear contradictory: Dissatisfaction with life and one's past, and satisfaction with oneself and one's appearance. The two themes actually tap different dimensions, both of which are characteristic of these men. Dissatisfaction with life relates to their negative evaluation of their past and/or their present life situation, as well as future prospects. On the other hand, these men indicate that on the whole they are satisfied with themselves—their traits, appearance, mental state and outlook on life.

Another cluster of themes that appears in the interviews suggests a dread of becoming dependent, and a strong desire to remain active. In addition to appearing as a major theme in several of the protocols, dread of becoming dependent underlies worry about health, and is probably related to the theme of wanting to remain active. Importance of family, another major theme in the protocols, seems to be related to the desire to remain independent as well. Of the family constellation, wives play the most central role. In addition to the obvious factor of companionship, these men perhaps realize the importance of their wives in their ability to maintain their independence as they grow older.

An underlying and recurring theme for these men is that of stoic acceptance. They tend to be more or less satisfied with themselves, given the circumstances in which they found themselves. But stoic acceptance is suggested by a brooding undertone of resignation and, in some cases, despair. Not that they fear death—in fact, acceptance of the inevitability of death is perhaps the main fruit of their stoic philosophy. Rather, there is a bittersweet attempt to extract as much dignity and satisfaction as possible out of life, given the realities of existence as they perceive it.

Comparing Cultures

Before considering the question of "successful aging" in these two samples, let us first look at the cultural differences reflected in the responses of these men. Although chosen to represent similar strata from their respective societies in terms of education and professional background, the groups differed considerably in their basic attitudes toward aging, as well as other beliefs and practices.

Clearly emerging from the overall summaries there is a marked difference in the place that religion plays in the lives of these men. For the Indians religious beliefs and practices constitute one of the major overarching themes. And as indicated in Table 5, concerns for family and society are related to the larger religious framework to which almost all of these men subscribe. One respondent summarized this point of view when he observed that the terms "secular" (in relation to India being a secular state) and "India" are contradictory terms. "Every Indian," he explained, "is religious at heart." We observed this phenomenon throughout our interviews. In a few instances men who had devoted their lives to science expressed doubt about the existence of God, but on further probing even they expressed belief in the notion of re-incarnation.

Not only does a religious world view provide a pervasive framework in which the Indian men live, religious practice is an important part of the lives of many of the men. For example, nineteen of the twenty Indian respondents indicated that they pray or meditate one or more times a day. A majority of the men in the English sample, on the other hand, indicated that they seldom or never engage in prayer or meditation.

Even for those in the English sample who were engaged in religious activities there was not the sense of immersion in a taken-for-granted religious reality. The religiously involved indicated that they saw their beliefs as an individual choice, made in the face of other options that could just as well be made. This was illustrated by the comment of a devoted churchman, who had undergone a profound period of depression following the loss of his hearing. Still active in his church, and heavily involved in caring for his family and other elderly in the community, he was continuously wrestling with religious doubts. "I hold on to my faith with both hands, because I know how easily it is lost," he confided.

Another area in which there were marked cultural differences was in the place that family played in the lives of these men. Family loomed large in importance in the lives of men from both cultures, to be sure. Closer inspection indicates more difference than similarity, however. For the English men the major family theme is related most often to his wife, particularly concern for the wife's health. For the Indians, on the other hand, concern relates more to children, or to the family as a unit. A suggestion of the role that larger family plays in the lives of the Indian men is given by the demographic data in Table 1, which indicates that a majority (55%) live with extended family, either with their wives or singly. None of the English sample, in comparison, lived with extended family.

Differences in family dynamics are as impressive as differences in living arrangements for the two cultures. Whereas wives play a central role in the lives of the men in the English sample, wives were much less salient in the lives of the Indian men. This difference is illustrated by the fact that it was often impossible to determine from the open-ended interview responses whether or not wives of the Indian men were still living, whereas this was apparent throughout the English interviews. Children, particularly sons, loomed large in the lives of the Indian respondents. Children were important to English respondents, too, but compared to the emotional attachment to wife (or grief on the loss of their wives), these relationships were relatively diffuse.

Probably the greatest cultural difference between these two groups of men relates to the theme of individualism. Dumont (1977) suggested that individualism is a prevalent ideology of the West, in contrast to a sense of corporateness found in India. This can be seen not only in the differences in religious identification and family relations noted above, but in other concerns and interests expressed in the interviews. For example, the extent to which individualism permeated the world view of the English sample is suggested by the fact that for them family, at least as far as children are concerned, seemed to be viewed as a voluntary organization. Indian men, by comparison, were embedded in a family network of obligations and privileges that absorbed much of their attention and energy.

Several other themes that emerged from the English interviews attest to this individualistic ideology. The most obvious is the dread of dependency which was prevalent in many of the interviews, suggesting a desire to maintain one's individual identity and life space. The themes of concern for health and the desire to remain active are also clearly related to the individualistic orientation of these men. The high importance placed on wife in the English interviews, in contrast to the importance of extended family among Indian respondents, also suggests a heightened sense of individuality. And concern for the continued health of wife among the English men is probably not unrelated to their awareness of the importance of their wives in making it possible for them to maintain their independent living arrangements.

It should be noted that this difference in desire for independence relates to religious beliefs, as well. The Hindu concept of *asrama*, or "life stages" postulates different agendas for the successive periods of life (Malamoud, 1982). In the later two stages, those of "householder" and *sanyasin*, the individual is not only freed from family and societal obligations, but is expected to progressively disengage from previous roles and activities. Though few lives actually correspond to these prescriptions (Vatuk, 1980), Hindus accept stages as normative (Das, 1979). On the other hand, Western society fails to provide a cultural alternative to the ideal of activity and engagement of the earlier years of life (Clark and Anderson, 1967). Lacking normative guidance for transformation of value-orientations, the English men tend to frantically try to maintain previous activity and independence levels, and anything which limits their ability to do so is perceived as a threat to their very being.

Two words might be used to provide a highly abbreviated summary of the differences in the cultures of these two groups of elderly men: *dharma* and "stoicism." *Dharma*, the Hindu word for duty, refers to the religious obligations to family, society and to God, which one is expected to fulfill in the course of one's life (Wayman, 1970). Implied in the concept is the notion of one's interdependence with both one's extended family, as well as membership in larger society. And on a more comprehensive level, one is related to God and the cosmos in fulfilling one's dharmic responsibilities.

Stoicism, on the other hand, at least as exemplified by these respondents, places the focus on the individual and his existence in an intractable world. Cut off from a viable religious tradition, the English respondents tend to see themselves as isolated individuals, alone in the world except for what ties they maintain with family and a scattering of friends. Declining health and reduced activity level threaten to remove even these bonds. Faced with this perceived reality, the strategy that has been adopted by many is that of stoic acceptance or resignation. (Cf. Shanas, et al., 1968, for further evidence of this stoic trait in British elderly.)

It would appear, then, that these men reflect the cultural characteristics which were sought in choosing the Indian and English samples for this study. That is, the Indian culture reflects variant value-orientations from those dominant in Western societies. If Clark and Anderson (1967) are right in their suggestion that elderly who age most successfully have come to subscribe to the value-orientations that emphasize co-operation, congeniality, etc., then it should follow that the two samples of elderly would exhibit different levels of adaptation to the aging experience. Let us now examine the level of "successful aging" reflected in these two samples.

Imposing a Western Template

We are faced with a curious set of data concerning life satisfaction for the two samples. As noted in Table 6, the English respondents expressed dissatisfaction with life and their past, but satisfaction with themselves. Although appearing to be contradictory, the former seems to be related to their negative evaluation of their past and future life situations, while the latter indicates satisfaction with themselves—their present traits, appearance, etc. Satisfaction with self probably taps a general moral dimension for these men, while their dissatisfaction with life likely taps a more generalized view of the world. The Indian men, on the other hand, indicate that they are satisfied with their lives, past and future, as well as being pleased with themselves and their appearance.

Given the different configuration of responses, it is difficult to compare the Indian and English men on "life satisfaction"—the term clearly means different things in the different cultural settings. It should be noted that as part of a larger study, these men were given the LSI scale, and were found to have almost identical scores on this structured instrument (Thomas & Chambers, in press). If we had not conducted a phenomenological analysis of the protocols, the qualitative differences in the two groups would have been completely lost.

Even if it is impossible to judge a cultural difference in "life satisfaction" on the basis of self report, qualitative differences are quite apparent in the interviews. Overall there seems to be more acceptance of life and contentment among the Indian respondents. They are certainly more integrated into their families, and seem to feel themselves integrated with the larger cosmic order. Let us turn to a consideration of how successful the respective samples were in terms of negotiating the developmental tasks identified by Peck (1968).

In relation to the task of coming to terms with the inevitable physical decline of aging, "body preoccupation" refers to the extent to which a person continues to focus on bodily/physical comfort and well-being. The successful resolution of this task involves moving from such preoccupation with one's body and the physical level, toward "body transcendence." Indications of transcendence are concerns that go beyond the physical, involving outside interests, such as social, creative or spiritual concerns.

From the themes which emerged in the analysis (Table 5 and 6) there is clear evidence of bodily preoccupation in the English sample. This is indicated not only by the relatively high frequency of personal health concerns in their interviews, but concern for their wives' health loomed large as well. Further, interest in and concern for physical appearance was common in the "satisfied with self" theme. Body preoccupation is further suggested by the theme of concern about dependency and the desire to remain active. Turning to the Indian sample, there is much less evidence of body preoccupation. To be sure, there is concern for personal health, but this is relatively minor in comparison to the evidence of bodily transcendence, particularly concern for family and society.

Peck identifies "ego transcendence vs. ego preoccupation" as the final developmental task in the later years. Here the cultural differences are even greater. Indian respondents not only place greater importance on religion and spiritual practices, which suggests that they see themselves as part of a larger reality, but they also give evidence of transcending the bounds of their individual egos in their concern for the welfare of the larger society. For the English group there is strong evidence for ego preoccupation. The underlying stress on individuality, as evidenced by concern for independence, suggests a "narrowly ego-centered clinging to one's private separate identity" (Peck, 1968. p. 91). And they show scant awareness of being part of cosmic reality that is larger than themselves, though this awareness pervades the awareness of the Indian sample.

Conclusion

In the previous section the words "imposing a Western template" were deliberately used to call attention to the fact that it is impossible for Western researchers to discuss so value-laden an issue as successful aging without imposing their own values. Clark and Anderson (1967) suggest that although adaptive tasks are culturally specific, the developmental tasks faced in the later years of life are "pan-cultural." Even this is doubtful: if a dedicated Hindu *sanyasin*, for instance, were doing such a study (assuming he were to find it worth doing), can we assume that he would reach similar conclusions? Indeed, would he ask the same research question in the first place?

We can't really answer this question, but historical and cross-cultural perspective suggests that we at least view the issue as problematic. Coan (1977), in his systematic survey of definitions of "optimal personality development" in different cultures and historical periods, came up with an array of competing terms, including: hero, artist, sage and saint. He concluded, however that the various terms are not entirely unrelated. In fact, there is considerable overlap in the basic concepts used in different cultures and in different historical periods, suggesting that definitions of what constitutes optimal personality are not entirely relative, despite the different titles that may be attached to these qualities.

Returning to Clark and Anderson's (1967) adaptive tasks of aging, and Peck's (1968) developmental tasks of the latter years, there is clear convergence here as well. The adaptive tasks of a) acceptance of physical and social limitations, and, b) revision of goals and values into an adequate philosophy of life are remarkably similar to Peck's developmental tasks of body and ego transcendence.[5]

It is something of a puzzle, then, to find such a divergence in self-evaluated life satisfaction and degree of success in grappling with the developmental tasks of aging for the English sample. By contrast, the two are highly correlated for the Indian sample.

Perhaps the reason for this discrepancy relates to differences in other cultural values held by the two groups. As noted earlier, Shanas, et al. (1968) observed that British elderly tend to deny concerns about poor health, reflecting the same stoic stance that we found with our English respondents. In interviews we have conducted with middle- and upper-middle class elderly in this country, we have noted a similar reluctance to talk about health problems. It just isn't the thing to do in "polite society."

Likewise, it may well be that the almost grim insistence that they are happy with their lives may be a culturally-conditioned tendency on the part of the English men to "keep a stiff upper lip" in spite of adversity. At any rate, such a possibility fits well with our data. And it suggests the danger of relying on self-report life satisfaction or morale as a single measure of "successful aging" among elderly. As Carstensen and Cone (1983) remind us, social desirability can be a serious problem in self-rated measures of well-being with the elderly.

The question with which we began, "Are there differences in 'successful aging' in two widely diverging cultures?" would seem to be answered in the affirmative. At least if objective evaluation of success in coming to grips with major developmental tasks can be taken as an indication of success in aging, there is evidence of cultural differences.

There are several factors that could account for the observed difference in aging between the two cultures. At least three factors come immediately to mind: 1) Hindu culture provides value-orientations which are more congenial to the aging process (e.g., less individualistic, less competitive, etc.); 2) Indian society provides more clearly defined guidelines for adapting to the late years of life (specifically, legitimizing dependency needs); or 3) the presence of extended family support may aid in facing the psychological challenges of the latter years of life.

There is no way to tease out which of these factors are most relevant for the observed differences. Indeed, the three may be highly inter-related—e.g., diminished individualism may be a concomitant of immersion in an extended family system. Or it may be that the most important variable is the fact that the Indian culture provides a context of meaning and purpose that enables its elderly to face the latter years with equanimity. Whatever the factors involved, it is clear that they couldn't be imported wholesale into this country, even if we knew what they were.

Cole (1986), analyzing the situation of the elderly in Western societies, particularly the U. S., observed, "Unless we grapple more openly with the profound failure of meaning that currently surrounds the end of life, our most enlightened view of old age will amount to perpetual middle age" (p. 130). Although the Indian culture can't be imported to contemporary Western society—and many of its components we would not want to incorporate if we could—the experience of their elderly suggests some directions that may contribute to the quality of life for the aged in this country.

Clark and Anderson suggest that our society needs to provide institutional alternatives for our dominant value-orientations in order to reduce the tension faced by the elderly in Western society. Naranjo (1981) goes even further, looking to the Hindu model in suggesting that our centers for the care of the aging become spiritual schools, to help them find meaning in life. Whatever prescriptions one may make, research that takes us beyond simply the study of aging in Western societies should help us gain perspective on the problems and possibilities of development in the latter years of the life cycle, and perhaps give us clues to the ingredients that help one "age graciously."

Support for this research was provided by the American Institute of Indian Studies and the University of Connecticut Research Foundation.

Notes

1. Clark and Anderson (1967) provide a good example of this tendency. In Appendix B of their book (pp. 449-450), they indicate that they asked a number of questions of their respondents concerning affect, interest in life, optimism, etc. These forty-five questions were subjected to a cluster analysis, which yielded eight oblique clusters. The authors selected one eight-item cluster, a "Depression/Satisfaction score," as the measure of morale which they used throughout the volume. Cf. Taylor (1977) for a thoughtful critique of the use of morale as a variable in gerontological research.

2. Clark and Anderson (1967) make a distinction between "adjustment" (criteria which are external to the person) and "adaptation" (which involves internal and external accommodation). The schizophrenic mentioned above might be seen as a case of adjustment to a particular environment, but would not be considered to have adapted. Life satisfaction, in the sense it is being used here and by Clark and Anderson, involves both external adjustment and internal adaptation of the individual to the environment.

3. This is, of course, not entirely possible. The assumptions and values of the interviewer are embedded in the whole research enterprise, from framing the research topic to deciding on the questions that are to be asked (or not asked) of the respondent. But within these parameters, which the researcher should make as explicit as possible in making public the results of the study, every effort should be made to bracket one's biases and allow informants to describe their own lived experience.

4. We coded the data independently because this was the first time we had used this technique. Such a practice is not considered necessary for phenomenological research (Colaizzi, 1978). Reliability is achieved not so much by means of "objective" intercoder uniformity as by means of completion of the hermeneutic circle. That is, the

original data is not discarded when the data reduction has been completed, but at each stage of the analysis the researcher refers back to the original data. The use of this strategy for enhancing reliability in qualitative research is discussed more fully in another paper (Thomas & Chambers, in press).

5. These are a summary of the five adaptive tasks that Clark and Anderson (1967) identify: 1) perceptions of aging and definition of instrumental limitations; 2) redefinition of physical and social life space; 3) substitution of alternative sources of need-satisfaction; 4) reassessment of criteria for evaluation of self; and 5) reintegration of values and life goals (pp. 402-412).

References

Cartensen, L. L. and J. D. Cone.. (1983). Desirability and the measurement of well-being in elderly persons. *Journal of Gerontology* 38: 713-715.

Clark, M. M. and B. G. Anderson. (1967). *Culture and aging: An anthropological study of older Americans.* Springfield: Charles C. Thomas.

Coan, R. (1972). *Hero, artist, sage, or saint?* NY: Columbia University Press.

Colaizzi, P. F. (1978). Psychological research as a phenomenologist views it. In R. S. Valle and M. King (eds.) *Existential-phenomenological alternatives in psychology.* NY: Oxford.

Cole, T. R. (1986). The 'enlightened' view of aging: Victorian morality in a new key. In T. R. Cole and S. A. Gadow (eds.) *What does it mean to grow old? Reflections from the humanities.* Durham, NC: Duke University Press.

Das, V. (1979). Reflections on the social construction of adulthood. In S. Kakar (ed.) *Identity and adulthood.* New Delhi: Vikas.

Dumont, L. (1977). *From Mandeville to Marx.* Chicago: University of Chicago Press.

Glaser, B. G. and A. L. Strauss. (1967). *The discovery of grounded theory.* Chicago: Aldine.

Kakar, S. (1982). *Shamans, mystics and doctors.* New Delhi: Oxford.

Kvale, S. (1987). Validity in the qualitative research interview. *Methods* 1: 37-72.

Madan, T. N. (1982). The ideology of the householder among the Kashmiri Pundits. In T. N. Madan (ed.) *Way of life.* New Delhi: Vikas.

Malamand, C. (1982). On the rhetoric and semantics of Purusartha. In T. N. Madan (ed.) *Way of life.* New Delhi: Vikas.

Minturn, L. and J. T. Hancock. (1963). The Rajputs of Khalapur, India. In B. B. Whiting (ed.) *Six cultures: Studies in child development.* NY: Wiley.

Naranjo, C. (1981). Meditation and maturity: In God we trust. In J. R. Staude (ed.) *Wisdom and age*. Berkeley: Ross Books.

Neugarten, B. L., R. J. Havighurst and S. S. Tobin. (1961). The measurement of life satisfaction. *Journal of Gerontology* 16: 134-143.

Nydegger, C. N. (1980). Measuring morale. In C. L. Fry and J. Keith (eds.) *New methods for old age research*. Chicago: Center for Urban Policy, Loyola University.

Peck, R. C. (1968). Psychological development in the second half of life. In B. L. Neugarten (ed.) *Middle age and aging*. Chicago: University of Chicago Press.

Shanas, E., P. Townsend, D. Wedderburn, H. Friis, P. Milhaj and Stehouwer. (1968). The psychology of health. In B. L. Neugarten (ed.) *Middle age and aging*. Chicago: University of Chicago Press.

Tambiah, S. S. J. (1982). The renouncer: His individuality and his community. In T. N. Madan (ed.) *The way of life*. New Delhi: Vikas.

Taylor, C. (1977). Why measure morale? In C. N. Nydegger (ed.) *Measuring morale: A guide to effective assessment*. Special Pub. No. 3. Washington, DC: Gerontological Society of America..

Thomas, L. E. and K. O. Chambers (in press). The phenomenology of life satisfaction among elderly men: Quantitative and qualitative views. *Psychology and Aging*.

Vatuk, S. (1980). Withdrawal and disengagement as a cultural response to aging in India. In C. Fry (ed.) *Aging in culture and society*. NY: Praeger.

Wayman, A. (1970). Varnasrama-dharma: Ends and obligations of man. In J. Elder (ed.) *Lectures in Indian civilization*. Dubuque, IA: Kendall-Hunt.

White, R. W. (1966). *Lives in progress*, 2nd ed. NY: Holt, Rinehart.

Chapter 12

Social Relationships Among the Rural Elderly: A Multimethod Approach

LINDA A. WOOD

There is an abundance of research on various types and aspects of social relationships among the elderly, for example, on friendship, family relationships and social support. This research has helped to identify the connections among social relationships and specific aspects of well-being (e.g., health), and it has extended our understanding of how the social relationships of the elderly are implicated in their well-being. But the literature includes relatively little description of relationships. We have information about how many relationships people have and with whom, and various ratings of the perceived quality of the relationships, but we do not know much about their nature. This lack is probably an inevitable reflection of the overwhelming focus of the literature on quantification and statistical analyses. We also have no satisfactory theory of social relationships and therefore do not know precisely how relationships affect and are affected by well-being.

In this chapter, I want to suggest that we require a more descriptive, detailed and qualitative approach to research and a more systematic approach to theorizing if we are to understand how relationships permeate everyday life. Secondly, I want to propose that we give careful attention to defining and distinguishing between "relationships" and "interactions" if we wish to understand relationships and how they unfold in and are constituted by everyday social activities.

These arguments will be elaborated in the context of data from a study of loneliness and life satisfaction among the rural elderly. The orientation of the research is multimethodological, with an emphasis on qualitative data and analysis. I first describe the study and consider the data on interactions, on relationships and on the connections between them. I then discuss some theoretical implications and methodological issues raised by research in this area and make suggestions for future research.

The Study

The major purpose of the present research was the intensive study of loneliness among a small group of rural elderly. The aim was to develop an ethogenic theory of loneliness among the rural aged that would integrate previous approaches to loneliness and provide the basis for a general social-psychological theory of loneliness (Wood, 1983, 1985). The research as originally conceived was not intended to address specifically the relation between social interactions and social relationships except as these figured in the analysis of loneliness. The intensive study involved several phases or cycles, during which a number of different techniques were employed to collect different types of data on different topics related to loneliness and life satisfaction (see Wood, 1981). Most of the data were collected in three of four sessions by two female interviewers. Final interviews were conducted by the author.

The participants were drawn from a large sample of 392 elderly who had taken part in a survey study of life satisfaction in rural communities (Michalos, 1982). They were selected to represent different levels of life satisfaction, different marital statuses, different types of rural environment and approximately equal numbers of men and women. The analyses reported below are based on the data from fifteen participants who completed all or almost all of the various phases. Basic demographic characteristics of the sample are reported in Table 1. The participants are identified by pseudonyms.

Table 1
Demographic Characteristics of Participants

Participant # Pseudonym	Sex	Age in 1982	Marital Status	Work Status	Residence[a]	Education[b]
1 Arthur	M	79	married	retired	2	2
2 Bill	M	72	married	retired	2	3
3 Carl	M	76	widowed	semi-ret	1	1
4 Donna	F	72	widowed	semi-ret	2	3
5 Emily	F	70	married	homemaker	2	1
6 Flora	F	76	widowed	homemaker	4	2
7 Gloria	F	81	widowed	homemaker	2	1
8 Helen	F	72	married	homemaker	2	3

Table 1—concluded
Demographic Characteristics of Participants

Participant #	Pseudonym	Sex	Age in 1982	Marital Status	Work Status	Residence[a]	Education[b]
9	John	M	75	married	retired	1	1
10	Kevin	M	82	married	retired	2	2
11	Lorna	F	69	married	retired	3	2
12	Martha	F	70	married	housewife	5	3
13	Nancy	F	66	widowed	semi-ret	6	4
14	Robert	M	70	widowed	semi-ret	1	4
15	Ted	M	78	married	semi-ret	4	1

[a]1 = village (population < 500); 2 = town (500-1000); 3 = town (2000-2500); 4 = town (3000-3500); 5 = city (> 5000); 6 = open country
[b]Highest level reached: 1 - Grade 8; 2 = Some secondary; 3 = Some post-secondary; 4 = University degree

The analyses of social interaction draw largely on the diaries; for social relationships, the major sources are the questionnaires on life satisfaction and social networks and the interviews about loneliness. The specific techniques are described in detail below. In most instances, the numerical data obtained for individual participants were treated as nominal, that is, as qualitative. For example, a participant might select "6" from the scale of satisfaction to describe her feelings about friends; this was treated as a categorical judgment corresponding to the label on the scale, in this case, "Very satisfied." I emphasize therefore that in comparing these data, I did not employ any statistical tests. Rather, references to "lower" or "more positive" ratings reflect my judgment that there is a difference in the context of all of the information available about the participants. Space limitations preclude the presentation of all of the data and analyses on which this chapter is based; these are available from the author. (See also Wood & Johnson, 1989.)

Social Interactions

Participants were asked to keep a diary on audiotape for thirty consecutive days and to describe each day in terms of their activities and mood, with a particular focus on their interactions (contacts) with other people. The general strategy employed for the analyses was driven in part by the large amount of information generated through the diaries. The data were coded according to a set of categories. For the most part, they will be presented in the form of counts for each category, rather than in qualitative terms. Counts are employed not only because of space limitations, but also because the data needed to be condensed in some form in order to compare them efficiently with the data on relationships. It is important to note, however, that the numbers do not represent ratings, but simply a count of the number of interactions per category, that is, a count of the "countable." The counts are not averaged over individuals.

Method of coding

Each day of the diary was divided into morning, afternoon and evening periods. For each period, a research assistant coded all social interactions according to how they were made (phone, letter, in person), where they took place (participant's home or elsewhere), the identity of and relationship to the person(s) involved and the reason for contact. Activities in which social interactions are possible or implied (e.g., going to the bank or shopping) but for which interaction was not specifically described by the person were excluded. Interactions with more than one person were coded as one interaction for each type of relationship involved. Thus, if the person had dinner with two neighbors, this would be counted as one interaction; if the person had dinner with family and friends, this would be counted as two. The coding was checked by a second rater; any disagreements were resolved through negotiation with the author. The author and the assistant then developed a set of categories of types of interaction: *Casual* (Unplanned, informal; contact "in passing," "drop-in," "over-the-fence," "passing the time of day"); *Planned* (More formal or extended interaction; contact that is planned or centered on a particular activity (e.g., a meal and a game of cards, a luncheon)); *Spousal* (Interaction between spouses that is not associated with a particular social event or activity being done together); *Visiting* (Visiting people in a hospital or other institution); *Assistance* (Interaction for the purpose of giving or receiving help); *Business* (Interaction for purposes that are primarily practical, for example, exchanging goods or information, accomplishing a task).

Results

Table 2 presents the number of social interactions for each participant by type of contact and type of relationship. To save space, data have been collapsed across children and other family, and across friends and neighbors; data for other interactions are included only in the totals. Types of interaction are not shown where there were virtually no entries for a particular relationship.

Table 2
Social Interactions: Reports from Diaries

Participant #		1	2	4	5	6	7	8	9	11	12	13	14	15
# of days		37	34	31	38	27	36	16	22	30	30	33	29	35
Spouse	Spousal	2	6	NA	6	NA	NA	19	2	18	14	NA	NA	—
	Planned	4	—	—	—	—	—	—	1	1	—	—	—	—
	Assist	8	2	—	6	—	—	—	6	—	5	—	—	4
	Bus	—	2	—	—	—	—	—	—	—	24	—	—	—
Total		14	10	—	12	—	—	19	9	19	43	—	—	4
Family	Cas	11	1	4	18	4	3	9	—	—	7	24	17	9
	Planned	9	14	9	9	4	7	3	2	—	1	3	10	5
	Assist	13	—	3	2	4	10	3	4	—	—	10	8	3
Total		33	15	16	29	12	20	15	6	—	8	37	35	17
Friends[a]	Cas	2	11	4	12	9	1	13	2	8	12	33	16	—
	Planned	11	15	4	2	—	5	4	—	4	12	3	11	—
	Visit	16	—	—	—	2	—	—	2	—	5	2	—	—
	Assist	1	2	—	2	1	—	1	—	3	18	7	4	—
	Bus	1	—	—	—	—	—	5	—	—	1	—	—	—
Total		31	28	8	16	12	6	23	4	15	48	45	31	—
All: Total[b, c]		96	75	41	59	37	38	79	23	38	119	122	115	29
Average/day		2.6	2.2	1.3	1.6	1.4	1.1	4.9	1.0	1.3	4.0	3.7	4.0	.8
% Family[c]/Total		49	33	39	69	38	53	43	65	50	43	30	30	72
Average/day[d]		2.2	1.9	1.3	1.2	1.4	1.1	3.8	.6	.6	2.5	3.7	4.0	.7
% Family[d]/Total		34	20	39	49	38	53	19	26	0	7	30	30	59

[a]Includes neighbors
[b]Includes all interactions (spouse, family, friends and others)
[c]Includes spousal category
[d]Excludes interactions with spouse

We should note that these results represent what participants chose to report and not necessarily an accurate reconstruction of events. Further, omissions may reflect not only a participant's view that an interaction is not important to report, but also other factors, for example, how tired the participant was when making the report. I would therefore emphasize patterns rather than the absolute values of the counts. Overall, however, the counts are roughly consistent with other information provided by the participants. For example, Helen said that people might not think that she was lonely because she "sees lots of people every day."

I will not discuss the patterns that readers can see readily for themselves in Table 2, for example, the variation in types of interaction across partici-pants. Rather, I comment briefly on the nature of interactions for each type of relationship. In general, interactions with family members seem most likely to be casual and least likely to involve assistance. The data not reported in the table suggest that overall contacts, casual contacts and contacts involving assistance are relatively less frequent with children than with other family members, whereas planned contacts are slightly more frequent with children. (But there are fewer children than other family members, and they tend to live further away.) As indicated by the percentages shown in Table 2, interac-tions with family constitute a substantial proportion of all interactions for many of the participants.

Interaction with friends seems for most participants to be primarily cas-ual, and then planned, along with a few contacts involving assistance. The emphasis on casual contacts reflects the small size of the communities in which most participants live and the considerable overlap between friends and neighbors. Interactions with friends are approximately as frequent as interactions with family members, but are more likely to be casual and less likely to involve assistance.

The data for interactions with people other than friends or family mem-bers (not reported separately in the table) suggest that these interactions are only slightly less frequent than interactions with family or friends. Approxi-mately 40 percent of these contacts are casual, with planned, assistance and business contacts each accounting for approximately 20 percent of the inter-actions of the total sample.

Social Relationships

Participants completed a number of structured and open-ended tasks from which it is possible to construct a variety of assessments of their views of relationships. I consider first the various ratings of relationships and then discuss some of the findings from the qualitative analysis of all of the data.

Ratings of Satisfaction and Support

METHOD

First, on the Life-Satisfaction Questionnaire, participants were asked to select a scale value from 1 ("terrible") to 7 ("delightful") to describe their level of satisfaction with their relationships with each of spouse, family and friends. Second, participants were asked to generate a list of the people who were most important to them. Participants were then asked to rate each person listed on five categories of social support (financial/material, emotional, companionship, information and counseling) on a scale from 1 (little or no support) to 5 (a great deal of support).

Third, participants completed the Schmidt and Sermat (1983) Differential Loneliness Scale.[1] The scale consists of fifty-nine statements about relationships (e.g., "Members of my family give me the kind of support that I need") and is intended to yield subscores describing dissatisfaction with each of four types of relationships (romantic, family, friends and community) as well as an overall score. I shall take the DLS scores as indicating dissatisfaction and the scores on the Life Satisfaction Questionnaire as indicating satisfaction. Fourth, participants completed the UCLA Loneliness Questionnaire (Russell, Peplau, & Cutrona, 1980). This scale consists of twenty items that address general feelings about social relationships (e.g., "I feel left out").

RESULTS

Table 3 presents the scores from each of the above measures for each type of relationship for each participant, collapsed across categories of support. As in Table 2, scores are not reported for "other" relationships, except for the DLS score for Community. The table also reports the number of people in the categories of family and friends who were listed by participants as important.

Table 3
Ratings of Relationships: Satisfaction and Support

Participant #															
	1	2	3	4	5	6	7	8	9	10	11	12	13	14	15
Spouse															
Sat	7	7	NA	NA	5	NA	NA	5	5	6	5	5	NA	NA	6

Table 3—concluded
Ratings of Relationships: Satisfaction and Support

Participant #

	1	2	3	4	5	6	7	8	9	10	11	12	13	14	15
AS	5	4	NA	NA	3.2	NA	NA	3	4.2	3.8	4.4	4.4	NA	NA	3.8
DLS	1	1	NA	NA	4	NA	NA	4	3	3	6	1	NA	NA	2
Fam(n)	11	11	3	14	13	7	6	18	8	2	3	21	6	9	11
Sat	7	7	7	6	5	4	7	7	4	5	4	5	6	6	5
AS	3.5	2.1	4.5	2.9	3	3.3	3.6	3.3	4.2	2	3.4	4.4	3.3	2.7	2.9
DLS	1	0	1	0	3	8	0	0	5	2	3	0	1	0	0
Fds(n)	3	5	6	4	0	3	3	3	2	7	2	5	1	1	0
Sat	6	7	4	5	4	5	6	4	5	6	4	6	6	4	5
AS	2.5	2.1	3.2	2.9	NA	2.6	3.7	3.7	4.2	1.3	4.1	4.6	3.6	2.6	NA
DLS	1	0	2	0	1	6	0	8	3	5	5	0	0	8	1

Community

	1	2	3	4	5	6	7	8	9	10	11	12	13	14	15
DLS	0	2	6	1	4	5	0	8	8	8	5	2	2	5	1

All Relationships

	1	2	3	4	5	6	7	8	9	10	11	12	13	14	15
AS	3.1	2.2	3.6	2.9	3	3.2	3.6	3.4	4.2	1.6	3.8	4.3	3.3	2.8	3.1
TDLS	3	3	9	1	12	19	0	20	19	18	19	3	3	13	4
UCLA	0	0	4	1	3	7	0	17	12	3	8	0	0	15	1

Note: Sat = Satisfaction (7 = High); NA = Not Applicable; AS = Average Support (5 = High Support); DLS = Differential Loneliness Scale (High scores = High dissatisfaction; All scales 15 items except Friends (14)); TDLS = Total DLS/59; UCLA = UCLA Loneliness Scale/20 (High Scores = High Loneliness); Footnotes = number of items missing (NA).

I comment only briefly on participants' relationships as revealed by the scores; these are discussed further in the next section. In general, the ratings of satisfaction could be described as relatively positive for all relationships. The lowest rating given is "4," indicating a "mixed" judgment. There are various criteria that one could employ to assess scores on the Differential Loneliness Scale and the UCLA Loneliness Scale, although none are very satisfactory. For example, we can consider how many participants score above the mid-point. On the DLS, only one participant (Flora) answered more than half of the applicable items in the direction of dissatisfaction. On the UCLA scale, three participants scored higher than 10 out of 20. The average score on the UCLA scale using the original scoring procedure is 41.5, which indicates that the sample is not particularly lonely.

The ratings for support are also in general fairly high, in that most are above the mid-point of the scale. As I discuss below, lower ratings of support do not necessarily indicate dissatisfaction with a relationship. In any case, there does appear to be some consistency in the various ratings of satisfaction and feelings about relationships, although it also appears that some participants can be somewhat dissatisfied, but not particularly lonely.

The scores for the different relationships reflect these overall patterns. The most positive scores are for spouse, as one would expect on the grounds of the importance of this relationship, and the associated social desirability of evaluating it positively. The scores for satisfaction with family are almost as high as for spouse, although the scores for support appear to be somewhat less positive.

Finally, the scores for friends appear to be only slightly less positive than those for family, most likely because of the nature of these friends. In most instances, the number of friends is far fewer than the number on which the data in Table 2 are based. This reflects the tendency of participants to describe neighbors and others as friends for the purpose of the diary, but not to include them on the list. Based on other information provided by participants, it seems most appropriate to describe the friends included on the lists and in Table 3 as "close" friends.

Qualitative Analysis: Case Studies

The scores on the various scales do reveal some general characteristics and patterns of relationships for the sample as a whole, but this information is relatively limited and perhaps superficial. We need to examine what is revealed by combinations of scores and more importantly, to consider how they can be elaborated by information from other sources.

METHOD

There are several such sources in the present study in addition to the diary. First, participants completed a Biographical Information Questionnaire and a Lifeline. The questionnaire covered basic demographic and biographic information as well as participants' identification of the most important and satisfying events in their lives. For the Lifeline, participants were given a graph with age on the abscissa, marked in ten-year periods, and "good times," "bad times" on the top and bottom of the ordinate respectively. They were asked to draw a line that would indicate how they viewed their life over the years, labeling the high and low points.

Participants were also asked to complete Kelly's Repertory Grid for the ten most important members of their network (see Collett, 1979). Briefly, the participant is asked to think about three members of the network and to describe how two of them are like each other and different from the third. The participant then considers another combination of three members, generates a second dimension, and so on until he or she has generated as many dimensions as there are network members. The participant then rates each member on each dimension, using a scale from one to five. In this way, participants construct individualized measures that represent the particular characteristics of individuals and relationships that are important to them. Finally, participants were interviewed extensively concerning their experiences of loneliness both in the past and in the present.

In view of the multiple sources of information and the different types of information involved, the most useful way to assess relationships is to consider all of the information for one participant at a time. However, the presentation of such an analysis requires more space than is available. I will therefore discuss only three cases, selected to represent positive and negative relationships as well as different sexes and marital statuses. This should be sufficient to identify the most important issues and to serve as an illustration of how this analysis was done.

RESULTS: THREE CASES

Bill has very positive views toward all of his relationships, as indicated by scores on satisfaction, dissatisfaction and loneliness, but the ratings for support are much lower. However, these low ratings seem to represent Bill's general attitudes about relationships rather than a contradiction of the positive scores. For example, his ratings of support from his wife are lower than those given by some other participants, but all of the information indicates that this relationship is both very satisfying and very important to him. He described his wife as "an outstanding partner" and said that she "loves everyone and is loved by everyone"; meeting her was the most important event in his life. But his attitudes seem to reflect an individualistic rather than relational orientation, so that his needs or expectations of relationships, and therefore of support, may be relatively low. For example, he described himself as "by nature a loner." On the Repertory Grid, he identified only one negative characteristic, but also mentioned several characteristics that are not particularly relevant to relationships (e.g., industrious, inventive, organized). His ratings were also relatively more negative than those given by other "satisfied" participants. This does not imply that relationships are not important, but that they are not to be "taken for granted." For example, he stated that, "Family relationships are very important and must be worked at." In general, Bill is highly reflective about relationships, a characteristic that was revealed in several sources, particularly the loneliness interview and the diary.

The ratings given by *Flora* for satisfaction, dissatisfaction and loneliness are in general relatively negative, and reflect in part her recent widowhood. Her ratings of support from family members are relatively high, while the ratings of satisfaction and dissatisfaction for family are somewhat lower. For friends, however, ratings of support are lower than for family, and ratings of satisfaction and dissatisfaction more positive and somewhat more consistent. Other information seems to support the idea of higher expectations and greater disappointment with respect to family members compared to friends. For example, her ratings for satisfaction with family are not reflected in the Repertory Grid, which consists entirely of positive characteristics and of high ratings for the seven family members included. And she comments in the loneliness interview, "I miss my daughter not coming around very much."

Relationships are a very important focus as well as a problem for *Helen*. Her ratings of satisfaction for family are very positive, although they are not matched by the ratings for informational and counseling support. But her ratings on these forms of support are low for all relationships, and are probably more indicative of her perception that "others think she is strong and confide in her" than of dissatisfaction. She feels strongly that family contacts are important and that she should support and help her relatives. Her view of her relationship with her husband is very much colored by his illness, which requires that she spend a great deal of time and energy attending to his needs, and also creates difficulties for her because of his erratic behavior. Her frustrations with the current situation are exacerbated because it contrasts strongly with the positive and satisfying relationship she reports for the time up until her husband's illness. She identified marriage as the most important event in her life.

The least positive relationships for Helen are those with friends and community; her ratings on the DLS for both friends and community indicate high dissatisfaction, and she endorsed almost all of the items on the UCLA measure of loneliness. However, her global rating of satisfaction for friends is mixed rather than negative, and the overall rating of support from friends is above the mid-point. The information from other sources indicates that although she desires better relationships, she does not believe that it is possible to achieve them. She does have friends, but she also reports a history of disruptions in relations with friends. She describes herself as a very lonely person, who is not able to communicate with people easily. She is particularly dissatisfied with her relationships to the larger community; she feels isolated and "out of step" with others. In virtually all of the material, she presents herself as reflective, sensitive and concerned about her relationships.

Further issues concerning relationships are considered below. At this point, I would note only that although it is quite possible to find consistency among the various indicators of relationships, it would be misleading in most instances to focus on any one measure. Such consistency as there is appears only when sufficient material is considered, and even where an indicator is consistent with other information, its meaning is not readily apparent if it is viewed in isolation.

Relationships, Interactions and Life as a Whole

How does the nature of people's relationships relate to their interactions and to their life as a whole? Again, the analysis required to address this question involves the consideration of all of the information available for each participant, including much that cannot be presented here (e.g., participants' ratings of self-esteem and happiness). I have space only for a brief further consideration and contrast of the three cases discussed above.

Bill's high ratings of satisfaction with relationships are consistent with the generally high ratings he gave to other domains, particularly life as a whole and happiness. In contrast, Flora and Helen both gave low ratings for life as a whole and happiness, ratings that are consistent with the negative views expressed in at least some of the ratings of relationships (satisfaction, dissatisfaction and loneliness). In particular, Helen's low rating for self-esteem is reflected in her UCLA score, as well as in the numerous comments she made about her own characteristics and abilities.

How well do the participants' ratings of their relationships correspond to the kinds and numbers of interactions they have with family and friends? We must keep in mind that the numbers are only suggestive and that we are not dealing with statistical correlations. But there do seem to be patterns that would help to explain participants' expressed satisfaction or dissatisfaction, particularly in conjunction with the other information we have. For example, Bill and Helen both express high satisfaction with family relationships, whereas Flora views these as mixed. Bill and Helen have, on average, more contact with their children than does Flora. However, Flora has more contact with other family members than does Bill, so that in terms of total family contact, the averages per day are about the same for each of them.

But the numbers do not reveal one critical type of information, namely the location of family members. Both children and siblings live a minimum of two hours' drive from Bill and Helen. In contrast, Flora has one daughter, two brothers and two sisters (both institutionalized), all of whom live in the same town of approximately 3000. From the interview material, it is clear that her relatively infrequent contact with family members is a major aspect of the dissatisfaction she experiences with family relationships, particularly because she is recently widowed and living alone. It appears likely that this dissatisfaction is a considerable contribution to her general unhappiness and dissatisfaction, because almost 40 percent of the contacts she has are with family members. Similarly, Helen's general dissatisfaction and unhappiness reflect that 57 percent of her interactions are with people with whom she does not have particularly positive relationships. In contrast to Flora, however, these people are not family members.

The average number of interactions participants have per day is not clearly connected either to satisfaction in general or to their feelings about particular relationships. It certainly seems to be unrelated to loneliness as expressed by UCLA scores or directly by participants. We do not know how long these interactions are. I would suggest however, that except at the extremes (i.e., very brief or very long interactions, neither of which is involved here), time per se is not as important as the fact that an episode involving interaction has occurred. In any case, it may be the type of contact that is particularly critical. Bill has on average approximately twice as many "planned" interactions as Helen, and approximately four times as many as Flora. Perhaps more importantly, over 52 percent of all of Bill's interactions fall into this category; the corresponding percentages for Flora and Helen are nineteen and fifteen respectively.

There are clearly sources of the general satisfaction or dissatisfaction of these three participants other than their relationships. For example, Flora has fewer resources than Helen with respect to education and income, and Flora's relative dissatisfaction with housing reflects its relatively poor objective characteristics. But Helen also expresses relatively low satisfaction with housing that appears unrelated to its objective characteristics; other information suggests that this low rating reflects her feelings about the community as much as about the housing itself.

These brief analyses suggest that our understanding of older persons' satisfaction and happiness would increase substantially if we can gain sufficient information not only about relationships and social interactions, but also about the ways in which these are interwoven. Before offering some specific suggestions for how this might be done, I summarize the findings of the present study, based on all of the analyses that have been conducted.

Summary of Findings

The Importance of Relationships

It seems reasonable to conclude that even for those participants who are most unhappy in general or whose relationships are least satisfactory, the overall picture of relationships is fairly positive. There is no one, for example, who is particularly isolated in the sense of having very few relationships, nor is there anyone whose relationships could be described as largely negative. Much the same could be said of social interactions; that is, there is no one who is highly restricted in terms of contacts, or who does not have at least some positive interactions. For this sample, there are no noticeable signs of disengagement, either in terms of activity, or in terms of relationships.

I believe that there is no question about the importance of relationships and interactions with family members, particularly if we consider the participants' own statements on the matter. In general, these relationships are relatively positive and interactions with family members constitute a fair proportion of overall contact for most participants. With respect to support, there is a range of scores, which is to be expected because the scores are averages across all family members and because some forms of support (e.g., companionship) would not be available from family members with whom a person may have infrequent contact. But the scores on emotional support are above the midpoint for all but two participants. Relationships with family members are not sufficient however. All participants discussed the importance to them of having relationships with friends; this was not necessarily a reflection of dissatisfaction with family relationships or of the state of their friendships.

Sources of Satisfaction and Dissatisfaction with Relationships

What factors seem to underlie participants' judgments that their relationships are satisfying or dissatisfying? It has been suggested that satisfaction depends on expectations (e.g., Michalos, 1982), but there has been little work on the precise content of those expectations. The present study was not focused on this particular question, but the results do give us some suggestions about what might be important. They also emphasize that there is likely to be a great deal of variety across individuals concerning what contributes to satisfaction with relationships. Expectations about particular relationships will obviously depend upon the other relationships that a person has; for example, several participants noted that they did not expect their friends to listen to their problems because they talked to their children. But expectations about particular relationships also reflect general orientations to the possibility of relationships. For example, for some people, the "default" state is individualism and separation from others; one has to "work at" relationships, and loneliness is always a possibility. For others, however, the "default" state is relational. It is "natural" to be connected to others. Loneliness is almost inconceivable—or is thought of in other terms, for example, as boredom, rather than as the lack of relations with others. Further, these different orientations seem to be related to whether or not discontent with relationships is experienced as loneliness (cf. Wood, 1983).

Although relatively little attention has been given to expectations about relationships, there has been a good deal of work on the provisions of relationships. I cannot address that literature here. I would simply note that there appears to be no simple relationship between perceptions of various forms of support and participants' views of the quality of their relationships, whether we consider the ratings on the support scales, or the views expressed by participants in other sources. There is more to these discrepancies than simple variations in expectations or needs, although we have seen that these may play a role, for example, in connection with the value a person places on "independence." It is also important to emphasize the role of relationships in providing opportunities for giving as well as receiving. This aspect of relationships seems central for some of the participants in the present study.

The Role of Interactions

How are interactions related to the nature and quality of relationships? Again, there appear to be no simple relationships between interactions and satisfaction with relationships, such that, for example, high satisfaction is clearly associated with frequent interactions or with interactions of a particular type. Nor is there evidence that satisfaction and happiness in general are related in any simple fashion to frequency or type of interactions. Nonetheless, frequency of contact does appear to be important. The use of seemingly superficial and quantitative indices such as frequency of contact has often been criticized. However, I believe that the real issue is that such indices are less meaningful if they are considered in isolation, that is, without also attending to the nature of the contact and the type of relationship involved. For example, it is surely difficult to sustain the notion that one has satisfactory relationships with one's family when contact is infrequent, and one can generate no adequate excuses (e.g., geographic separation). But when contact is frequent, it may not have to be more than casual, at least not all of the time.

Discussion

As I noted in the introduction, I believe that the above findings support two arguments that can be made with respect to research on social relationships among the elderly. I consider first the distinction between interactions and relationships, illustrated by a comparison of my findings with those in the literature. I then discuss the methodological issues.

Interactions versus Relationships

Implicit in the approach taken in the present research has been a distinction between "interactions" and "relationships." What I would like to suggest is that we need first to sharpen this distinction, and then to attend to each of these both separately and together, both conceptually and methodologically. By interactions, I refer specifically to social action (behavior) that occurs in real time and real space, and that unfolds in specific social episodes (e.g., a meeting) in specific settings (e.g., a church basement). Interactions are concrete and contextualized. In contrast, relationships are concepts— cognitions about other persons and about the interactions one has with them. Relationships are abstract and decontextualized categories. We can view relationships as "emergent properties" or representations of interactions; in turn, we can view interactions as manifestations of relationships.

This is not to suggest that interactions are necessarily "accurate" manifestations of concepts of relationship, nor that such concepts are accurate representations of interactions. Our concepts of relationship may well represent other sorts of experience, and our interactions will reflect many other factors. But there is a reciprocal and evolving interplay between the two that must be considered if we are to understand either. Further, it is important to note that relationships are an abstract concept not only for researchers, but also for participants. This point has important implications both theoretically and methodologically. I consider the methodological implications below after discussing the distinction in the context of previous research.

COMPARISON WITH PREVIOUS RESEARCH

How do my findings compare with those in the literature? The comparison is difficult because there are no similar studies; other research has been largely quantitative, has used different indices, etc. But it is worthwhile to attempt the comparison because it raises important conceptual and methodological issues. There are several studies that suggest that relationships with friends are more important than relationships with family (e.g., Arling, 1976; Lee & Ishii-Kuntz, 1987; Wood & Robertson, 1978). My findings cannot address this issue directly, although I would say that both types of relationship are important in different ways depending on the individuals involved. There are also a number of studies that conclude that family relations are not related to well-being (e.g., Glenn & McClanahan, 1981; Lee & Ihinger-Tallman, 1980; Lee & Ishii-Kuntz, 1987). Although I have identified relationships with family as important, this is not quite the same as asserting that positive relationships with family are correlated with well-being. Nonetheless, it seems to me that my results are different from those reported in a number of previous studies. Why the differences? I believe that they involve more than the matter of sampling (my sample is clearly unrepresentative) or the level of analysis (group vs. individual results); they also reflect the distinction between interactions and relationships. I will focus on the study by Lee and Ishii-Kuntz to elaborate this point. It is a recent and sufficiently representative example of a number of previous studies; it also includes an examination of loneliness.

It appears to me that those studies finding family relations to be unconnected to well-being have mistaken assessments of interactions for assessments of relationships. In the Lee and Ishii-Kuntz study, for example, "Relations . . . were measured in terms of frequency of interaction" (p. 478) (primarily by "frequency of visiting"). While the authors state that they are assessing interactions, their conclusions are drawn in terms of relationships. What is particulary interesting about this study is that Lee and Ishii-Kuntz postulate that the effects of interaction on well-being are mediated by loneliness. Their analysis shows that interactions with friends are a strong predictor of morale, but family interactions have no effect. Loneliness is also a strong predictor of morale; when it is included in a path model, it suppresses the direct effect on morale of interactions with friends, although this effect is still significant. I would argue that in assessing loneliness, Lee and Ishii-Kuntz have in fact assessed relationships. And in demonstrating that loneliness has an effect on morale, they have thereby demonstrated the importance of relationships for well-being. In my data, satisfaction with relationships (as assessed by ratings of satisfaction, scores on the Differential Loneliness scale and qualitative indicators) is also related to well-being.[2]

Methodological Issues

I believe that we require a multimethodological research strategy that combines both quantitative and qualitative approaches if we are to address such questions as the meaning of frequency of interaction in a participant's life. It is reasonable to use numbers where the numbers are meaningful (counting the countable) and to examine relationships between numbers, as long as we do not mistake the patterns for the phenomenon of interest, nor delude ourselves into thinking that we have thus generated explanations.

Methodologically, we require different strategies to study relationships and interaction. Because they involve abstractions, relationships are particularly difficult to address directly. It seems to me that in asking participants to rate their relationships on a scale or to agree or disagree with a set of statements about relationships, we are asking them to do too much—in effect, we are asking them to do our work. We should rather be asking them to do what they do in everyday life; that is, to talk. But we cannot simply ask them to talk about relationships—that is likely to generate data as banal and superficial as those obtained by the use of standard scales. Rather, we need to conduct extensive in-depth interviews about concrete incidents and episodes if we wish to obtain accurate and useful information about their abstract concepts of relationship and support. Such self-reports are essential to an enterprise that stresses, or should stress, meaning.

How can we obtain information about interactions in our attempt to pen-
etrate beneath the abstractions of relationships? In some respects, this is an
easier task than assessing relationships, although it is fraught with practical
problems. The ideal strategy would be observation, although this is costly in
terms of both time and money, and not always possible. A compromise solution might be "self-observation," that is, systematic self-report done (more or
less) in real time rather than retrospectively. Diaries and modified time-budget
methods recommend themselves.

There are a number of other methodological problems that should be
addressed, although I cannot do so here. I would note, however, that many of
the methodological issues that we face in work of this sort also involve substantive issues. For example, it is clear that the sample in the present study (more
specifically, the participants for whom there is complete information) is biased
in favor of participants who are willing and able to talk to the researcher
about personal issues. But linguistic capacity and willingness to enter conversations are not only requirements for participants in research, they are
also important social skills for establishing and maintaining relationships.

In conclusion, I believe that the findings from the present research will
make a substantive contribution to the study of social relationships. More
importantly, I hope that they will make the point that in order to improve our
understanding, we require both a multimethod approach that includes
detailed, qualitative description, and careful attention to conceptual distinctions. If we are to do justice to the complexity and richness of people's lives,
we can neither think about them in simple one-dimensional terms, nor study
them in simple, uni-methodological ways.

The research described in this chapter was supported by grants from the
Social Sciences and Humanities Research Council of Canada and the Research
Advisory Board, University of Guelph. I acknowledge gratefully the comments
and suggestions of Rolf Kroger and the assistance of Julia Johnson.

Notes

1. The version used was developed specifically for older adults; it overlaps considerably with the published scale.

2. This reconceptualization requires further elaboration. I cannot do so here, but
would make one theoretical point. Several authors (e.g., Lee & Ihinger-Tallman, 1980)
have suggested that friends have a (presumed) stronger effect on well-being than does
family because family relations are ascribed, whereas relations with friends are achieved.
Social identity theory (see Wood, 1983) also distinguishes between family relations as
ascribed and relations with friends as achieved. But in this view, the fact that family

relations are not "chosen" does not mean that they are less important; rather, the consequences of satisfactory relationships with family are different from those of satisfactory relationships with friends. In essence, satisfactory relationships with family are not a positive contribution to identity, but unsatisfactory relationships are a negative contribution. In contrast, satisfactory relationships with friends are a positive contribution, whereas unsatisfactory relationships are not a negative contribution.

Ethogeny (Harré, 1980) provides a useful approach for thinking more generally about social interactions and relationships. The ethogenic framework for conceptualizing social episodes includes two parts: the phenomenology of action generation, and the analysis of episodes of social action. We can think of these two parts in terms of competence (knowledge), and performance (behavior), and incorporate within them the notions of relationships and interaction respectively. The phenomenology of action generation refers to a cognitive matrix that includes definitions of situations, personas, judges and rules. Relationships can be conceptualized as the intersection between personas and judges (self and others), and "rules" can incorporate ideas concerning expectations about relationships. The ethogenic framework itself does not specify content, that is, particular relationships and particular rules. These can be supplied however from other substantive theories about relationships such as social identity theory.

References

Arling, G. (1976). The elderly widow and her family, neighbors and friends. *Journal of Marriage and the Family* 38: 757-768.

Collett, P. (1979). The repertory grid in psychological research. In G. P. Ginsburg (ed.) *Emerging strategies in social psychological research* (pp. 225-252). New York: Wiley.

Glenn, N. and S. McClanahan. (1981). The effects of offspring on the psychological well-being of older adults. *Journal of Marriage and the Family* 43: 409-421.

Harré, R. (1980). *Social being.* Totawa, NJ: Littlefield Adams.

Lee, G. R. and M. Ihinger-Tallman. (1980). Sibling interaction and morale: The effects of family relations on older people. *Research on Aging* 2: 367-391.

Lee, G. R. and M. Ishii-Kuntz. (1987). Social interaction, loneliness, and emotional well-being among the elderly. *Research on Aging* 9: 459-482.

Michalos, A. C. (1982). The satisfaction and happiness of some senior citizens in rural Ontario. *Social Indicators Research* 11: 1-30.

Russell, D., L. A. Peplau and C. E. Cutrona. (1980). The revised UCLA Loneliness Scale: Concurrent and discriminant validity evidence. *Journal of Personality and Social Psychology* 39: 472-480.

Schmidt, N. and V. Sermat. (1983). Measuring loneliness in different relationships. *Journal of Personality and Social Psychology* 44: 1038-1047.

Wood, L. A. (1981, November). *Loneliness and life satisfaction among the rural eld-erly*. Paper presented at the joint meeting of the Canadian Association on Ger-ontology and the Gerontological Society of America, Toronto.

Wood, L. A. (1983). Loneliness and social identity. In T. R. Sarbin and K. E. Scheibe (eds.) *Studies in social identity* (pp. 51-70). New York: Praeger.

Wood, L. A. (1985). *Loneliness: A lifespan perspective*. Unpublished manuscript, Uni-versity of Guelph, Gerontology Research Center..

Wood, L. A. and J. Johnson. (1989). Life satisfaction among the rural elderly: What do the numbers mean? *Social Indicators Research* 21:59-88.

Wood, V. and J. Robertson. (1978). Friendship and kinship interaction: Differential effect on the morale of the elderly. *Journal of Marriage and the Family* 40: 367-373.

Commentary

Chapter 13

Gerontology with a Human Face

HARRY R. MOODY

A book about aging and the human sciences is more than a summary of research findings. It is also an announcement of an agenda for the future and, finally, a philosophical statement about the meaning of aging and about the appropriate methods of inquiry in the social sciences. The human sciences in gerontology, as the articles in this book confirm, exhibit a wide diversity of technique and topics of interest. More than anything else, the human sciences represent a new terrain or, better, a different kind of map-making that allows us to chart the terrain we see arounds us, a terrain so new and yet so familiar.

Reconstructing the Map of Knowledge

What is it that the new map discloses to us? Some points on the map are familiar. Long established landmarks of social gerontology, such as life satisfaction or family relationships in long-term care, are still present. But there are also some obscure features on the landscape—the tangled underbrush of life histories and the distant peaks of late-life creativity. On these distant summits the map becomes more tentative in its marking of the terrain. Like other investigators and map makers, those who fashion a qualitative map of human aging will not finish their work in a single generation. The map of knowledge is the product of patient labor and, above all, a passionate commitment to leave no part of the terrain unexplored. It is, in short, a commitment to the fullness of truth.

It is this last point—the uncovering of a recognizable but unmapped terrain—that gives human science methods in the field of aging their greatest claim to attention. After all, no subject is more ordinary, more familiar to laypeople and to gerontologists alike than the experience of growing old. The insights of the human sciences into aging will, of necessity, have a familiar resonance to them. Indeed, perhaps the greatest compliment that can be

given to the application of the human sciences to the study of aging is what
W. D. Ross once said about the metaphysics of Aristotle: that it gives us "daz-
zling glimpses into the obvious."

One of the strengths of qualitative research is the ability to look behind
quantitative data to discern differences lost according to commonly used methods of data reduction (Reinharz and Bowles, 1987). Where quantification
offers the power of abstraction, qualitative data returns us to "the things themselves" and to realities that elude conventional scales and instruments. This
point must constantly be rediscovered and reemphasized in every field of
human endeavor, if only because of the enormous persuasiveness and allure
of quantified data today. One must begin by saying out loud what we all
understand about status among both academics and the public at large. Quantitative formulations carry prestige and an aura of credibility among the naïve
and methodologically unsophisticated. But there is a dark side here as well.
Quantitative methods also involve a greater possibility of domination because they embody an instrumental-manipulative attitude toward the object
of inquiry.

Domination is made easier because of a legitimation conferred by quantitative methods of all kinds. Once the numbers have spoken, we cease to
question, even cease to think. Mystification by numbers is by now a commonplace, but it is no less insidious in the social sciences than in politics or in
practical life (Andreski, 1972). Yet the power of domination is far from complete. Practical people know all too well that they can't trust to numbers alone
when important decisions are at stake. For example, the skilled investor in
the stock market knows that quantitative data supplied by accountants must
be supplemented by qualitative understanding of management style and patterns of corporate behavior. These intuitions are not easily captured by finan-
cial data alone. But an amateur investor will be led astray by the numbers
alone because the amateur lacks any qualitative framework for interpreting
what those numbers mean. Indeed, it is precisely qualitative,and not naïve
quantitative, thinking that is the hallmark of the hard-headed pragmatist who
can look beneath the surface of reported data.

We need to apply these lessons to thinking about the place of qualitative
methods in the field of aging. The most obvious temptation comes from the
fact that the most widespread index of aging is quantitative: the chronological measure of years. In her article in this volume Susan Eisenhandler shows
how the purely quantitative qpproach to aging is inadequate, how age is "more
than counting years." Critical life events, above all chronic illness or a change
in health status, can interrupt ordinary patterns of interaction and thus produce discontinuity in both social time and individual identity. Typically it is
the experience of disease, either in oneself or in one's spouse, which prompts
identification with "old age." In other words, subjectively experienced health

status, not quantified measures, becomes a proxy for old age. Without this qualitative dimension, the quantitative measure of years is misleading.

Gerontologists of course have gone much further in extending the dominion of quantitative thinking, above all by devising measurement instruments. It is one of the tasks of qualitative gerontology to supplement, and at times to critique, the limitations of those instruments. For example, Thomas and Chambers, in their cross-cultural samples, show how identical life-satisfaction scores mask profound differences that can be entirely lost without phenomenological analysis. Going further in this direction, Robert Rubinstein takes issue with the fetishized and quantified notion of well-being ("life satisfaction") so prevalent in social gerontology. What we need instead, he argues, is a concept of well-being discoverable from the way informants discuss the quality of their own lives. In contrast to a categorical or "top down" approach to narratives of the self, Rubinstein wants a "bottom up" approach which works from what informants actually say in order to elucidate the variety of structures embedded in narratives. This grounded approach is not simply more textured or inductively rich. It also demonstrates certain structural features such as subjective inter-temporal comparisons and a distinction between pre-reflective and "second-order" responses to a larger pattern of meaning in life. It turns out that the meaning of well-being is, through and through, a temporal construct and that patterns of affect management are far more complex than might have been imagined.

Bias versus Objectivity

Another point of great importance for aging and the human sciences is the problem of value biases (McKee, 1982). Proponents of the human sciences sometimes feel vulnerable on just this point—as if qualitative methods must inevitably lead to distorted or biased results. But quantitative approaches, such as scales or measurements, by no means avoid value biases. On the contrary, the mystification of quantitative data may even make it more difficult to detect bias, as we have seen in the vexed history of intelligence testing. Quantification brings with it a degree of reification: a tendency for findings to take on the aura of "truth" or "fact." Ordinary critiques of validity and reliability do not entirely eliminate this problem. As Thomas and Chambers argue, in cross-cultural research on a value-laden issue like "successful aging," it is perhaps impossible to avoid imposing values.

As all the articles in this volume richly illustrate, the methods of human sciences stress the importance of *interpretation* in social life—a motif of longstanding importance for symbolic interactionism in sociology. In effect, this stress on interpretation marks a decisive epistemological shift away from an objectivist or instrumental orientation in favor of a more richly varied concept of human action. We move away from a concept of pure objects of understanding and toward a concept of praxis in the human world. This move is not merely a point of theoretical interest. On the contrary, it underscores one reason that qualitative research can have attraction for people beyond the academic world: namely, because of the practical payoff from research which is already amenable to practical applications of all kind. For that reason we should not underestimate the ability of qualitative research to generate *usable knowledge*: that is, findings that have practical significance precisely because they are drawn from the interpretive world of practical action in the first place (Lindblom, 1979).

The potential impact of this renewed link between knowledge and practice is recognizable in this volume in the article by Jaber Gubrium in which he considers a topic treated widely in the literature of gerontology: namely, nursing home placement. What Gubrium demonstrates is the pivotal role of interpretive concerns in answering two questions: the question of what a good nursing home is (e.g., a facility's claim to a "homelike atmosphere") and the question of when a caring household is no longer home—that is, when "it's time" to place an elderly relative in a nursing home. Both are questions of intense interest for policy and clinical practice.

Gubrium demonstrates that the response to the question "What is a good nursing home?" is far more complex than is likely to be grasped by existing measures of "quality of care." Conceptualizations about quality of care in nursing homes tend to adopt an overly rationalized, behavioristic model in defining quality. This approach in turn leads to regulation and monitoring of nursing homes that is seriously defective: for example, to exaggerate the importance of superficially countable interventions with residents while neglecting the *meaning* of these interventions to residents (Gubrium, 1975; Pearlman and Speer, 1983).

In understanding the problems of caregivers we recognize a related question largely neglected by contemporary bioethics, that of describing an equitable distribution of care-giving burdens among family members caring for an impaired relative. "Everyday" understanding of aging issues—the folklore of gerontology—recognizes how this question of equity in the distribution of burdens is fundamental to understanding family dynamics or the nursing home placement decision. But the conventional, quantitatively-oriented approach to measuring "caregiver burden" does not begin to capture these dilemmas adequately.

Still another example of practice implications from qualitative research in gerontology is found in the study of Alzheimer's Disease and the memory loss associated with that syndrome. Karl Scheibe in this volume argues that the traditional experimental study of memory systems should be complemented by the study of memory as a means of developing and sustaining personal identity. We cannot isolate the properties of individual memory from the web of social relationships in which personal identity is embedded. For example, among families of Alzheimer's patients, their own identities are affected by the gradual disappearance of memory and identity of a central figure in their lives. It is not isolated properties of individual organisms that are significant here but social transactions in which narratives are constructed or validated through human relationships. Even, as in Alzheimer's Disease, when the narrative self has eroded, something else remains, and thus the distinction between semantic and episodic memory may become important. The "self as narrative" is an important theme in a variety of disciplines which is likely to have implications in the future for clinical practice (Sarbin, 1986; Polkinghorne, 1988).

Along the same lines, Linda Wood, in her article in this volume, argues that in the literature of social gerontology today we have no satisfactory explanation or theory of relationships. On the contrary, empirical research tends to confuse discrete, quantifiable "interactions" with ongoing "relationships." A case in point is the body of research into the question of how family ties influence well-being. It turns out that a purely quantifiable approach to the number of *interactions* measures only the most superficial, and often meaningless, aspects of daily life, while ignoring the deepest ties among family members. I may see my elderly mother every week while my sister, living at a distance, sees her only several times a year. But the sheer frequency of interaction tells us virtually nothing about the relationships among the people involved. The convenience of quantitative comparison is what misleads us. This confusion between interactions and relationships not only produces inconsistent findings and incoherent accounts of the family life of old people still worse, if the purported findings are used by practitioners as a basis for action, the result could actually be harmful.

I stress the implications of human sciences research for practice because the demands of practical reasoning may turn out to be the strongest ally for qualitative methods in gerontology today. Of course both quantitative and qualitative methods lend themselves to distinctive forms of practice: in the one case, clinical or individual based, in the other case, policy or collectively based, in scope. This is not so much a difference between disciplines—say, psychology as against sociology—as it is a difference in the anticipated context of application of the knowledge gained. It is a difference in the form of practice and, above all, in the scale at which knowledge can be applied. The law-like statements in the social sciences are, almost invariably, statistical in their formation and therefore they apply to large numbers, not necessarily to individuals.

Clinicians deal with this problem by invoking "clinical judgment" and, more often than not, preferring case study approaches where the claims of clinical judgment are bolstered by qualitative methods. What I want to suggest, then, is that the rivalry between qualitative and quantitative methods is as much a struggle over practice as it is over theory and method. By debating the merits or qualitative or quantitative methods at the level of method or theory alone we neglect the pragmatic context of application or practice.

That neglect is inexcusable in a field like gerontology which has been practically-oriented since its inception, on both the medical and the social side. Along with the adoption of a qualitative or quantitative methods, there goes an implicit *action-orientation*, a covert stance toward the possible uses of knowledge in changing the world. Here theory and practice are not to be separated but rather subjected alike to critical reflection in terms of hidden interests, as Habermas has shown (Habermas, 1971; Habermas, 1974; McCarthy, 1978). It is one of the merits of the human sciences approach in gerontology that it offers us a way of making these human interests more explicit both in our discourse about research and in the methods used for inquiry. Values and strategies of action are no longer hidden but become explicitly thematized subjects of critical debate and collective deliberation.

Methodology and Relativism

How then can we achieve new methods of recovering this lost dimension of meaning in the lives of older people who are the subjects of gerontology? Can other disciplines provide methods useful for the social sciences? An increasingly influential approach in the humanities today is found in *hermeneutics* (Shapiro and Sica, 1984). As J. Gordon Harris in his article in this volume makes clear, hermeneutics involves systematic reflection on rules of interpretation and, as such, it holds a fundamental place in the human sciences. Hermeneutics grew up originally in scholary work on problems of interpreting the Bible and other scriptures. It was subsequently extended to problems raised by other texts such as legal documents and works of literature. As Harris indicates, Biblical hermeneutics brought an awareness of the multiplicity of interpretations of the same text and the need to recognize the relationship between interpreter and culture.

The hermeneutic enterprise is not confined to literary texts but extends to all acts of interpretation, including those in the human-sciences. Karol Ferguson, along with other contributors to this volume points to the importance of dealing with data derived from case studies, which offer the researcher an opportunity for subjects to become more vivid and lifelike for the reader. In transposing data from qualitative to quantitative terms, we are essentially reducing it to denumerable categories, therefore reducing its complexity to more manageable form. The case study method, by contrast, offers a way of retaining greater depth and complexity. But there is often a price to be paid. On the one side, there is the danger of abstraction through data reduction; on the other side, the danger of piling up facts which lose their meaning. Thomas and Chambers refer to the difficulty facing one who gathers qualitative data: namely, the threat of drowning in data. The hermeneutic balance lies in resisting both dangers.

The hermeneutic approach is commended by some not only because of its greater fidelity to the subject matter but also, allegedly, because of its superior ethical claims. For example, in this volume, Karl Scheibe cites the life stories collected by Eclea Bosi and praises this work as a rare example of the psychologist simply "surrendering to her material, so that the material is in no sense subject to her, but is instead invested with full human dignity." It is not unusual to ee methods of the human sciences praised as a means of recovering those human qualities that elude measurement, in contrast to the supposedly dehumanizing spirit of quantitative investigation. The contrast is well conveyed by Colaizzi's comment: "All research is either human research or dehumanizing research."

In this way of thinking, the "humanistic" dimension of qualitative research becomes not merely a matter of methodology but of ethics as well. Qualitative research is seen as a way of breaking down boundaries between subject and investigator and thus demanding, if it not inspiring, a measure of empathy in the act of research itself. Yet as Leon Rappoport (1980) observes, empathy alone is only a virtue, not a methodology. Still, he too suggests, following Meacham, that social science investigation might adopt a paradigm of *dialogue* rather than *interrogation*: that is, a process of *mutual* definition and data collection (Rabinow & Sullivan, 1979).

Both the promise and perils of this approach are illustrated by the article by Mary Gergen included in this volume. Mary Gergen offers an illustration of the "dialogic method" of social research based on the metaphor of a conversation in which both speakers and listeners play a part. She praises "mutuality" as a cardinal trait of "authentically" used dialogic methods. In her view, dialogic methods include the interpretation of performative use of language, interpretation of individual motives, and the effort to induce change among participants. These constitute, respectively, the intersubjective, participatory and emanicipatory interests of the qualitative research enterprise. The first interest aims at interdependence and mutual involvement of subjects and investigator. The second interest aims at eliminating hierarchical or authoritarian attitudes. The third interest explicitly introduces values, in contrast to positivist attachment to value-free inquiry. It is commendable here that the researcher is being quite explicit about the human interests that stand in relationship to the activity of knowledge building.

But there are also dangers worth watching for as we move down this path. The first is an element of epistemological relativism that seems to enter wherever interpretive methods gain ready acceptance (Neugarten, 1984; Collin, 1985). If social reality can be interpreted in an indeterminate number of ways, if a reality "out there" is finally just a shifting agreement or convention among observers, then what standard remains for accepting or rejecting one or another interpretation of social reality? A social constructionist framework rejects in principle the idea of what Durkheim called "social facts." This tendency toward relativism seems to lead to a gradual blurring of boundaries between fact and value, investigator and subject. Often enough, along the way there is an erosion of truth-claims in favor of social action inspired by a specific ideological agenda: Freudian, Marxist, feminist and so on. Ironically, relativism and dogmatism can coexist, as they do in modern culture generally.

I believe that the "relativistic turn" promised by interpretive and hermeneutic methods should not be accepted too quickly. It is one thing to argue, with post-positivist philosophies of science, that empirical facts are always theory-laden or contextually defined in relation to instruments or explanatory schemes. It is quite another thing to suggest that any claim to truth—a relationship between propositions and the world—is to be relativistically de-constructed and tossed overboard (Ackermann, 1985). Conventions or social agreements about phenomena are not on the same level as revisable constructions of theory or interpretation. There may be no absolute boundary line here, as there is none between night and day when twilight comes, but anyone who fails to recognize the difference is likely to stumble into a relativistic night in which all cows are black (Bernstein, 1983).

Certainly, social science has seen enough of self-fulfilling prophecies and interventions by investigators who, wittingly or unwittingly, produce the effects that they want to see. And these results are obviously not always an exercise in emancipatory growth; they may simply be cases of self-delusion. An easygoing relativism ("All facts are socially constructed") blinds us to the difference. Dialogic study can end up undermining the concept of objective knowledge. If human sciences in the study of aging becomes simply a covert code word for "action research" or ideologically motivated inquiry, then we run serious risk for the future of this style of research. The danger, unfortunately, is present today in those varieties of the humanities and the social sciences which have eagerly and openly embraced a political or value-based agenda. The result is dogmatism and intolerance of opposing viewpoints.

Still, what Gergen and other proponents of dialogic methods remind us is that other seemingly objective, quantitative methods all too often contain deep value commitments and biases of their own. Conventional social science is not without ideology of its own, but the ideological content is obscured and mystified by the superficial rigor of quantitative methods. If dialogic methods can break down that mystification and introduce lived experience into the research enterprise, then the risk of dialogue, and of other methods where the investigator relinquishes control, may prove well worth it (Fischer, 1987).

Human Development as an Emancipatory Interest

Let me conclude with some comments about the role of the human sciences as a new source for understanding what we think of as human development itself, a subject discussed in more detail elsewhere (Moody, 1988). In his essay in this volume Harry Berman argues that "For human science researchers interested in the study of the life course, interpretations should serve not only to clarify the text in its own terms, but should also show how the text relates to developmental theories." This claim leads us beyond the hermeneutic circle into difficult questions of theory and truth.

But this claim raises a further question. Are interpretations to be assessed in terms of whether they themselves can be satisfactorily explained by a specific life-span developmental theory? Or should interpretations be judged first by their fidelity and adequacy to the text—in other words, a so-called hermeneutic standard? If the former, then interpretations of texts, life stories and qualitative data generally become a kind of second order data set—something in turn to be accounted for by theory. If the latter, then how will the diversity of interpretations be integrated into any over-arching developmental theory? It is hard to see exactly how some limited set of qualitative data could actually disconfirm a theory. Would, say, the fact that the life history of a particular individual contained no signs of Erikson's ego integrity-versus-despair or demonstrated no evidence of Butler's life-review be taken as in any way disconfirming those theoretical ideas? Or would we rather be more likely to adopt some interpretation—that it, some way of making sense of that individual story—which effectively removes it from a chain of predictions and disconfirmations?

Putting the problem this way makes us aware of some of the ambiguity conveyed by that elastic word "interpretation." After all, through the Middle Ages astronomers came up with "interpretations" of the data of planetary motion that allowed the Ptolemaic system of astronomy to become ever-more refined and elaborate, thus avoiding disconfirmation of the Ptolemaic theory. Could it be that interpretations in the human sciences at times play such a role—in effect, shielding developmental theory from disconfirmation (Popper, 1972)? Or, on the other hand, must one adopt a standpoint in which theory (but *which* theory?) becomes somehow an arbiter of the adequacy of interpretations put forward on the basis of qualitative data sets?

Berman's point about the relation between textual hermeneutics and developmental theory also opens up another possibility for the role of qualitative research: namely, the prospect of widening our image of what development itself consists of in the first place (McCullough, 1981; Moody, 1986). This is both a critical function—calling attention to limits in current formulations, say, of late-life cognition—and also a heuristic function—suggesting new lines of research.

Both the critical and the heuristic function are raised by questions about the sampling procedures used in qualitative research. Gubrium, for instance, acknowledges that, when research is dominated by questions of interpretation, it is strategic, not representative sampling that should be the rule. If the purpose of data gathering is not descriptive but critical or heuristic, then strategic sampling is eminently justifiable, even if the number of individuals involved is very small. We are concerned, after all, with human possibilities, not with descriptions of average behavior.

It is just this point which opens up new vistas for understanding what human development may mean in its unexplored potential (Peck, 1968; Philibert, 1968; Maslow, 1971; Staude, 1981). These new vistas could give concrete content to what Habermas has called for in describing an emancipatory interest in the progress of human knowledge. We obviously have an emancipatory interest in the repression-free psyche promised by psychoanalysis (Freud) or in the social justice favored by theories of moral development (Kohlberg). To these examples of emancipatory social science we should add the ideals of late-life creativity and wisdom depicted by a full account of life-span development psychology. Freedom, happiness, justice, wisdom: these are human interests that can inspire the enterprise of research as much as the interest in domination of nature or human society. These emancipatory interests, and not mere methodological debate, are what is finally at stake in the human science approach to gerontology.

The value of this approach is illustrated in Allen Chinen's article offering a developmental approach to quantitative and qualitative reasoning over the life-span. Chinen looks at two twentieth-century philosophers, Wittgenstein and Whitehead, but the broad conclusions he reaches are roughly the same as those reached by students of late style of older artists (Munsterberg, 1983). In the careers of both Whitehead and Wittgenstein Chinen finds a shift away from abstract, reductive reasoning characteristic of quantitative science in favor of pragmatic, concrete, relativistic, contextual and dialectical forms of reasoning. Late-life thinking, at least in its most creative phase among exceptional individuals, is more accurately described as intuitive, holistic and even transcendent.

By recognizing this tendency, or at least this possibility, in life-span development, and by giving greater legitimacy to strategic sampling, we open up an enlarged role for the humanities in gerontology (Spicker et al., 1978; Van Tassel, 1979; Cole and Gadow, 1986). But the implications here extend beyond older people who happen to be philosophers or artists. The depth dimension of experiential knowledge and wisdom has implications for practice and practical reasoning. It is another instance of what Polanyi called personal knowledge (Polanyi, 1958), which has an evident kinship with qualitative modes of understanding.

Of course, practical judgment, when it is focused on immediate problem-solving, remains distinct from literary or phenomenological understanding where imagination or empathy is an end in itself. But what is most important here is to see how qualitative studies of pure theory (art, philosophy or science) converge, at the structural level, with the lived wisdom of pragmatic judgment. The same dialectical structures arise in both theory and practice. It is this dimension of praxis and action, emphasized repeatedly throughout this discussion, which returns us to a shared human world where actions have consequences and where our full humanity and sense of responsibility are engaged.

Conclusion: The Mirror and the Map

It is a common experience that in growing older we come to glimpse, whether dimly or in full awareness, the imponderable consequences of actions reaching over the entire span of life. This is a fact that we experience as either fate or wisdom. In any case it is an intuition about life that cannot be grasped in other than qualitative terms. And it is not simply that qualitative methods allow us to grasp unseen dimensions of aging. It may be equally that the study of life-span development, including cognitive development in its higher manifestations, will give new depth and validity to qualitative modes of thinking for people of any age. In short, the study of aging through the human sciences will become a kind of mirror for ourselves in which we may hope at least to see a gerontology with a human face.

And yet, once again, we must raise the question Eugene Thomas raises in his introduction to this book: "But is this science?" Science is more than looking in a mirror: it is a community enterprise in which each generation contributes to the common act of discovery (Rorty, 1979). The achievement of discovery requires that we have accurate maps to guide us. The need for these maps is part of the "knowledge-constitutive interest" so that we can navigate through the human world. And, once again, the map of the human sciences must be, preeminently, *practical* knowledge.

Here I return to the original metaphor: the human sciences as a way of reconstructing the map of knowledge. It is worth pondering a moment on how different are these two metaphors I have invoked: a mirror, in which we see our own face, and a map, in which we discover a landscape outside of ourselves. The first is a metaphor of subjectivity: looking at ourselves or at our own image. The second is a metaphor of objectivity: the map is only a tool by which we move through a world outside of ourselves. By itself the mirror leads to a post-modern desert of relativism in which we never get outside of ourselves. And by itself map making leads to a ever-more refined navigation in which we are in danger of forgetting what the journey is all about.

The paradox of research in human aging is that we need both kinds of metaphors to describe how we sould orient the task of knowledge-building. We need the reflective knowledge of "mirroring" the experience of aging in ourselves and in first-person accounts of all kinds. That means looking in the mirror because aging is finally, just ourselves and not an "object" beyond ourselves. But we also need the abstractive knowledge that is "mapped" by a symbolic network (theories, explanatory constructs) inevitably different both from ourselves and from the landscape which the map represents. For both kinds of tasks the human sciences can contribute immeasurably to our understanding of aging in the future.

References

Ackermann, Robert J. (1985). *Data, instruments, and theory: A dialectical approach to understanding science*. Princeton: Princeton University Press.

Andreski, Stanislaw. (1972). *The social sciences as sorcery*. London: Basil Blackwell.

Bernstein, Richard. (1983). *Beyond objectivism and relativism: Science, hermeneutics, and praxis*. Philadelphia: University of Pennsylvania Press.

Cole, Thomas and Sally Gadow (eds.). (1986). *What does it mean to grow old? Views from the humanities*. Durham, NC: Duke University Press.

Collin, Finn. (1985). *Theory and understanding: A critique of interpretive social science*. London: Basil Blackwell.

Fischer, C. (1987). The quality of qualitative research. *Theoretical and Philosophical Psychology* 7, 2: 11-22.

Gubrium, Jay. (1975). *Living and dying at Murray Manor*. New York: St. Martin's Press.

Habermas, Jurgen. (1971). *Knowledge and human interests*. (trans. Jeremy J. Shapiro) Boston: Beacon Press.

Habermas, Jurgen. (1963/1974). *Theory and practice* (trans. John Viertel) London: Heinemann.

Lindblom, Charles. (1979). *Usable knowledge*. New Haven: Yale University Press.

Maslow, Abraham. (1971). *The farther reaches of human nature*. New York: Viking Press.

McCarthy, Thomas. (1978). *The critical theory of Jurgen Habermas.* Cambridge: MA: MIT Press.

McCulloch, Andrew W. (July 1981). What do we mean by 'development' in old age? *Ageing and Society*, Vol. 1, Pt. 2.

McKee, Patrick L. (1982). *Philosophical foundations of gerontology.* New York: Human Sciences Press.

Moody, H. R. (1986). The meaning of life and the meaning of old age. In Thomas Cole and Sally Gadow (eds.). *What does it mean to grow old? Views from the humanities.* Durham, NC: Duke University Press.

Moody, H. R. (1988). Toward a critical gerontology: Contributions of the humanities to theories of aging. In James Birren and Vern Bengston (eds.). *Emergent theories of aging.* New York: Springer.

Moody, H. R. (1988). *Abundance of life: Human development policies for an aging society.* New York: Columbia University Press.

Munsterberg, Hugo. (1983). *The crown of life: Artistic creativity in old age.* San Diego: Harcourt Brace Janonovich.

Neugarten, Bernice. (1984). Interpretive social science and research on aging. In A. Rossi (ed.) *Gender and the life course.* Chicago: Aldine.

Pearlman, R. A. and J. B. Speer. (1983). Quality-of-life considerations in geriatric care. *Journal of the American Geriatrics Society* 31: 113-119.

Peck, Robert C. (1968). Psychological development in the second half of life. In B. Neugarten (ed.). *Middle age and aging.* Chicago: University of Chicago Press.

Philibert, Michel. (1968). *L'Echelle des Ages.* Paris: Le Seuil.

Polanyi, Michael. (1958). *Personal knowledge: Towards a post-critical philosophy.* Chicago: University of Chicago Press.

Polkinghorne, Donald E. (1988). *Narrative knowledge and the human sciences.* Albany, NY: SUNY Press.

Popper, Karl R. (1972). *Conjectures and refutations: The growth of scientific knowledge* (4th ed.). London: Routledge & Kegan Paul.

Prado, C. G. (1986). *Rethinking how we age: A new view of the aging mind.* Westport, CT: Greenwood Press.

Rabinow, Paul and W. Sullivan. (1979). *Interpretive social science: A reader.* Berkeley: University of California Press.

Reinharz, S. and G. Bowles. (1987). *Qualitative gerontology.* New York: Springer.

Rappoport, L. (1980). Renaming the world: On psychology and the decline of positive science. *Journal of Social Reconstruction* 1 (2): 33-57.

Rorty, Richard. (1979). *Philosophy and the mirror of nature.* Princeton: Princeton University Press.

Sabia, D. R. and J. Wallulis (eds.). (1983). *Changing social science: Critical theory and other critical perspectives.* Albany: SUNY Press.

Sarbin, T. R. (ed.). (1986). *Narrative psychology: The storied nature of human conduct.* New York: Praeger.

Shapiro, Gary and Alan Sica (eds.). (1984). *Hermeneutics.* Amherst, MA: University of Massachusetts Press.

Spicker, Stuart et al. (1978). *Aging and the elderly: Humanistic perspectives on gerontology.* Atlantic Highlands, NJ: Humanities Press.

Staude, John Raphael. (1981). *Wisdom and age.* Berkeley, CA: Ross Books.

Van Tassel, David (ed.). (1979). *Aging, death and the completion of being.* Philadelphia: University of Pennsylvania Press.

Contributors

Harry J. Berman Ph.D., is Associate Professor of Child, Family and Community Services at Sangamon State University in Springfield, Illinois. He has written several articles on the analysis of older people's diaries and has also conducted research and written articles on retirement decisions and on the management of nurse aides in nursing homes.

Kim O. Chambers, a doctoral student at The University of Connecticut in the school of Family Studies formerly studied at the University of Florida concentrating on humanistic psychology, counseling, and higher education administration. He has done work on the experience "privacy" and is currently involved in marital and family therapy study and gerontological research.

Allan B. Chinen, M.D., is a psychiatrist on the Clinical Faculty of the University of California, San Francisco, and in private practice. He has published numerous research papers on adult development, psychotherapy, and folklore, and is the author of two volumes on fairy tales and the psychology of aging.

Susan A. Eisenhandler Ph.D., is a sociologist who teaches at the University of Connecticut—Waterbury. She is a former Administration on Aging trainee whose research interests center on the social construction of old age by community elders. Her current work explores the relationship between driving, old age and identity.

Mary M. Gergen Ph.D., is a member of the Psychology Department and the Women's Studies Program of Penn State University. Her major scholarly involvement has been in applying feminist perspectives to social and developmental issues in psychology and to methodological issues in the social sciences more generally. In 1988 she edited *Feminist Thought and the Structure of Knowledge* for New York University Press.

Jaber F. Gubrium Ph.D., is professor of sociology at the University of Florida and research associate in its Center for Gerontological Studies. He has written and edited a number of books on aging and the social organization of care in human service institutions. A growing interest in the

241

semiotics of family has led to the publication of a series of papers on the subject and a forthcoming book, *Public Family, Private Household*, which critically examines the descriptive culture of domestic life. Gubrium is the editor of the *Journal of Aging Studies*.

J. Gordon Harris Ph.D., is Professor of Old Testament and Vice President for Academic Affairs at the North American Baptist Seminary, Sioux Falls, SD. He is author of the recent book, *Biblical Perspectives on Aging: God and the Elders*. He teaches a graduate course on "Ministry and the Aging Adult," and has conducted seminars on aging for professional and lay audiences.

Harry R. Moody Ph.D., is Deputy Director for Academic Affairs at the Brookdale Center on Aging of Hunter College in New York. A philosopher, his interests include reminiscence, late style in art, education and public policy for older people.

Robert L. Rubinstein Ph.D., is Senior Research Anthropologist and Head of the Anthropology Program at the Philadelphia Geriatric Center. He has conducted research (in the U.S.) and published books and articles on older men and the home environments of older people and is currently involved in a study of childless older women. He has also undertaken field research in Vanuatu, in the South Pacific.

Karl E. Scheibe Ph.D., is Professor of Psychology at Wesleyan University. He is a social psychologist who has written extensively on a wide range of theoretical and experimental topics. He has edited *The Social Context of Conduct* (1982) and *Studies in Social identity* (1983), and is author of several books, the latest of which is *Mirrors, Masks, Lies and Secrets* (1979).

Karol J. Sylcox Ph.D., is a qualitative researcher, gerontologist, and writer. Her research interests include creativity, aging, and children's books which deal with issues concerning old people and aging. She has published several articles about creativity and aging, and is writing textbook exercises and trade books for children.

L. Eugene Thomas Ph.D., is Professor of Human Development and Family Relations at the University of Connecticut. He has conducted research with young adults and the middle-aged, as well as with elderly, examining the effect of beliefs on psychological well-being and behavior. He will be returning to India in the fall to interview elderly religious

religious renunciates in Varanasi, in order to compare them with his sample of elderly Indian and English "householders".

Linda A. Wood Ph.D., is Associate Professor of Psychology and Research Associate, Gerontology Research Centre, at the University of Guelph, Canada. She has published on various aspects of loneliness and methodology in social psychology. Her current research concerns language and social interaction, particularly politeness. She is a director of an ongoing panel study of the quality of life and social relationships of older people in Ontario.

Index